D1346816

Silent Story
Domestic Abuse and Depression from a
Male perspective

Leon Matthew-Doorman was born in Birmingham 45 years ago. He is a dedicated father of three and has one grandson. Having joined the forces at 16 he travelled extensively for some years. On leaving the RAF Leon pursued his quest for knowledge and took a Degree course in History and Political Science at The University of Birmingham. He has always loved words and use of the English Language. Having studied for his Degree, he went on to do a Post Graduate Certificate in Education. Leon worked in Schools in Birmingham encouraging pupils to develop an interest in Culture and History throughout the ages. Leon continued to attend night school and pursued his interest in Photography and Theatre Studies. He also wrote a play which was performed on radio. The play has now been translated into a short story and published. Eight years ago he decided to make a career change and trained to become a Paramedic, a job both intense and committed. Leon has a passionate outlook on justice and equality. The book was written as a true reflection on society, policing, equality and the law as it stands today.

Silent Story
Domestic abuse and depression from a male perspective

Leon Matthews-Doorman

Arena Books

First published in 2018 by Arena Books
Arena Books
6 Southgate Green
Bury St. Edmunds
IP33 2BL

www.arenabooks.co.uk
Distributed in America by Ingram International, One Ingram Blvd., P.O. Box
3006, La Vergne, TN 37086-1985, USA.

Leon Matthews-Doorman
Silent Story *Domestic abuse & depression from a male perspective*

British Library cataloguing in Publication Data. A Catalogue record
for this book is available from the British Library.

ISBN-13   978-1-911593-29-4

BIC classifications:- BTP, VF, VFJS, BGXA, BGA, VFV, VSPM, VXA.

Printed and bound by Lightning Source UK

Cover design
By Jason Anscomb

Typeset in
Times New Roman

DEDICATION

To those who have been falsely accused of a crime. I also want to consider those who have been or are still suffering in an abusive relationship. Finally, I want to dedicate this book to those who live with the daily pain of depression and other mental health illnesses.

ACKNOWLEDGEMENTS

There are so many people I could mention but particular thanks goes to Lizzie for her support and common sense and my children for being who they are and of course, never forgetting little "Dolly.'

CONTENTS

FOREWORD

I was recently asked by a close friend why I called this book *Silent Story*. The answer is quite simplistic really. Initially I answered by saying it 'just was'. The truth lies in the fact that the contents and feelings within these pages are based on things that are not talked about. Firstly, people with depression are often ashamed to admit that mental health plagues their everyday life. Depression is often associated with lack of control or weakness. This is further compounded when it is associated with horrific crimes such as shootings and murders. For example, President Trump said in a rambling interview (August 2015) that gun laws aren't to blame for the deaths of two young journalists, appearing eager to shift back to issues more in his comfort zone as he struggled to offer any substantive answers.1

"This isn't a gun problem, this is a mental [health] problem,".

At the time Trump also said limited mental health infrastructure was in part to blame and should be fixed, spending much of the interview portraying gun violence and mental health as a "complex" and "tough" issue. To a degree he is right. There appears to be less and less support for mental health provision. But he is both wrong and ignorant to make such a sweeping statement with regard to something he clearly had no knowledge of. Furthermore, and there is no indication of importance here, domestic abuse is often carried out behind closed doors. Domestic abuse (in any form) is not acceptable. But when it happens to those of whom appear least likely to be victims, the shame carried is immeasurable, therefore, untalkable.

To the outside world I was a middle aged man with a good career and a happy family life. Yet behind the façade I was a victim of domestic, emotional, financial and sexual abuse by my female partner. This is the story of how I was let down by the authorities and how I've managed to attempt to build my life again once I had the courage to leave.

It had and has been a battle of what it means to be a male in an abusive relationship and the suffocating struggle with depression. I wanted to share my feelings and thoughts and help anyone out there to realise they are not alone.

As a result, you may find that the book has been broken down into clear separate segments. Of course, although they are defined separately they do indeed have an element of overlap. They need to so the reader can see the relationship between each factor of abuse and depression. However, let me be clear here. This book is not an anti-female rant. Far from it. I want domestic abuse recognised in all of its forms. It's just that when I realised I was a victim I struggled to find anything for me – anything for a male victim. Yet, the internet, leaflets and support groups are all female centred. Of course I must accept that females hold the greatest proportion when it comes to victim status. But statistics mean nothing when you are the victim and living the abuse day in day out. In effect, I needed something to help me and I found nothing. So here it is my support structure being offered to you whether male or female. But this is the abuse from a male perspective. And this is the depression from a man who hated to recognise there was a problem. It took something like this to push me to seek help. And on reflection, I type these words with no shame at all. I am what I am and it had taken me most of my life to accept this.

Of course, I have not used my real name as there are still people who need to be protected. I am sure that you appreciate where I am coming from with regards to that matter. Although I am not ashamed of what I am telling you and there are parts that are direct and painful, but unlike an abuser I need to protect the ones I love.

Okay, so where do I begin? Well I had been arrested. Wrongfully. But what was I to do or say when I was in the middle of a system that was tailored to persecute the real victim? I am a male. And with this comes a number of facts. I had nowhere to go for shelter or protection when I realised I was the victim of an abusive female partner. I had been assaulted both physically and sexually. She had stolen from me and belittled me in front of my friends and family and even in my own home. But the mental torment was far worse. As a male I felt there was nothing I could do about it and she used this to its full effect. She knew she could claim anything and people would jump. She knew this was the case as she had done it before. Twice before in fact. And the precedent of her actions showed there had been no consequences to her wrongful activities.

But it's very hard to bare your sole to the world when the world has preconceived expectations of what it is to be a man. But no one should be made to feel frightened, inadequate and scared in their own homes and especially by their partners no matter what sex they are. I have now learnt and witnessed that it is so hard for men to believe they would be listened to and treated equally in such cases. But at some point, the balance needs to be addressed. I am fully aware that this little one-man crusade would never change the victim status being a gender specific occupation. But when it is you in the middle of it, statistics mean nothing, and preservation means everything. When you live a life of fear and uncertainty and that your home is no longer a safe haven, the life you thought you could live turns to dust. It is further trampled on when you know there is nothing you can do about it regardless of the rhetoric given out by the authorities. The fact remains that men cannot seek shelter at a local refuge. Men cannot automatically take the children. And it now appears that men would not be believed when they make a counter claim. It is wrong to assume that the female would nurture and love any more than a male, yet we are stereotyped in so many ways. The abuse I experienced was nothing more nor less than my female counterpart but I had not received equal support or consideration following my revelation.

As previously stated, this is by no means a male only agenda. Abuse in all of its forms is wrong and can happen to anyone. It needs to stop. In fact, after releasing my story to the world the support I had received from females had outweighed that shown by men. It appears that the common denominator lies with the fact that men refuse to admit it exists even if they are the victim. I had refused to admit it to myself, it was the easier option to take as I had lived in hope that it would change. I was doing the manly thing and behaved in a manly fashion. Time and again she promised she would stop her abuse. But her mental structure could not distinguish between what was and what was not acceptable. She had no-one to answer to for her abuse, therefore, it became okay to act in such a fashion. This was, alas, enforced by my failure to acknowledge the abuse I had received and so it continued.

I am not excusing her actions. I am sure at some point in her life the dawning of what she did would eventually hit home. But domestic abuse goes on regardless of what new policies the government of the day rolls out. I am afraid to tell you all that domestic abuse will continue beyond our lifetimes, but the system lets the victims down. And if I can be as bold to say at this stage – especially if you are a male victim. As time developed and the depth of the hole I had found myself in deepened, I was unable to control my lifelong depression. I had suffered depression from an early age but for a majority of my life it was controlled. It had taken years to develop skills to keep it in check. But when life started to unravel I was unable to manage my illness either. As a result, my depression took hold at a greater grip than ever before. After all, I had lost everything within a single moment. At that specific point I had no purpose. I had no home, no job to attend (I had been suspended based on a presumption [company policy by all accounts]) and contact with my children had become difficult. In my logical mind there was no reason to continue. Ending my life seemed the only logical conclusion. It became physically painful to live as the pain I was experiencing was utterly unbearable. I had become at ease with this decision as the past had gone and I could see no future. It felt easy to accept (to me) this logical conclusion.

Throughout this book I want the reader to find this vein within the text. It may not be obvious at times, but I was struggling to grab the reins again. There is nothing worse than finding that not only had you lost control of your physical life but to lose control of your mental strength is beyond comprehension. But I hope that you, as the reader, would find some glimmer of hope. I had said within the text that the world is a big place, but it is smaller when broken down into smaller communities. The communities within this book is a home for victims of; domestic abuse (regardless of gender), people who had experienced a wrongful arrest and people suffering the pain of a problematic mental health condition.

I suppose by surrendering my maleness and refusing to accept the idea of 'manning up' I had welcomed a new approach to everyday life. I was hurting, and I was ill. I therefore, needed help. There is no shame in anything I had said or done. I decided to accept medication and the support that counselling had brought. But mostly I was man enough to tell everyone that I was being abused by my female partner. After all, I had nothing else to lose especially when I had no personal value of myself anymore. I had refused to take responsibility for another adult's poor behaviour. Ultimately, I demanded an apology from those who should have supported me more. I knew I was right although I had been wronged. And this is my story.

PART I
ABUSE

CHAPTER 1
How it all began

The morning was bright and sunny when I awoke. Perhaps for many people it was just another Sunday morning but for me it was different. This particular Sunday morning was, for me, the first day of an unexpected new future. I had decided the day before that I would tell my ex-partner that I had had enough. For months I had been subjected to her unreasonable actions and life had now become unbearable living under the same roof as her.

Threats had become a regular occurrence and she had showed her true colours many times beforehand. She had become an expert in manipulation of not only myself, but others around her. By her own admission she had become an abuser without restraint. But to the outside world it appeared that I had it all. A good education, a nice home, and a job I enjoyed. I never complained to others about what was going on and I gave a persona of being strong and in control.

But, normality took an evil and wicked turn based on a single phone call. Furthermore, this phone call was carried out whilst I was out of the house and so at that moment, I was unable to understand the consequence of what she had done. In effect this was her last roll of the dice as she knew I was leaving and so no longer had control of me anymore. She knew what she was doing and knew the full effect of the damage she would cause. But this didn't stop her, as it transpired she had done this so many times before to previous partners.

The events leading up to that day:-

Sunday 7th May 2017 – After spending the morning with my ex-partner I took my daughter back home to her mother. Whilst returning, I stopped off at a local supermarket to buy a few provisions. Once back at the car I called my ex-partner to tell her I was heading home. During the call she became hostile. She instantly accused me of having an affair. This was normal behaviour for her and so was, therefore, treated as another accusation in a long list of other accusations. I arrived home at about 13:00hrs and she was verbally abusive claiming that I was having an affair with a work colleague. Previously, I had mentioned that the colleague required a reference, and so my partner was aware that there had been various forms of contact. I explained to her that this occurred only during staffroom 'chat' but she refused to accept it. She then sat in her car clearly on her phone. I decided to leave her out there to let her come to her senses and calm down. The rest of the day/evening was spent with me explaining who my work colleague was and that I was not having an affair. Throughout the evening both she and her middle daughter (aged 17) were in the bedroom discussing things (of which I was not a part of). The atmosphere was dreadful with the usual silent treatment being aimed at myself. I decided to spend the night on the sofa as I knew I would be at risk of physical violence from her based on previous experiences should I try to sleep in my own bed.

Monday 8th May 2017 – I decided to work an overtime shift at work (0700-1900hrs). I worked for the health service as a Paramedic. When I arrived home the silent treatment continued with the occasional derogatory comment directed at myself mainly by my ex-partner.

Tuesday 9th May 2017 – I worked a night shift (1830-0630). This was a period of relief as my ex-partner was at work whilst I spent the day in bed un-harassed and safe.

Wednesday 10th May 2017 – I worked another night shift (1900-0700). I finished 45 mins late due to a large job of which I was always expected to book at home in front of her to prove I had completed the extra hours. Once she had left for work I felt safe and was able to sleep in the bed.

Thursday 11th May 2017 – Another night shift. However during the day, I booked two property viewings as I had decided that I had had enough of living in the present regime. I had booked both viewings for Saturday (10am and 14:30hrs).

Friday 12th May 2017 – Following my night shift I woke and collected my daughter at about lunch time. My daughter's mother stated that she had not been well. As a result I cancelled the Saturday viewings as it was irresponsible to take my daughter out viewing property when she felt so ill. My ex-partner was still being unreasonable and it was clear that her daughter was also carrying out the silent treatment towards me. Her daughter eventually decided to stay out that night at a friend's house.

Saturday 13th May 2017 – My ex-partner seemed more reasonable on the Saturday and so as a result we opted to take my daughter out for a walk in her push chair. We walked to the village church which was about a half hour's walk from home. Whilst heading home I told her that I could no longer live under these conditions and that I was, therefore, looking for a new home. I asked her to start contributing more to the household expenditure, so I would be able to save money towards a deposit for a new property. As a result, she became verbally abusive (she also pointed her finger in my face) shouting all kinds of derogatory things. Her behaviour was so bad a couple in their garden looked up to see what all the commotion was about. I was deeply embarrassed by her behavior and actually considered that she was going to hit me at one point.

Later in the evening I settled my daughter down on the sofa as I had little intention of going to bed. I stayed up until about 2am watching a range of TV programmes. Prior to this my ex-partner came down stairs asking me to come to bed. I did not wish to share the bed as I knew she would be temperamental following the earlier conversation. However, as my daughter was ill, I decided to put her in her cot and try to settle myself in the said bed. At about 2:30am I felt my ex-partner kiss my neck and so I pretended to be asleep. She held my genitals and so I rolled onto my stomach still pretending to be asleep. She knew I was not asleep and whispered into my ear that I was "going to pay for this".

Sunday 14th May 2017 – I told my ex-partner that I had considered her actions to be inappropriate and that I had previously sought advice about male domestic abuse. I had also told her that I still intended to leave her at the earliest opportunity. I went downstairs and discovered the living room covered in rubbish and half eaten food. Her youngest daughter (she had 3) had left the living room in a shocking state. I asked her to speak to her as it was unfair that my daughter should be exposed to this in her present condition. As a result, she became abusive and threatening towards me. She screamed in my face and squared up to me. She stated that I was an unfit father and she wished me dead (this was not unusual as it was often said). Due to her behaviour and my daughter's sickness I decided to take my daughter home earlier than was originally planned.

Whilst driving home I called 101 (a non-emergency number for the police in the UK) to report my history of abuse at the hands of my partner. They gave me a crime number and invited me to make a statement at Worcester Police Station on Wednesday 17th May 2017. I was also told that my partner could not stop me returning to collect a few belongings as I was planning to stay with my son for a while. I then called my partner to tell her that I was coming home to collect a few things and was going to stay with my son. She told me that I was not welcome home anymore and the police were there. Of course, I went home in the hope that the police would protect me and assist me with gathering my belongings and leave. I arrived home and was met by two policemen. They informed me that I was under arrest for assault. I was, to say the least, shocked by this claim, but fully compliant with the police. It was reasonable to consider that they would also help me with my accusations and reported assault and abuse.

The police took me to Worcester Police station and from that point I realised that the police had absolutely no interest in what I had to say. As a result I was locked in a cell and I appeared in the Magistrates Court the following morning (Monday). In total I spent 30 hours in police custody and at no stage was I given the opportunity to express my experiences of abuse at the hands of my partner. And I suppose that was that. But it wasn't. Shortly afterwards my whole world turned on its head. Everything I had considered to be right and normal became wrong and hostile and I was at the centre of it. It was from this moment I felt that being a male was a crime.

Firstly, it now appeared that I was not allowed to be abused by my female partner. It was perceived as being unreasonable to talk about it – especially admit that I was a victim. Secondly, it looks as if sexual abuse is a one-way street. If I had informed on my ex earlier I felt I would had been scoffed at or even ridiculed. It seemed ridiculous to be both a male and a victim of sexual abuse at the same time.

Once I had the courage to admit what had happened, it felt as if everything had fallen apart. Throughout my life I was informed and instructed that I should have faith in the legal system of my country. Yet, alas, this had all been denied me. The one and only time I had needed the help of the police, they set out to dismiss my claim and pursue a prosecution based on a lie by a woman who had a previous record of malicious claims. But this wasn't in an undemocratic country. My country's historical claim was based on the rights of man and the fair balance of the law. This simple test smashed that theory apart. It could have happened to anyone in any street in any town. This was England and I was not only abused by my ex-partner but I was also now a victim of a blinkered legal system. As stated, following my arrest on the Sunday, I appeared at the Magistrates Court the following morning. The previous night had been dreadful. Although I had been treated well by the custody staff I was still aware that each and every one of them had dismissed my counter allegation. For them it was a simple conclusion. A female had made an allegation; therefore, it was not only true but the male must have been the perpetrator. It was only following my arrest that I had been informed of her allegation. It was claimed that I had spat at her four weeks prior to my arrest. But there was no evidence. There was no truth in her allegation. As a result I opted to plead not guilty and was bailed to appear before them again at a later date. Although there was no evidence and my facts contradicted her tale, the Crown Prosecution Service (CPS) still thought they had a case.

Following my release on bail I opted to stay with friends whilst I sorted myself out and tried to work out what on earth was going on. Within a blink of an eye I had lost my home, my daughter and was now suspended from work on a presumption of guilt. Work claimed that this was based on policy, yet I thought they knew me better than what had been alleged. This hurt deeply and I felt betrayed especially as I knew attending work would give me some form of normality in a world that had gone crazy. It emerged that work had been informed of the arrest prior to my release. As a result I was suspended whilst this awful mess hung over me. It got worse.... I was informed that I was not allowed to see my daughter due to the nature of the claimed incident (domestic). Still to this day I had not formally been informed why this approach had been taken. It appears that I was considered guilty on the whim of a bitter woman who called 999 as she knew I was calling the police via 101 that same morning. At no point had I ever been given the opportunity to defend myself. What made matters worse, was regardless of my good character and work ethic I was seen as guilty and treated as such.

There is a level of shame admitting that you are being abused regardless of what sex you are. Furthermore, in my case I did not even realise it until I came across an article highlighting what abuse is. Whilst working one evening prior to this incident, I was called to attend an assault. On arrival it transpired that the victim was a middle aged male who had been attacked by his wife. Although it was clear that some form of physical assault had taken place the conversation I had with the victim opened my eyes. In the presence of the police he stated that he had experienced a range of abuses at the hands of his wife. This conversation sent a shiver down my spine. He went into depth about what had happened to him prior to the attack that he had endured a few months prior to the assault. Nearly everything he mentioned I was able to identify with, as having had first hand experience myself. Once I had arrived home that following morning, I decided to spend a few moments trying to identify the true meaning of abuse. I discovered plenty of examples and explanations. But I found the following;

The cross Government definition of domestic violence and abuse is (2):

"Any incident of controlling, coercive, threatening behavior, violence or abuse between those aged 16 or over who are, or had been intimate partners or family members regardless of gender or sexuality. The abuse can encompass, but is not limited to:

- ≅ psychological
- ≅ physical
- ≅ sexual
- ≅ financial
- ≅ emotional

CHAPTER 2
How come I didn't even realise I was a victim?

Throughout my career as a paramedic I was trained to identify anyone who had been, or was at risk of being abused. At no pint had I ever considered that I was also a victim. After all, how could I be? I was seen to be strong and dependable amongst my workmates and friends. Furthermore, the abuse was a slow growth and I never realised that it was happening. However, it was not until I came across another victim and followed it up by reading articles on hidden abuse that I realised I was ticking most of the factors. My ex had previously reported her ex-partners for a sting of alleged abuse and assaults. She had informed me that her previous partner – a policeman, had, she claimed, assaulted her on numerous occasions. She pursued an assault claim against him but it was not pursued due to insufficient evidence of which she was still highly bitter about. She openly discussed with my friends, family and other acquaintances about her so-called abuse at the hands of men. Furthermore, she managed to obtain a PIN (Police Intervention Notice) against her ex-husband to try and enforce reduced contact between him, his daughters and herself (do you now see a pattern forming?). My ex claimed that at some point I assaulted her two weeks previously to the 999 call operator. She stated to the police that I loosely strangled her with her scarf and spat in her face whilst in the bedroom.

But consider this..

If such an event had happened why were the police not called at the time? Her only witness (her middle daughter) stated that she saw spit in her mothers' hair. If she did have spit in her hair she would have wiped it off by the time she was in the living room – where her daughter supposedly saw it. My ex became aware the day before the police were called (13th May 2017) that I was planning to leave her and had refused to have sex with her on numerous occasions. She further informed me that I was "going to pay for this". She was aware that I was intending to get advice from an outside source for help and advice on domestic, emotional and sexual abuse. As a result she dialled 999 while I was returning my daughter to her mother, therefore, I was conveniently out of the house.

As a point of record, I had reported some of these events to my line managers at work back in October 2016. Both had documented these reports following the telephone conversations and face to face interviews I had had with them. On reflection this was probably the best thing I had done. I had not gone into great detail with my managers but I had mentioned that things were not right at home and I needed somewhere to stay. As time went by following the arrest these records became invaluable to aid my case and secure my defence. Many of the new found abuses I was experiencing came under certain headings. I was being controlled, manipulated and abused by the one person I had expected more from. I discovered that her actions had specific labels of which I would go into greater detail below.

Controlling behaviour

My ex demanded that I called her when I arrived at work. I was then expected to tell her if I was either on an RRV(rapid response car) or DMU (large ambulance). If I was on a DMU I had to tell her if my crew mate was either male or female. Depending on gender my ex would then try and find my crew mate on Social media. Once found she would sometimes contact the female crewmate and send them threatening messages. During the shift (mainly a day shift) I was expected to contact my ex at least 3 times a day either by phone call or text. Furthermore, I would be expected to let her know when I was returning home. If, and it regularly happened as a paramedic, I was late finishing I had to book my over-run at home in front of her with the associated job number. I was not allowed to see friends or family without her permission. Yet she had no concern if she went out herself. I was never allowed to see friends or attend work functions and as a result I missed friends leaving drinks and team bonding evenings. I slowly became an outsider within my workplace. Once I had left the home it transpired that my ex had threatened female friends with violence and name calling of which my friends didn't tell me about until they felt safe to do so.

Coercive behaviour

My ex often called me names and made threats to my general

safety. She once said that because of her ex being a policeman he would have connections to either having me beaten up or got rid of. Yet this was the same ex she had tried to have arrested previously to me meeting her.

Financial abuse

I was expected to pay for all the household bills (except for TV license and council tax). As a result I had no money of which to save and leave her. My ex took full control of the housing expenses. I was expected to pay £880 rent, £300 food and so on. Therefore, I was left with no money for myself. Furthermore, I was also expected to buy her clothes and shoes on a monthly basis. But it is important to note that financial abuse comes in many forms beyond an expectation that you would pay for everything. For example, it can involve your partner spending your jointly-earned money, taking out loans in your name, making you pay the utility bills, or scrutinising every penny you spend. Furthermore, it can be the fore-runner of even more serious emotional, or physical, abuse. A recent report called Unequal Trapped and Controlled (Marilyn Howard and Amy Skipp) (3) identified the ten most frequent signs to look out for are a partner who:

- ≅ takes important financial decisions without you
- ≅ uses your credit/debit card without asking
- ≅ controls your access to money, through credit cards or a bank account
- ≅ takes your benefit payments, or wages
- ≅ refuses to contribute to household bills or children's expenses
- ≅ puts bills in your name, but does not contribute to them
- ≅ takes out loans in your name – but does not help with repayments
- ≅ takes money from your purse/ bank account
- ≅ stops you working
- ≅ uses you as a free source of labour

I had experienced a few of these (not all) but my ex would often take my car (without asking – which is an offense in itself) and never replace the fuel that was consumed. This may seem like an inconsequential act but I was expected, therefore, to contribute to further expenses that were not my own. I really struggle to see any benefit at all in joint accounts. It may have started out to be all 'romantic' and feeling that you had become 'one' by having a joint account. But I had witnessed from friends in similar situations that this becomes a financial nightmare once the break up begins. My ex suggested a joint bank account within days of moving in together. I instantly dismissed this idea but said I would consider it. Thank heavens I didn't open a joint account as I would still, no doubt, be suffering with the consequences now. Following simple online research, banks either didn't seem too interested or had little clout with regards to joint account difficulties. In essence, they are not able to intervene in such disputes. HSBC, for example, would only put restrictions on a joint account if it had advice from the Police to do so. Royal Bank of Scotland (RBS), Lloyds and NatWest would block an account if they are formally notified that there is a marital dispute. Financial abuse had become recognised in various front line services such as the police and within the ambulance service. Furthermore, other organisations such as the Citizens Advice, The Mankind Initiative, The National Domestic Violence Helpline and many others had developed specialist knowledge on this matter. There is an importance to keeping records especially in cases like financial abuse as this is (as I found out) strong evidence that you may rely on later. The controlling of any monetary incoming and outgoing was initially seen as caring. But such habits built up into controlling behaviours. This financial abuse crept into all other areas of the relationship. For example, in my case I had to justify anything that I purchased and I had to supply receipts if I visited a coffee shop on my own on my day off. Furthermore, as she had full control of my finances I was unable to save to leave her.

She regularly went through my phone and my work diary questioning every late shift or early start. Very often she would write my shift details within her own diary. If I was off during her work day and went out I was expected to let her know where I had been and to supply evidence – usually a receipt with time and place of where I was at a specific time.

Accused of being unfaithful

The irony lay in the fact that I was often accused of having affairs yet was not allowed to be out of the house without her and if I was I had to regularly report in. Yet, my ex had been having an affair in the early part of our relationship. My ex was constantly jealous and possessive. Furthermore, she constantly accused me of being unfaithful with either work colleagues or friends. She constantly scanned my social media account, diary and phone. Although I would state that my ex was not, what I would call a heavy drinker she became angry and sometimes violent when drinking alcohol. These occasions would result in her threatening me with violence or a weapon, usually a knife.

Sexual assault

My ex often forced me to have sex against my will. My objections to sex arose when I decided I wanted to leave her in October 2016. To combat her advances I would either pretend to be asleep or get drunk prior to going to bed. I sometimes used the excuse of having thrush to avoid penetrated sex with her. It was not unusual for her to hold my sexual organs against my wishes. If sex took place it was always in the dark with my eyes closed. Sex was never an enjoyable occasion with her. But most importantly, I acted beyond my will or consent. My ex always found a way to blame me for her violent behaviour and told me that all men were "bastards". She also wished to punish me for the fact that, in her opinion, her ex (the policeman) got away with assaulting her.

Of course, I often didn't recognise the signs and often made excuses for them or accepting the behavior as 'one of those things.' It is only now that I can see them for what they were. They were wrong and I deserved greater respect and dignity that I was experiencing at the time. Of course, we all accept that hindsight is always a good thing, but I was offering an explanation to unreasonable behavior which seemed right at the time. Being sexually assaulted by your partner is perhaps the most difficult fact to admit or even share. But I found that it happens at a greater rate than is initially expected. There is an expectancy that men should accept any sexual advances set by a female, but this is wrong. Men who have been sexually assaulted or abused also face some additional challenges because of social attitudes and stereotypes about men and masculinity. Nearly 20 per cent of victims of sexual abuse are male and one in five males would experience some form of sexual abuse in their lifetimes, but these numbers could be much higher, because we only have the statistics that are reported to go on (4). The fact remains that as men fail to report it these statistics may be drastically wrong and erroneous. It has been found that 11 per cent of rapes being reported are by men. But men are also 10 times less likely to report rape (5)

Consequences of sexual abuse

Listed below are some of the consequences of sexual abuse. These of course are not exclusively male consequences (6)

- Use of alcohol or other drugs.
- Suicidal thoughts and behaviour.
- Flashbacks and invasive thoughts.
- Nightmares and insomnia.
- Anger.
- Anxiety and fear.
- Depression.
- Mood swings.
- Mental health difficulties.
- Self-blame.
- Difficult feelings of guilt, shame or humiliation.
- Numbness.
- Helplessness, isolation and alienation.
- Low self–esteem, self-doubt, diminished self-belief.
- Difficulties with relationships and intimacy.
- Problems related to masculinity and gender identity.

The media tends to focus on unwanted attacks by men on women, but the reverse is also a factor. Some men feel shame believing that they should have been "strong enough" to fight off their partner. Many men who experienced an erection or ejaculation during the assault may be confused and consider that they are no longer a victim for allowing this to happen. It had now been established that having an ejaculation does not equate to consent. These normal physiological responses do not in any way imply that you wanted, invited, or enjoyed the assault. My ex often forced me to have sex against my will. As previously stated, my objections to sex arose when I decided I wanted to leave her in October 2016. Denial in abusive relationships is a coping skill. At first, denial for me was a mishearing, "did she really say that?". But this turned into an ease as if I pretended to mishear it there would be no consequence to challenging it. Denial, therefore, became a major characteristic of our relationship.

My step mother was an alcoholic. And it killed her. The denial for her addiction stopped her from getting any form of treatment and it became destructive. I once suggested that she had a problem and I got the sharp side of her tongue. Her denial was pathetic as the physical signs (both to her body and the empty bottles all over the place) gave it away. But in a none-physically abusive relationship it is much easier to hide and deny. During the relationship, I found that I was on a continual cycle of denial. One minute my ex was loving and reasonable, then the next she started to break the trust and promises again. As always, apologies and promises were made and I found that I accepted and believed her because I loved her and made excuses for her – it was also the easier option to take. In my case I fed the need for affection by feeding it denial. If I allowed it to happen I would get the acceptance I desperately needed. As the affection reduced I fed it more denial and so the circle continued to a point of destruction. The irony is that as I had perfected the art of denial it had become a part of my character and a character of the relationship.

Denial is the first defence that we learn as a child. I recall my son (when he was about 4 yours old) having eaten a whole packet of jaffa cakes one morning. It was a whole lot of nothing, but he vehemently denied having eaten them, even though the opened packet was still on the floor and chocolate was smeared around the edges of his mouth. It was cute and that's why I remember it so well because it was funny. But for him it was his first line of defence – 'it didn't happen so there can be no justification for a consequence.' In my case I would consider that the abuse didn't happen so still love me – it was okay to say or do that. And now I know that this was wrong.

My denial came in four stages; Firstly, I denied that the problem existed. I refused to accept that there was a problem within the relationship. Like so many other men I stuck my head in the sand in the firm belief that the problems would just simply go away. Secondly, I minimized or rationalized. I could justify why she did what she did. She had come from a disruptive family and so she was a product of that. Furthermore, 'I was a bloke and I can take what she was dishing out'. In effect, I made excuses for her faults and rationalized the behaviours. Thirdly, I found that when I admitted it, I denied the consequences. I came to accept that it was my duty to report in to her three times a day, or to have sex against my would and better judgement. I came to accept that if I took the easy option of doing what was required, I would not face the nasty consequences of what would happen otherwise. Fourthly, I was unwilliing to seek help for it. This was a difficult option to justify but the easiest to carry out. Initially, I just simply refused to accept that I was being victimised by the woman I loved and who I thought loved me back. She had manipulated me so badly that I found the edges blurred and I couldn't see the levels of abuse I had been suffering. She had taught me to accept that it was either my fault (of which I found myself apologising for) or it was a normal part of the relationship. Therefore, why would I need help when I was adamant that I was the problem? When I finally realised that things were not right it came as a shock. How could I have been so stupid to have allowed this to have happened and for so long?

This denial shaped so much of my characteristic. I had perfected the art of locking things away. Or as I often called it 'boxed and shelved' it. I dealt with things at home and left them at home. Likewise, I dealt with things at work and left them at work. I think this is what men do to cope with things in different ways. I had discussed this with other men since and it seems to be a common factor, although some, like myself, never realised it. The consequences of this was that my closest friends at work just had no idea of what was going on. Therefore, were unable to help. Under no circumstance should any shame or blame be left at anyone's door for not seeing it. The fault was mine (although she was ultimately to blame) for being a 'blokey bloke' and not being prepared to admit there was a problem that I could not handle. My denial at work, therefore, created a persona of being a reliable, hardworking (because I never wanted to go home) paramedic. I was known to have a good sense of humour because the art of denial was to either change the subject, become dismissive or to turn it into a joke and therefore, minimise the true horrors within.

Denial within the relationship worked. Making excuses for what was going on became second nature and I often did it without a second thought. The problem, therefore, is further compounded with a trust of myself. During the relationship, I made some decisions that were (and I can only see it now) wrong. I justified her behaviour and made excuses for them. So how can I be sure that the decisions I make now are right. How can I be sure that these are my true feelings if they had been caged and restricted for so long. This new freedom had a bitter taste at times because if I am unsure of trusting myself, how can I trust others? Men refuse to admit that there is a problem (either as the victim or perpetrator). I can honestly admit that I had a history of refusing to accept any problems or warning signs. This is both within an emotional sense (abuse) but with physical ailments too. But by applying varying degrees of denial, I applied a rationale. We might deny that we have a lump; and so make ourselves believe that it's probably a cyst; but it may have been cancer so it could be treated. Sticking our heads in the sand and denying a problem could lead to death – either physically or emotionally. Yes, this is directly aimed at physical and emotional abuse in all of its forms.

CHAPTER 3
Bullying

Before you read any further, I must stress that I am no expert on this subject and do not hold a psychology qualification beyond 'A' level. The conclusions drawn in the following pages are based on how I saw the problems within my own relationship and is not scientific in any way.

My relationship with my counsellor developed slowly at the beginning. I know this was mainly my fault as I was always hostile to the idea of talking about my problems to a stranger. However, on one of the visits we talked about a whole range of things. The main thrust of the conversation was how well I was starting to feel and how things had developed positively over the previous few weeks. However, there was one thing that stuck in my mind once I had left. My counsellor raised the question as to whether abusers are born that way or not? I am sure this whole question had been considered for generations. The whole 'nature and nurture' debate had never really been concluded in my eyes. Furthermore, it is too big and wide to really discuss in these pages. However, with some thought I believe that we are a product of our upbringing. But there comes a point in our lives when we have to make a conscious decision. Do we follow the path based on our experiences? Or do we attempt to break away from some of the negatives that we may had witnessed? Are we able shape our own destinies and characteristics? When I think about some of the school bullies there was no common social characteristic. Some had come from good back- grounds and some from broken homes. They were either male or female but there was some evidence of low self-esteem in pretty much all of them. As an adult these people usually had some kind of professional insecurities that they used to deflect away by focusing on other work colleagues. This is to make themselves look better than they are and so can secure their employment for longer than it is worth. What is agreed on, is that people who abuse are weak and feel powerless so they had to bolster themselves by making others feel weaker and even more powerless. Whether this is something they are born with or not, it is almost always the case.

Having been brought up in a strict, old-fashioned household, I intended that I wanted to be less likely to bring my own children up in the same fashion. My father was a stiff upper lipped, middle class Englishman who never showed much in the way of emotions. This was typical of his generation and certainly his own background. Whereas, my mother was a harsh physical disciplinarian. She had also been brought up in a strict regime by her own parents. I knew just how horrible it felt and how much of a negative impression it had left on me. I decided to take a new path away from my own experiences and made conscious decisions to act in certain ways. Perhaps this was why my self-esteem was already low as I had not really fully formed my true characteristics by the time I ventured out into the world as an adult. When my ex was confronted with problems or difficult circumstances, she would become uncompromising and verbally offensive. I think that she had become so focused on her own

frustrations and inabilities that she was able to deflect them very well. After all, she had had years of practice and experience and a whole host of failed previous relationships to draw experience from. She had turned this into an art. My ex had a very poor relationship with her father (her mother had died many years before). I can now see the pattern emerging that her first male role model shaped her view on all men (she often stated that all men were 'Bastards'). Neither was good. I could almost feel sorry for her. But as an adult, she had made grown up choices and so she was responsible for those actions. I find it difficult to consider that she was 'born' to abuse but developed the ability from her own experiences. It's just that in her case she chose not to break away from it. She was weaker than she had considered herself to be which, as you know, is a key characteristic of abusers. I was sure genetics do play a factor in some abusers. I also believe that some are created. If we are good people, we have a conscience and care about other people's feelings and views. But if you consider psychopaths for example, they have no conscience, and certainly no empathy. Abusers do know right from wrong, and this is perhaps why much of the abuse is held behind doors whereby nobody else can witness it going on. By doing this they can also maintain a public persona which everyone adores. Brian Masters, who had written biographies of several mass murderers including Rosemary West and Dennis Nilsen, identified that humans have the ability to commit evil acts. The purpose of society is to restrain these evil tendencies by laws and social constructions. I also feel that we have some form of inner barometer of what we consider to be right or wrong. It's just that our abusers have them set wrongly.
(7)

I can now see that my ex felt that her desires were more important than the people she hurt and that she was doing nothing wrong. This characteristic is dangerous and destructive not only to other people but to herself. Her actions would become embedded in her daughters view of the world and so the suffering would continue. This can only evoke pity, but I refuse to be an apologist for her. Let's get greater clarification here. Not all criminals, for example, produce children who commit crimes (although they are perhaps more susceptible to do so). There is a point when we learn right from wrong. But it is down to the individual to decide how far our moral boundaries are set and no one is responsible for an adult's actions when they finally decide to take a certain path. Generally, I believe that abusers learn their skills and maintain them for their own profit. I recently read a question whereby it asked if abusers were attracted to certain kinds of people. It transpired that they seem to like people in a caring profession. I cannot profess to know why but I assume it is because a caring person can feed the abusers ego. Perhaps carers are always trying to find the best in people and so, therefore, forgive any negative attributes that they may initially find in an abuser. When I gave this some deeper thought it dawned on me that during the trial it transpired that my ex had a history of abuse towards her partners. What I also found relevant was that a majority of us worked in a uniformed public service. Namely I am a paramedic and her previous was a policeman. Okay, it may be a coincidence but there is certainly enough there to feed a thought process. Of course, before I write anything about this story I do a little research to either prove myself right with my thoughts or to find an alternative view. However, I had discovered that many victims of psychological abuse are often strong, confident, and successful people.

When I've thought about some of the people I've met following my abuse (or for that matter people I had known to have been abused) I had found people to be broken both physically and emotionally. In fact, some (ignorant) people (and I had recently had the displeasure of meeting a few) think of someone in an abusive relationship as being someone weak. From my point of view based on my own experiences this may well be the end result of being shaped and abused, but in reality, they probably didn't start that way. If you would have asked me at the start of my abusive relationship if I considered myself to be abused I probably would have said "no". From the outset, I had had to fight for what I had achieved. I was never given a positive start in life but what I had achieved I had done through my own hard work. Would I ever have considered myself to be strong and successful? I probably would have said "yes". Obviously, this would have been under certain situations. But I was successful. I had attended University three times, I had held a commission in the Royal Air Force and I always seemed to have done well at things I had put my mind to.

But according to Shannon Thomas, a therapist and author of the book "Healing from Hidden Abuse," success and strength are actually what attract abusive narcissists and psychopaths to their targets (8).

Shannon further states that..

"Psychological abusers are attracted to what is going on within the person's life that is shiny, glamorous, or exciting, or successful, or dynamic, or vibrant,"

I see it therefore, that the abuser feels that they are also entitled to this reward and so latch themselves to their victims like a moth to a flame. Why should they work for it when it can be handed on a plate to them? This is certainly a characteristic I now recognise as being a part of my ex. I could list the things and benefits she had obtained from me and her many ex's. However, when her world was about to be turned upside down (ie when I told her I was leaving her) she could only turn to the one defence mechanism she had, and that was a full frontal attack of which she tried to destroy what I had worked for. In effect, if she couldn't have me then no-one could. I had written many topics about what it feels like to be depressed or to be abused. I had also reflected on personal characteristics of a victim. But now it is clear to see. The perfect victim had to be successful and strong, but they also had to be very sympathetic to other people which allows the abuser to abuse unchallenged for so long.

Abused and abuser live under a 'mutual understanding'. This is similar to the master and slave relationship mentioned by Plato many centuries ago. The master was dependent on the slave's loyalty and the slave dependent on the master's maintenance and humane treatment of him. While slaves had to bow to their master's wishes under the constant threat of punishment, they could also become indispensable to them, function as their confidants, and be party to their secrets. The abuser abuses because they can. But if the victim stops it, they no longer have the power and so may move to their next victim. The abuser now thinks that their new victim/partner understands them better than you did and so the cycle continues. As I now see it, perhaps being a paramedic was the perfect ingredient to create the perfect storm. But many other people can put themselves down on this list. Success is subjective, and when each victim compares themselves to their abusers they had had success in life by recognising the decency of themselves and not enduring the relationship anymore. My abuser is left with nothing. Her youngest daughter moved out shortly after her lies were exposed. She does not have the capacity to understand what it is like to treat people with respect and her ride would continue until the metaphorical wheels fall off. The problem is that we may over-give. And when we continue to over-give we find it very hard to say no. Therefore, we have become their chattel. They have complete ownership of our thoughts and emotions. The stereotype is that abusers prey on the weak, because they would be easier to manipulate and bully. This has perhaps been portrayed by victims in soap operas and films. However, this isn't the case because a vulnerable target isn't appealing. They are weak and have not achieved anything from which they can milk from. My abuser wanted someone who was already doing well in life, and also someone who had their emotions under control. My ex, like so many other abusers wanted a "challenge" which would reward them for their efforts. From conversations I have had with people who knew her she enjoyed winding me up because I was seen as laid back and not wound up very easily. She saw it as her challenge to get that reaction and when I no longer fell for the bait the challenge was too much. This made her a very toxic and vicious individual. For her, it's all about feeling superior. Like I have said, it was the 'master and slave' relationship. But without her slave she couldn't be a master anymore. People who engage in abuse of their partners, are often narcissistic and believe everyone is beneath them.

Bullying is a negative behaviour regardless of how it is identified. Bullying in an adult relationship tends to be identified as being 'toxic' or 'narcissistic'. But I wish to discuss how we come to accept this behaviour as adults. When I look back to my school days I can honestly say I was never really bullied. I had the odd skirmish after I started at a new school but that was soon 'nipped in the bud'. But why am I considering writing about 'bullying' in a book dedicated to depression and domestic abuse? Well, I think there is an overlap that is worth considering. When I visited my local library one morning to do some research I came across a book that talked about anxiety and depression. Within those pages came a chapter about how the behaviour of other people can resonate for years afterwards. I thought, therefore, that this of course, is highly appropriate to what I was writing. What I didn't understand is that if my children had come home from school (for example) showing any signs that they were being bullied, I would have been down to the school demanding a meeting with the head teacher. So why didn't I do it for myself? Well a part of my reasoning is down to the fact that I eventually accepted that my ex partner's behaviour as normal and I felt unworthy of her attention. Therefore, grateful of any form of affection that was occasionally shown.

According to the Oxford English Dictionary (2009) Bullying is;

"use[ing] superior strength or influence to intimidate (someone), typically to force them to do something."

Through my own stupidity I had a settled view of what bullying was based on what I saw in my school days. During my relationship I was not punched, kicked or slapped. But I was forced to do things against my better judgement and would. I was manipulated to do things that left me empty or worthless and I was often called names. From generic and basic research I discovered that people who are bullied are more likely to experience:

- ≅ Depression and anxiety,
- ≅ increased feelings of sadness and loneliness,
- ≅ changes in sleep and eating patterns,
- ≅ loss of interest in activities they used to enjoy.

Do you see this as a familiar tick list? If you are in an abusive relationship then you would answer 'yes' to most, if not all of the above. I can certainly relate to these outcomes even after the relationship ended. The experience of being bullied can end up causing long term damage. I found that it is not necessary to be physically harmed in order to suffer lasting harm. Words and gestures are quite enough. I now consider that bullying is an attempt to instill fear and self-loathing into the victim. Being the repetitive target of bullying damaged my ability to view myself as a desirable, capable and effective individual. I considered that during my relationship, if my faults were constantly highlighted, then they must be real. I found that I became thankful to the abuser who was happy to identify them (yet couldn't even see her own). With all of this in mind I now consider that there are two potential outcomes that stem from being bullied. It becomes more likely that you would become increasingly susceptible to becoming depressed and/or angry and/or bitter. I started to believe that I was undesirable, unsafe in every avenue of my life and that I was relatively powerless to defend myself. When victims are forced, again and again, to contemplate their complete lack of control over the bullying process, they are being set up for a learned process which in turn sets them up for hopelessness and depression.

Eventually I started to accept that I was helpless and my situation was hopeless. By virtue of the way that identity tends to work, I was being set up to believe that these things she was saying about me were true. Many years ago I attended a school reunion (I always said I wouldn't go to one, but I did). Whilst there I started a conversation with a girl who was (I would consider to have been) a victim of bullying. Yet this girl was attractive, came from a good home and was intelligent. During the conversation about life following school she identified some key points that had stuck with me ever since. Firstly, she discussed her inability to have ever maintained any long term loving relationships. It became clear that this was due to her own self-worth and insecurities. Her inability to trust anyone was shaped by the way she had been treated. Not only by the classmates she fell victim to, but the types of men she eventually attracted. She had clearly come to accept everything that was told to her with regards to her position within the school society (and by subsequent ex partners). It appeared, therefore, that this self-perception was never shaken. She still carried this burden of worthlessness after nearly 25 years after leaving school. Secondly, because she hated school so much she never reached her full academic potential. I always considered her to be a bright girl whilst at school, but she informed me that due to the fear of attending classes she either skipped them or messed about to try and obtain some form of acceptance from the more popular kids. As a result of this her economic well-being was not great. Due to her lack of qualifications she had to accept jobs based on the minimum wage. Thirdly, her mental health was very fragile. She openly admitted to suffering with depression and anxiety. Medication was now a daily long term reality to support her in her failed accomplishments. She was a tragic figure of which did not fit with how she could have been had things been different for her. Perhaps she was everything the bullies desired. I consider now that they had set out to destroy her to address their own insecurities and failures. But this got me thinking that perhaps narcissist start from an early age and never really grow up or change.

I was thankful that I was not at school during the present cyber age. At least we could go home after school and feel reasonably safe. Technology clearly has a negative side when present day bullies pursue their victims online. I think boys have always had it easier. Boys (based on my own experiences) just have a fight and carry on as if nothing had happened afterwards. Whereas, girls linger the bitterness for months (if not years) and involve just about everyone else in (what starts off as) petty little arguments. I often saw this first hand during my career as a secondary school teacher. A 2004 Spanish college student sample study (https://www.mentalhelp.net/articles/the-long-term-effects-of-bullying) (9) suggested that there is a direct relationship between victim's perception of control over their bullying experience and the extent of long term difficulties they experience as a result of bullying. To put it simply the bullied students who believed they were able to influence and/or escape their bullies reported fewer negative long term effects from having been bullied than did students who felt helpless to influence their situation while it was happening. Rather than try to control the past (either being a victim of school bullies, getting over a toxic relationship or a victim of domestic abuse/violence), it might make more sense to focus on what you can control in the present. Of course for many it is easier said than done when you are living in that kind of relationship.

I believe that the road to recovery is to repair the damaged identity and self-esteem that has been broken by my ex. It's important to feel safe again and to learn that I had something positive to offer other people. Presently, I am still trying to have more control over my moods and accept that medication and outside support is what is required. I didn't think that these are modest aims, but easily accomplished goals that I can achieve in my own time. I've heard it said that the hardest relationships to get out of are the ones that are the most dysfunctional. This may be because you have been brainwashed into thinking that you could never survive without them or you are too weak to make any decisions of your own. It does take time for the mist of manipulation to lift and it is equally fair to say that your friends or family might be telling you this already. I would also like to say, take your time and read through these pages to see if you can identify with anything I have to say. I've considered that it is often more comfortable to stay in the broken relationship rather than risk the unknown. There are countless rational excuses that keep us in the status quo. They can range from being too...

- ≅ busy,
- ≅ tired,
- ≅ broke,
- ≅ needy,
- ≅ and so on.

CHAPTER 4
Leaving

But I now want to consider issues such as where to go, steps to take in preparation, financial issues and what to do when you eventually leave. Leaving your abusive home is legally not a problem. You are not breaking any laws only breaking the cycle of control and manipulation. This is going to be a new you. For me it had been an opportunity to discover myself and to be reunited with the things I used to enjoy. The main problem financially is usually the fact that you didn't have enough money to just leave, not that you won't survive or cope without them. You may have a joint bank account with your abusive partner. Apply for a new bank account as soon as you can. You may need a new permanent address, such as the safe place address, to apply for a new bank account. Doing this would cut you off from your ex and make it harder for them to find you.

I found that I was stuck because she took control of my money and constantly monitored my social media page. She also checked my emails and scanned my phone. Leaving for me was a now or never approach. However, in reality the police became involved and I was removed from the home (I am sure you have followed my story thus far) Finding somewhere to live can be problematic as it is the biggest choice to make before you are able to leave. I considered a shelter but I was unable to find a shelter for men that was local so I could still attend work and see my daughter. This was extremely frustrating on many levels. A great deal of advice both online and at police stations is aimed at female victims and so, as a male, I was excluded from the choice of safety and security. Furthermore, for obvious reasons I was unable to secure a place in a home for an abused woman. Renting my own home was my only realistic option. But again it depends on you having the finances to do this. As stated I had no control over my own money and so therefore, was unable to save for a deposit. As stated previously, if you have a joint bank account open one of your own instantly. Furthermore, avoid using debit or credit cards to pay for deposits etc as you can be traced via these transactions. Another option put to me was the idea of flat sharing. But I considered that this could lead to other problems associated with sharing a property. Furthermore, your problems can become theirs if your ex finds out where you are. It may also be problematic if you need to take your children. I eventually opted to stay with a friend. Initially I was going to stay with my son but I quickly realized that this would have been the first place she would look for me. For me, staying with friends worked really well as my friends were aware of what was going on. In effect they also became my counsellors offering me support beyond what I had been offered in a formal way. Though it may be challenging to find a safe place to go, leaving without a safe place can lead to a night or several nights spent sleeping on the streets. By any stretch of the imagination this could never be recommended. Often, the streets can be very dangerous and risky, regardless of age or gender.

Before leaving make a plan: When do you want to leave?

When can you leave? Is there a time frame when you're alone at home and can pack everything you need and leave? If there isn't because there's constantly someone at home (and you have to leave secretly), you'll have to try to get out everything you need step by step and escape from work or pretending to walk the dog (for example) -so you tell the abuser that you're going to work or walking the dog but instead go to whatever place you've opted for. Take all the official documents you can like the ID, passport, driving licence, birth certificate, work papers etc. If you can't take the originals try at least to make a copy. Take some cash if you can. Avoid using credit or debit cards as these can be used to locate you. Without a doubt, because my ex had access to my account details she could have roughly identified my new location.

If you have to leave secretly and can't leave directly, try putting (for example) two sweaters on and then leave one at work or at a friend's home. I was lucky enough to have a locker at work in which I managed to deposit some underwear and shirts. But be aware though that it shouldn't get obvious that suddenly your clothes are disappearing so only take some. You'll be able to buy new ones later. I was not too proud to admit that charity shops had been a fantastic place to restock some of my lost clothes. With regards to your mobile phone, remember you can block any unwanted calls or numbers you may or may not recognize. Although this may be considered as a counter-measure to disappearing I considered that it was important to inform some people I trusted. I informed my boss where I was staying. I also informed my union representative. But, and this is vitally important, if possible document the abuse with a diary and photos. You might need that evidence later. I found that when I had eventually left the abusive home I needed time to sort myself out. Or to be more accurate I needed time to 'sort my head out'. Whilst I reflect on it I would now say that this is perfectly fine. I found that in my first week of leaving I contacted various people to inform them of my whereabouts and planned actions. Firstly, as mentioned, I contacted my workplace. I felt it was important to do this as I kept work up to date with developments. For me this was especially important as they had wrongfully suspended me and I wanted them to follow my journey to prove my innocence.

As I was now at the lowest point of my life I resigned myself to the fact that I needed help. Contacting a doctor as soon as possible is a very important point to consider. I registered with a local doctor on a temporary basis. This new doctor was massively supportive and due to my openness about my abuse and depression took the time to listen and help. They instantly treated me for depression, PTSD and sleep problems. To ensure my safety and financial independence I contacted my bank to change my address as soon as possible. This is easy enough to do They didn't require identification (other than me inputting my PIN number in to the card machine. There were no unreasonable questions asked and it was done quickly and painlessly. It took about 10 minutes whilst I was on the high street. I found it important to take some time and in effect do nothing. If I recall I spent hours, if not days spent either in bed or just sitting in the bedroom. For me this was a process of recovery. I just wanted to slow things down to a stop just so I could get a grip on things again. But it never once crossed my mind to contact the ex. If I had it would have meant I was playing into her hands and enforcing her view that she controlled me. However, it goes without saying that she had made contact with my son during this period. Furthermore, I didn't want to test the patience of those of whom were not only supporting me but risking their own safety if the ex turned up. Unconsciously I was now finding myself again. I was able to go out for a walk whenever I wanted and took the time to do the things I wanted to do. I found myself returning to my love of reading and enjoying music again. This wasn't an instant process as my mind had to escape the invisible grip that my ex seemed to still had over me. But it was gradual. A day at a time, turning into weeks and eventually months. It was a slow process but one I needed to take especially as I had wanted to leave.

Sometimes, happiness comes from making tough decisions about our relationships. For me, ending the toxic relationship was important to create some form of happiness and self respect. Some people boost our energy reserves whilst others drain us dry. In reality, we each have choices. We often get to decide who we allow into our lives. Not everyone deserves all we have to offer or all of who we are. Therefore, ending a challenging relationship might just be what's needed. Being in a happy relationship is part of life's plan. Happiness is part of that plan. Health is part of that plan. Stability is part of that plan. But a constant struggle is not and shouldn't be something we have to deal with just to get by. Is it ever a good time to exhaust yourself mentally and physically? Is it ever a good time to operate from a place of shame or guilt? What about continually repeating the same behaviour that created the problems in the first place? By continually attempting to fix the unfixable may seem crazy but understandable when you find yourself in that position. It was probably a week before I decided to leave my ex that I started to question what I was observing. I knew things were wrong but I wanted to question how wrong things were. I asked myself the following questions;

- Is the pain too great to stay the same?
- Do I constantly picture an alternate reality?
- Is it impossible to make boundaries?
- Am I the only one that is willing to meet in the middle?
- Is getting an apology (when it's truly deserved) like pulling teeth?
- Does this relationship take more energy than it gives?
- Am I completely fatigued when I was with the person and energetic when they're gone?
- If it's a romantic relationship, are the sparks dead?
- Is the only thing holding me back is my fear of change?
- Am I afraid of what people would think of me if this relationship fails?
- Do I find myself missing the old me?
- How to say Goodbye to Toxic Relationships

Deciding to end a relationship might not be the same as actually leaving. The more entangled you are, the more logistics might have to be worked out. It's okay to take your time and plan the exit and the next phase. I've heard it said that the hardest relationships to get out of are the ones that are the most dysfunctional. The stress definitely takes its toll. That's why it's okay to get some help. By the time I had decided to leave there's no need to force the ex to see my point. If she was going to see it or change, that would have happened a long time ago. At the moment when I decided to go there had been a range of feelings. From a shattered heart to some serious soul searching. Sometimes I had wished I had more compassion and better communication skills; other times, I wished I had got out sooner. Clearly, it's not always simple. I now know that grief is good. Feel it. Heal it. It's natural and not expelling it can have a detrimental effect. Had my life really fallen apart now I moved on? Maybe. It felt like it considering what I was left with at that moment. But maybe that's exactly what was needed to build the life I've been meant to live.

CHAPTER 5
Violence

Violence of any kind is not acceptable, and violence against any gender or sex within the home should be stopped. I now want to argue the fact that violence is not a one way street. Women are violent too, and yet it seems as if it is still a 'dirty little secret' that those of whom are in authority seem to fail to accept this fact. As a result men would still be victims at home and continue to be failed by the police, CPS and the courts. Women who experience domestic violence are openly encouraged to report it to the police. It has been said that men who experience such violence often encounter pressure against reporting, with those that do face social stigma and questions about their masculinity. Furthermore, violence against men is generally less recognized than violence against women, which can act as a further deterrent to men reporting their situation. Some studies have shown that women who assault their male partners are more likely to avoid arrest than men who attack their female partners, (Lupri, Eugene; Grandin, Elaine (2004). "Intimate partner abuse against men". January 4, 2009. Retrieved June 21, 2014.) and that female perpetrators of violence are often viewed by the police, CPS and the courts as victims rather than offenders. As such, men fear that if they do report to the police, they would be assumed to be the aggressor, and placed under arrest.[10] In 1985, the U.S. National Family Violence Survey [11], carried out representative sample of 41 houses where 1 to 10 calls to the police had been made (24 female callers and 17 male callers), found that; When a woman called the police to report domestic violence, the man was ordered out of the house in 41.4% of cases. However, when a man called, the woman was ordered out of the house in 0% of cases.

When a woman called, the man was threatened with immediate arrest in 28.2% of cases; when a man called, the woman was threatened with arrest in 0% of cases. When a woman called, the man was threatened with arrest at a later date in 10.7% of cases; when a man called, the woman was threatened with arrest at a later date in 0% of cases. When a woman called, the man was arrested in 15.2% of cases; when a man called, the woman was arrested in 0% of cases.

In 12.1% of cases when the man called, the man himself was arrested (12)

More than 700,000 men are thought to experience violence from a partner every year – but new research has shown that they risk counter-accusations. The number of women convicted of domestic abuse has quadrupled in the last 10 years, going up to 3,735 in 2013/14 from 806 in 2004/05. It is not immediately clear how many arrests of male perpetrators of abuse against men there have been.(13) It has been suggested that under-reporting is an integral problem with domestic abuse. For example, in England and Wales, the 1995 "Home Office Research Study 191", carried out as a supplementary study to the British Crime Survey, reported 6.6 million incidents of domestic violence in the previous twelve months, compared with the 987,000 incidents found by the Crime Survey. The difference in the two reports was that Study 191 was a questionnaire of a random representative sample of people, while the Crime Survey attained its figures from crime records, i.e. actual reported cases of VIOLENCE.(14) Additional studies carried out in 2010 and 2011 found that whilst 27% of women who experienced domestic violence reported it to the police, only 10% of men did so, and whilst 44% of women reported to some professional organization, only 19% of men did so.(15) Too often it has been heard that "my wife or girlfriend has said if I leave, or tell anyone, she would say I was the one attacking her and she was just defending herself". In my case my ex made it clear that because I refused to have sex with her and was planning to leave that "I was going to pay for that". As a result she contacted the police knowing fully well that the law supports the woman in this case regardless of the truth or the evidence. In 1996 study of 1,978 people in England, only 21% of women who admitted to committing domestic violence gave self-defense as a reason.(16)

Is it too much to expect the authorities to recognize the fact that there are violent women out there? It has become recognized that rates of female violence reported in the UK has increased these past few years. Women are far less likely than men to commit crimes, but rates of female violence reported in the UK has increased. The number of girls and women arrested for violence has more than doubled between 1999/2000 and 2007/08.(17) The idea of a woman being violent, even murderous, is shocking. But why? Is violence at the hands of women somehow different to that at the hands of men? Regardless, we don't treat male and female violence the same. Society tries to justify their actions with a victim like status. Of course, murder is a rare crime within British borders but it cannot fail to acknowledge that females can be violent too. We can also witness first hand the behavior of females whilst out and about in any town or city. It is not unusual to witness a female punching, slapping or kicking her partner (or anyone else for that matter). Society either pities the women who commit terrible crimes or try hard to distance themselves from them. Perhaps it is easier to class woman who abuse or kill as exceptional. Specific cases are elevated to legendary status, and those who commit them are pitied or vilified, rather than understood.

Characterised as "the most evil woman in Britain", Mira Hindley made several appeals against her life sentence, claiming she was a reformed woman and no longer a danger to society, but was never released. Mira Hindley died in 2002, aged 60. The first example is Joanna Dennehy. Joanna murdered three men who all died from stab wounds. The bodies of all three men were discovered dumped in ditches outside Peterborough. Joanna Dennehy, was later sentenced to life imprisonment with a whole life order. Secondly there is Tracie Andrews who murdered her fiancé on 1 December 1996. Tracie was sentenced to life imprisonment after being found guilty of murder at her trial in July 1997 and served 14 years before being released from prison. Another way to deny female violence is to argue that women act only under the influence of evil men. All too often, women offenders are characterised as 'mad' (and so to be pitied, rather than blamed), 'bad' (set aside from women as a whole) or 'sad' (forced into violence by pressure of circumstance, in retaliation or by coercion). This leads to my third example of Rosemary Pauline "Rose" West. Rose was convicted of ten murders in 1995. Rosemary's husband Fred, is believed to have collaborated with her in the torture and murder of at least nine women between 1973 and 1987. Initially, like Mira Hindley it was considered that they acted under pressure or by duress from their male partners. I am not for a moment suggesting that my ex-partner had murderous tendencies, but it took a massive step to admit what had been going on at home. But it was a fact that she threatened violence and the easy disposal of my body. Throughout my relationship with my ex she often reminded me of how she could get any man eating out of her hand and often gloated about her achievements with members of the opposite sex. She made it quite clear that her blonde hair and blue eyes could help her get away with anything. This, I feel was endorsed by the police action on the day of the arrest. Of course, the police acted in her interest and she conveniently made the effort to shed fake tears. But this over shadowed the facts as they were presented. She had no injuries, I had no record of violence and there was no hard evidence to back up her claim. But the police opted for the idea that women are victims, thus, she must be right.

Whilst reading around this subject I came across an article about Caroline Aherne (Royal Family TV show fame). It transpires that Caroline inflicted all kinds of abuse on her husband Peter Hook (Joy Division and New Order bassist). Peter Hook married Aherne in Las Vegas in 1994 but the pair split three years later. What struck me was that the public persona clearly does not reflect what goes on behind closed doors. This was my case also. To family and friends she was seen as meek and polite. Unfortunately, my father fell for this facade and never made any form of contact with me to ask me what had gone on. In fact it was suggested to me that perhaps my father thought he had a chance with her – she would have loved that. Yet behind the scenes she was abusive, threatening and far from the image she had created for public viewing. Peter Hook came under criticism as he revealed what had been going on after her death. Yet I can appreciate the fact that he may have felt he would not have been believed if she had remained alive.

Peter wrote:

"Yes I loved her, yes she could be very funny, and there were times I felt privileged to have a private audience with such a great comic talent. But she was also a very troubled person and nowhere did that manifest itself more than in our relationship."

He further said Aherne, tried to "brainwash" him with negative comments before becoming physically abusive. Describing the start of the violence, he wrote:

"She attacked me, using her nails to scratch at my neck, tearing off my necklace and ripping my top. It was proper shocking stuff… And although she was really contrite the next morning it marked the beginning of some serious screaming-banshee behaviour – putting cigarettes out on my arm, attacking me with bottles, knives, chairs and other assorted furniture…It would be set off by the slightest thing – talking or looking at another woman was a favourite."

Having watched The Royal Family (although I was never really a true fan) you marry up the image of the character with how you perceive them to be. Perhaps this is where my concerns arise with the blonde hair and blue eyes of my ex. The public persona does not match the private character of a bitter and dangerous woman.

The dictionary definition of persona states;

The aspect of someone's character that is presented to or perceived by others.

I further came across this article whilst researching what was written by an ex policeman. It is interesting to note that even the author admits that the police had failed and continue to fail. Furthermore, it takes an "ex" policeman to admit it. Anyway, have a read. You will find the article at –

http://www.huffingtonpost.co.uk/bob-morgan/male-domestic-violence_b_3962958.html (18)

I was a Metropolitan Police Officer through the 1980s, 90s and up to 2006. Like most ex or serving Police Officers I had seen the reality of domestic violence in its many forms – from harassment to minor assault to rape and murder. In the 80's the Police were very bad at dealing with domestic violence but as the years went by I think we became slightly better at it – we got a bit better at supporting women victims – we got little bit better at arresting the male suspects even where we thought the victim may not want to go ahead with a prosecution – and this was right thing for Police to do. By being positive about taking action the victims often felt more able to see the matter through.

We followed the direction of the training we received and started to get better with dealing with the women as victims and men as perpetrators. However in one important way we failed almost entirely – that is in recognising and dealing with domestic violence against men. Having been out of the Police service for a number of years and having become more aware of the issue of violence against men I started to look back at the incidents I had dealt with and at first didn't remember a single case of it. Then I remembered one serious incident where a man was fatally stabbed by his girlfriend – and it occurred to me that I had not recognised this as a domestic crime with a man as victim. We had dealt with it for the serious offence it was of course – she was arrested and prosecuted. Then I started to think about what happened in many of the other cases of domestic violence and remembered how some men had complained that they had been attacked and said they had merely defended themselves but which had led to a wife or girlfriend being injured. Sometimes we would had believed the men – other times we would had arrested them because the strong emphadise then – as now – was on women as victims and men as perpetrators and it was often his word against hers. But we rarely – if ever – thought in terms as men as victims in the domestic setting.

I hate to think how we probably arrested some men who were actually the victim because we didn't believe them and in fact failed to deal with the real perpetrators in these particular cases. I should be clear about this – I definitely didn't recall any man saying that they were constant victims of abuse – but I bet some of them were. Too many women suffer dreadfully from domestic violence and we must do more – it is clear that women are more often the victims and suffer worse levels of violence overall and I would want any man who does violence to a women to be arrested – unless it was lawful self defence. But it is also clear to me that we had not said and done nearly enough to address the needs of men as victims of domestic violence and we still didn't.

According to the Crime Survey of England and Wales around 800,000 men and 1.2 million women were victims of domestic violence last year. Violence against men is a topic usually addressed only in passing before we get back to discussing domestic violence almost exclusively in terms of women as victims and the figures suggest this view does not reflect the reality of domestic violence. In debate and in reports and articles violence against men is often mentioned but usually only in passing before going back to talking about the matter almost solely in terms of women as victims. Of course words do matter because they later become the actions of the Police and others in the criminal justice system. We need to do more than merely recognise this as an issue we need to change perceptions and mere passing references to the issue of violence against men would not achieve that. To seek to strike a fairer balance on this should not detract from the work that needs doing to protect women. But to continue failing to recognise males as potential victims in anything but the very clearest terms is a problem. I am not sure how the Police approach these matters these days – but judging by the imbalance in the public debate I worry that this problem is still not recognised and men who may had been the victims of violence are not only not being supported but might well be arrested when they had defended themselves. The Labour Party had proposed a 'women's champion' to tackle domestic violence against women – and this could be useful in providing much needed extra support for women – but no mention of the 800,000 male victims!

We must do more to protect and support both men and women as victims but we are still not taking violence against men as seriously as we should and this needs to change.

You only have to type in a few words into google to discover that domestic violence against men has been going on for centuries. Although conceptions have changed the protection for men has not. Historically, any man complaining of being a victim of domestic abuse at the hands of his female partner, have left him open to ridicule and further abuse. As a result, many men have retired further into a shell of denial and continued victimisation. In my case I turned to the police who instantly opted for the easy solution and treated me as the criminal. Furthermore, the heavy handedness and blinkered anti-man approach of social services had stopped me from seeing my daughter (is this not legalised kidnap?). What is really upsetting is that all of this had developed from the word of one person (my ex) who set out to say she would "destroy me" if I left her. The authorities therefore, supported her behaviour. I've still not been able to speak to anyone to give my side of the story. Why would they let me, as I would be challenging their views on domestic violence (as men can be victims)? Of course, I fully intended to complain about my treatment to both the police and social services after the trial. However, I am also prepared that they would close their doors and deny that there was a problem. This of course, further compounds the reasons why men do not complain about their abuse.

In the 21st century when we claim to have real equality it doesn't stand up to scrutiny in these cases. I was a victim whilst in my relationship, I became a victim following my escape and this is perpetuated and maintained by the state and those I was supposed to trust. Whilst searching the internet I came across a dissertation by Khawaja Akbar, called "Law and the Male Victim of Domestic Violence." In it he comments about how the system had let men down both historically and presently. He touched on the fact that these services are completely out of their depth and opt not to improve their flawed system. It is flawed and I was living proof that it is.

CHAPTER 6
Scapegoating

I had just finished reading an article about how, throughout time, societies had focused their attentions on specific groups or individuals when blame is required. This form of negative focus is known as 'scapegoating'. By definition, the scapegoat is a person or people "made to bear the blame for others." The scapegoated individual or group is seen as a threat to the successful functioning of the group as a whole and therefore must be rejected. As far as the group is concerned, the scapegoat is the sacrifice needed to ensure survival.

Usually when I had a moment of inspiration I often sit and digest what it is I am considering. I consider that Scapegoating for me had a number of homes in which it resides. Firstly, it sits very comfortably within an abusive relationship. Secondly, having depression can have a negative effect upon some professions and finally, society uses it to focus its failings on. Scapegoating has led to violence against and the degradation of groups of people throughout history. It has been witnessed by genocide in the Sudan, "ethnic cleansing" in Croatia, the Holocaust in Nazi Germany, apartheid in South Africa, lynching's in the American South, honour killings of women in the Middle East and South-east Asia. It had often been run by a stronger section of society enforcing its power over a weakened group. This is, and can be mirrored within the family home. From my own experience abuse was developed over time without objection from me in the beginning. Power was handed to my partner by my apathy to rejecting it from the outset. I became the centre of attention when blame for something needed to be applied. For example, I would be blamed for incidental things such as running out of milk. Or I would be blamed for things I had no input over, like comments from her ex husband or events at her work.

Blame was easily proportioned to other people, namely myself, rather than her taking responsibility for her own actions. This removal of focus ensured her righteous persona to everyone else.

Ultimately, she could justify physical and sexual abuse on to me when it was I that objected to such behaviour. It became my fault for her actions, therefore, becoming her unreasonable justification for such violent acts. I, therefore, become the scapegoat for her inadequacies. The abuser justifies it by creating a reason to abuse that just does not fit with the reality.

So how did my abuse and depression create problems at work? During my time as a paramedic I came across at least three members of staff who were taken 'off the road' due to illness – to be specific, mental illness. Although it was justified as a chance to recover, it still sent a shiver down my spine. I considered that I would be seen as not good enough to do the job if I declared my illness. During my practice, I had never been disciplined for failing professional standards. I had a list of commendations from members of the public for 'jobs' I had done. Yet, I knew that if I had informed my superiors of my condition I would be seen instantly as unsuitable. In effect I would have been scapegoated due to my illness as being inferior to what my job required. I feel I would have been judged at work for having an illness. Would I suddenly be unfit for practice for having depression and/or PTSD? I would have been ashamed to step into the staff room with the label of 'depressive' hanging over me for everyone to see. Mental illness is still seen as a weakness of which I would have been ashamed to admit. Even now very few people of whom I worked with know that I had depression. How could I have gone from being a good member of staff one moment to being one of questionable abilities? My illness made me a scapegoat of peoples lack of understanding with regards to my abilities. Nothing changed in my abilities or character based on a false disclosure by the police. When scrutinized it makes no sense to do so. I was being judged for living in an abusive relationship and not getting out earlier. Not being able to leave was due to a range of circumstances out of my control. It didn't make me a failure. The lack of support ensured the continuation of my victim status. There are no male refuges within any proximity to where I was from and worked. Furthermore, scapegoating would be further enforced, as a male victim within an abusive relationship is still a social embarrassment. I would be a target to ignorance from outside quarters, but I was also a scapegoat within my own home. She could justify her abuse because she failed to recognise her own failings and so I took the blame.

Society still views people with mental illness as being emotional or crazy. They either didn't take us seriously or they fear/pity us. The media also does a discredit to mental health patients. Time and again when news stories hit the headlines about some murderer they always find a link with some form of mental illness. Is it not, therefore, labelling every mentally ill person as a potential murderer? Or are they scapegoating a section of society for societies failings? It is of courses easier to blame a section of society that are unable to defend themselves than face their own failures and shortcomings. People should not be discriminated against for mental illness. It is illegal to discriminate based on gender or colour yet, I had seen and witnessed discrimination based on depression. An illness of which is difficult to treat because people still see it as a stigma (I did for many years) and so the condition continues. It is easier to scapegoat these people rather than address their own failures. This is especially so within a relationship, the workplace and society as a whole. People can't control what they are born with and shouldn't be ignored or made fun of because of it. People should not be defined by their mental status. Some of the nicest, intelligent and strongest people I have ever had the pleasure of meeting had depression. However, people born with a mental illness such as depression face disbelief instead of support. Without help and support they may resort to self-harm, ridicule or even suicide.

CHAPTER 7
New Terms

During my research I came across a number of phrases that I had never heard of before. One of them is a term called 'gaslighting'. This term is used a great deal by our American relatives. So what is 'gaslighting'?

Gaslighting is another branch of mental abuse. Without realising, this is a powerful form of manipulation in its most awful form. If you are in an abusive relationship you would have been subjected to this type of exploitation at some time or other. Gaslighting seeks to sow seeds of doubt in a targeted individual or members of a group. The result is that the targeted then questions their own memory, views, understanding, and at worse; sanity. It is implemented by using denial, misdirection, contradiction, and lying. It finally results in the targeted individual to question their own beliefs and knowledge about a certain event or action of which they had previously been sure of. As a result, the abuser takes greater ownership of your understandings, knowledge and question-ability of their actions. Below are listed seven stages of how a gaslighter dominates their victim (the points below are excerpts from; How to Successfully Handle Gaslighters & Stop Psychological Bullying, by Preston Ni).

1 – Lie and exaggerate

My ex was proficient at being able to lie and exaggerate. She was able to create a negative narrative about me ("There's something wrong and inadequate about you"), thereby putting me on the defensive all of the time. I found that I was always being compared to her ex (incidentally, of whom she had tried to have arrested but her allegations were proven to be false – no charge was brought against her). She always had the ability to criticise my fathering role – although her own parenting skills were questionable also.

2 – Repetition

Joseph Goebbels was once quoted as saying that, "…. if you repeat a lie often enough, people would believe it." Repetition, like psychological warfare, is when the falsehoods are repeated constantly in order to stay on the offensive, control the conversation, and dominate the relationship. My ex would continue to criticise and find any opportunity to find a reason too. This action became her daily obsession and chore. She found a hook on which to constantly reel me in with. As my psychological well-being had been so downtrodden (with her dubious evidence), I came to believe her objections and began to agree with her views and opinions.

3 – Escalation

My ex was able to step up her offensive behaviour (escalation) when challenged. When called on her lies, she escalated the dispute by doubling and tripling down on her attacks on me. She was proficient at refuting the evidence with denial, blame, and more false claims (misdirection), sowing even more doubt and confusion. When I discovered that she had been messaging another man of whom she had been seeing regularly behind my back, she flatly denied it (even though I had spoken to the chap directly before I asked her). She had suggested that I had imagined the whole thing. She even went further to suggest that I needed medical help.

4 – Wear down

A favourite trick of my ex was her attempt to wear me down. She continued to stay on the offensive, until the point came whereby I was utterly worn down. I became self-doubting and anxious and I further started to question my own identity, and reality.

5 – Co-dependency

This behaviour formed a relationship based on co-dependency. The Oxford Dictionary defines co-dependency as "excessive emotional or psychological reliance on a partner." I can now see that I felt constant insecurity and anxiety based on what she told me of who I was. As a result, she seemed to have made most of the decisions. This was because I was made to think I was incapable of making such important choices. Furthermore, I was unable to see friends or family without her direct approval. This element created a relationship that was based on fear, vulnerability, and downgrading.

6 – A battle on two fronts

My ex had the ability to play Jekyll and Hyde so often it was difficult to see the edges of her personality. It became a battle on two fronts. She often gave me hope that she had seen the errors of her ways and would spend moments explaining her actions that would draw pity from me. Therefore, justifying her actions. Occasionally she would show me tenderness and kindness.

7 – Divide and conquer

Her ultimate objective was to control, dominate, and take advantage (divide and conquer) of everything around her including her own daughters. She maintained and intensifying her lies to continue the image of perfection to other people not in the relationship. She involved my father to try and gain numbers for her quest. This action was to increase her personal gain over my self-respect. With gaslighting, it feels as though the ground is always shifting beneath you. There is no centre of gravity or a single point that you are able to focus on. Throughout these pages I have suggested that you keep records as soon as you have doubts. These records showed me that there was a distortion of the facts as I knew them. This, although I didn't know it at the time was gaslighting. My records kept me focused on the fact that I was being abused. The reality is that you would never change a gaslighter. They are unsure themselves of what is black and white because their own distortions have weakened their own state of reality. They only gain success if they have drawn you into their whirlpool of self destruction.

Another term to understand is the one entitled 'love bombing'. Love bombing is an evil, wicked tool that builds their victims to a high. Then instantly brings them crashing down with disastrous results. Love Bombing is a tool mainly used by sociopaths or narcissists who try to control the relationship with bombs brimming with "love" right from day one. Narcissists and sociopaths thrive on drama and they didn't care what form it takes. 'Love bombing' is another weapon in their arsenal of abuse and manipulation. The heavy bombardment of love actions that may appear very similar to "love". But these actions are extremely overwhelming and deliberately executed. It is so intense that the bombing can effectively sweep people off their feet and cause high levels of infatuation, as the target is unaware that it is a manipulative means to gain attention. The perpetrators mainly focus on the weak or vulnerable in society. It is the main weapon of paedophiles or other sexual predators. These victims may be at a vulnerable stage in their life and the love bomber swoops in and naturally seems to fill all the voids. They play close attention to painful emotional wounds, weaknesses and insecurities. They would tell their victim everything they want to hear and they often express dramatic displays of affection. However, anyone can be taken advantage of and can become a victim, particularly people following a difficult break up or depressed state. Love bombing is initially carried out through excessive phone calls, text messages, emails, and so on. Also they express the constant desire to be in close contact whether virtual or physical and the desire to be connected almost every moment of every day. These three stages may not just happen once. The cycle can go round and round on repeat until either the abuser becomes bored or until the one who is the target sees through it. The stage of 'Idealization', is where the love bomber identifies the needs of their victims and attempt to fill that void with what they wish to offer their victims. Love bombers are masters at flattery. They constantly tell their victims how much they adore them, how beautiful they are, how funny, talented, special, precious and any other sweet nothing they can think of. Love bombers would make their partner feel as though they are the only person in the world. They talk about subjects such as; how grateful they are to finally be understood, what terrible previous relationships they had, how they had found the love of their lives and so on. The love bomber finds the process of 'Devaluation' stimulating and just as exciting as the early days. As their victim's self-worth has been determined by the bombers words and actions. From this point the love bomber begins to rip the victim apart. They have become proficient at knowing which buttons to press that would trigger the emotions the bomber requires. Finally, 'Discarding'. When the victim starts to feel strong enough to break away, the cycle of love bombing goes back to the start to the start and the vicious cycle starts all over again. This scenario is repeated and repeated until one or the other can bear no more.

Love bombing is similar to gaslighting. Love bombing is a predatory move. It is intended to lure and attract a victim so that they feel irreplaceable and fall unquestioningly into their trap. The love bomber doesn't need to make any real emotional commitment to their victim. Love bombing is a one-way game, with the simple goal of destabilizing and derailing the person being targeted so that they become very easy to manipulate. Gas lighting has similar attributes. The person convinces the victim that they have some form of problem that only they can understand and therefore, give the impression that they being helpful and supportive – perhaps the only one in the world who can. As identified, the one being bombed can quickly become co-dependent on the love bomber. This is especially when their confidence low and it comes at a time when they appreciate any form of approval. Once dependency has been achieved and the bomber has obtained what they set out for they would quickly lose interest and they would no longer find the relationship fulfilling. If the victim starts to question the 'realness' of the relationship, the bomber would attempt to cause maximum damage. They would be outraged that anyone has dared to challenge or question them. Especially if it's their partner of whom they had claimed to love and adore. As narcissists refuse to, or cannot, deliver such things as commitment, respect, honesty, authenticity or intimacy and so see this as a personal attack upon their character and ability to love.

After the challenge, the love bomber would retaliate by becoming emotionally distant, withholding affection, blaming their partner for the downfall of the relationship, using silent treatment, moods or even temper tantrums to cause emotional torment. All of the initial flushes of romance dissipate and the victim is left craving the intensity of what they once knew. It is also quite likely that the love bomber would disappear for days or even months at a time to deliver a timely and crushing blow.

The big wide world is full of pitfalls and trip hazards. The problem with 'love bombing' is that we feel the bomber is offering us everything we have ever desired. They seem to protect us from the evil and wicked world in which we live. These people are false and set out to use their victims for their own gratification. Love bombers sit alongside 'gaslighters' on the manipulative scale. If you are vulnerable, perhaps due to depression or a desire to be wanted following a disastrous relationship. You are clearly in their sites. I hope that these pointers have helped to identify these individuals (both male and female).

CHAPTER 8
Anxiety

Anxiety is a good thing. It stops you from heading into dangerous or unusual situations. It is a normal reaction to things that we dread. For example, as a teenager, I always felt anxiety before entering the exam hall. As an adult, I get anxious every time I have to have a blood test – I just hate needles. I have known other people become anxious if they spot a spider within close proximity. Every time I get anxious my mouth goes dry, my breathing increases and I feel light headed. Sometimes I sweat and I can hear my heart racing. But this is normally a short lasting period of panic. There is nothing wrong with any of this. It's good and it's natural. But what is life like when anxiety takes over everything? I have given this some deep and meaningful thought. The only example I can give is that after an earth quake (depression) there is always an after shock (the anxiety). After having my personality shattered I then started to question what I knew or understood. This led to having anxiety about doing normal everyday things that I had previously taken for granted. I found that my anxiety gave rise to other psychological problems. Such as:

≅ trouble sleeping
≅ lack of concentration
≅ feeling depressed
≅ loss of self-confidence.

These feelings became a problem when they were too strong to deal with. My anxiety generally made my life difficult and making choices even harder. Following a range of research carried out over a long period of time, it has been established that sufferers and survivors of domestic abuse experience increased levels of anxiety. Living in constant stress or fear can indeed create a constant raised level of anxiety. (19)

I always lived in fear of what I would expect to find when I got home from work. The above examples of how I felt (dry mouth, increased heart rate and so on) was often a characteristic of my journey home. However, I could also add the churning feeling inside my stomach. Once home, I would feel anxious about her ever-changing moods and behaviour. This anxiety was a result of living in fear. And this living fear became a habit which increased my anxiety and depression. And so, the constant cycle continued. When I found that my living conditions were stressful I had no opportunities to offload, other than going to work. I was not allowed out on my own and I had to contact my partner at least three times a day when I was at work (sometimes I had to include a photo so she could see I was in uniform). I had no opportunity to relax or de-stress. Also, I couldn't socialise with friends or family and so had no escape from the captivity I found myself in. What was worse was that a home should be a haven yet it became my prison. However, what I found once I had left was that the same levels of anxiety still existed. I had learnt that following the lack of support I had received, and the lack of help from the authorities the world is a dangerous place. I felt vulnerable and often experienced nightmares. In effect, the life I had led remained after leaving the environment. Now, I had become accustomed to the feelings of fear and vulnerability even though I was no longer living under that regime. It had also been found that people who are exposed to any form of abuse or persecution, tend to develop extreme social anxiety, or/and stress related illnesses. Sadly they can also develop confusion over their own identities. (20) Emotionally abused people can experience post-breakup symptoms similar to post-traumatic stress disorder (PTSD).

I worked out I had PTSD after taking a walk one afternoon. I heard a song that she used to like and my mind was rushed back to a moment I heard in the kitchen when she said she was going to have me killed. Other occasions also cause PTSD such as smells, colours and even types of cars. My mind would associate these 'items' with periods of stress and unhappiness. As a result it took me a while to try and do normal things like listen to certain songs. Even shop in certain supermarkets. I no longer visit certain places, not only for the fear of bumping into her but because these places had so much association with the cause of my problems. Anxiety had left me hesitant although I am able to often hide it well. My anxiety had taught me to be even more suspicious of authority or kind actions by others. I know that this would be overcome. It had to. I had a lot of support in place and I had created nice, easy personal goals to give me a level of achievements of which to reflect upon. The abuse left a long dark shadow that created, depression, PTSD and anxiety. With enough light and reflection this shadow would recede and I would be able to replicate the person I eventually want to be.

PART 2
DEPRESSION

CHAPTER 9
Depression

It was when I was doing one of my favourite past-times that I came to a realisation. I was sitting in a coffee shop at the time. Nothing special one might think. But it is when you think about it. You can sit in any coffee shop and you can cross the paths of people from every back ground. These people come with a wealth of experiences and knowledge. One group of people caught my eye. They were a group of young people, in their twenties. Watching them, they were clearly happy in each other's company. Although they could be heard laughing and sharing a range of stories, they were not imposing on the rest of us in the shop. What struck me after several minutes was that by the number of those who were sitting around the table at least (statistically) two or three of them would suffer some form of mental illness at some point in their lives. If it was suddenly revealed by any one of them around that table that they suffered with depression would the tone of the conversation have changed? Would they have alienated those individuals or embraced them? Since thinking about this I have had two trains of thought. Firstly, do we now have a new generation of people who are now more accepting than any generation prior? Secondly, what if there is still no change? Perhaps we have not moved on as well as we believe society likes to think it has.

Society, in my view has moved on with regards to so many aspects of life. Men and women are considered equal (although this can be challenged). Homosexuality is no longer a crime. There are laws in place to protect those of whom suffer a physical form of disability. Yet, I struggle to see equality within mental health concerns. I do accept that society no longer chains 'the mad' to the walls anymore, but there are some of whom are still subjected to medicinal chains and become restricted due to their side effects. Society is a fickle madam. It accepts concepts based on a fashion and understanding. Let me explain this better. I recall a lecture once whilst at university. It discussed how the female form within art had changed. At one point the voluptuous female figure was seen as more desirable as extra weight was seen as healthier and wealthier. Yet magazines today (and certain elements of art) reject this in favour of the stick thin model, who perhaps shows restraint from indulgence and control over image.

Mental health has also had its ups and downs of acceptance. George Fox for example, the founder of the Quaker movement, clearly suffered schizophrenia. George Fox openly stated that he heard voices which drove him to religious compulsions. After all, how many times have we heard about the return of the new messiah. Would Jesus be accepted today or would he be locked up? Who knows, he probably had returned but we had rejected him (or her) in the name of self-protection. And he/she is buried in a mental health ward as opposed to turning water into wine. It was during the 80s that certain things were not mentioned. AIDS was considered an illness for those who deserved it. Prior to that the condition of shame was cancer and was referred to as 'The Big C'. Yet, I do feel that depression is the new leprosy – it is considered shameful and hidden away. I have been open and candid during these writings. Perhaps, too open at times. But consider this, I have suggested that it is okay to be open about this condition yet not everyone of whom I know, knows that I had it. It is easy to share comments and views over the internet, within these pages or by word of mouth yet, I had been very selective about who knows any of this. When I told someone this, they asked why. They knew the answer to this before I even opened my mouth. I am still scared of being judged. We know depression is not contagious but I fear being cast aside and perhaps being identified as; 'Leon – the one with depression'. As opposed to 'Leon – the one with….. the cute smile, or something.' It's crazy to state this but I know this is the case. Other suffers had also told me this is so.

Depression has been a throw away comment used and often misused on a regular basis. I had often heard people say they are 'depressed' when in fact they are feeling 'slightly down' about a particular topic. I can recall a time when the news columns spilling their headlines after a particular boy band split up. The media has the habit of focusing on the inconsolable teenage girl walling like a banshee stating she is 'soooo depressed' about the end of the band. That's not depression, that's her not understanding what depression is and using the title to defend her stupidity. It exaggerates a feeling to suggest sympathy which is not justified. Instead of understanding depression as an illness, many people view depressed people as simply being sad or refusing to be happy to gain attention. This outlook can harm the esteem of depressed people, because these people may begin to feel guilty for their feelings if they accept this view. It has been said that depression is a western illness. I was once told that because we in the west has more leisure time we fill it with thoughts which lead to depression. Therefore, I believe that ignorance is more damaging and leads to segregation. It is easier to turn a blind eye than accept that our brothers and sisters are the same as everyone else in every other respect.

Any form of mental illness does not indicate mad, bad or sad. And so society has no right to reject that individual. Yet it does. I have previously stated that when a crime is committed the media instantly find some connection to a mental health condition. This is a tragic and dangerous conclusion. Mental health is not a prerequisite to a life of crime, but the true crime is the ignorance of people allowing the preconceptions to continue. For those without depression or any other form of mental illness I want to tell you this. It might be a shock but, some of the nicest people I have ever met have depression. I have found them to be far more considerate, polite and understanding than those of whom claim they didn't suffer. People with mental illness have had to be more understanding as they can appreciate what it is like to be judged or to feel unwell. They equally value each day as it comes and take absolutely nothing and no one for granted. I, therefore, applaud their strength by keeping their condition hidden to avoid the shame and ridicule that is heaped upon them. In an ideal world, I want to remove convenient labels that are placed on mentally ill people. Previous scapegoats such as homosexuality, Judaism, colour of skin or gender and so on are accepted without prejudice. Can this not be done for depression too?

So, returning to my group around the table. Are we now living in an age where those seated would reject those suffering or not? I would like to think they would accept the suffering into their arms. But alas, I am still sceptical. Society needs a scapegoat and those of whom are not protected are the easy prey. Mental illness is not protected therefore, the cycle of self-protection secrecy would continue. Depression needs to be celebrated not hidden. Many great historical people suffered with depression (Winston Churchill, Buzz Aldrin, Graham Green to name just three) but it is conveniently acceptable to forget that in honour of their greatness.

It recently dawned on me that I was part of an exclusive club. I didn't wear a badge or carry a membership card. But it requires a certain feature to be a member. Not many of my friends or family know of my membership, and I would rather it stayed that way (I was not a Mason either, before you jump to conclusions). Although, when I say it's exclusive – it isn't really, because it transpires that there are actually millions of us throughout the world. Let me try and make this a little clearer. I learnt to drive when I was 17 and at 45 I've never been without a car. I've had some fantastic cars, and some real shockers. But I've always had a car of some sort. Since having a driving license I have always adored 'Bentley's'. They are such beautiful cars. The curves are such that I want to run my hands over them. The interior is such that I would happily sit inside for hours on end. And as for the engine, the roar is like an untamed beast insisting on liberation. What is there not to like about such a thing? But, if I had all the money in the world I would never buy one. Why? One may ask. Well the answer is simple. I wouldn't want the attention. It would fill me with horror to think that people are looking at me. So, I was happy with my VW Golf. It does what I want (except the boot is too small). It got me from A to B and no one gives me a second look when I drive into town. It can absorb itself into its surroundings and can be easily forgotten by people who see it. It just doesn't shout out "look at me".

So, what has this to do with depression? This is complicated to answer but I hope that you, the reader, would be able to understand. I am proud to have survived this illness to date although I have had it all my life. Yet I would rather the people who knew me didn't know about it. I didn't want to be judged I want them to know me for the persona I am allowing them to see. I am happy to disappear in a crowd. But this is an exclusive club to be in because some of the nicest people I have ever known have depression. And we are quiet about it. Perhaps it is because we didn't want to draw attention to something we had been made to feel ashamed about. We didn't want people pointing and judging.

Since setting out to write this book I had often taken steps to see how other people with depression get through life. I had found many depressive types. For ease, I have broken them down into three different categories; There are people who think they had depression – but didn't. These are tragic types. They shout from the highest peaks telling everyone how much they deserve attention and how life has been 'so hard' for them. These types get over depression as soon as they become occupied – or get the attention they think they deserve. Then there are people who know they have depression and are willing to talk about it only if they feel they have too. They cope with life on a secret basis based on techniques they had developed but didn't have the energy anymore to hide it as well as they used to. Finally, there are people who had depression and take measures to hide it. They struggle with the suffocating pain but didn't wish to make a fuss in-case it creates greater problems. They had created a persona that fits with how they think they should be seen. These depressives are tired but are still holding on. For this book I want to completely dismiss type 1 depressive. They give depression a bad name and only suffer with their own vanity. Recently, I had been able to identify those types who try to hide it. When you are one it takes one to know one. But there are features I want us all to recognise. People with depression can identify someone's pain from a distance. What is worth knowing is that they can feel the pain others are experiencing. Depressives don't want to feel pain and as such feel the agony in others, yet know there is little they can do about it. I can think of people I know with depression and I had spoken to a couple of them. The relief on their face when I share my feelings and thoughts is immeasurable. They are relieved that someone understands. Yet I had only ever told them privately. It's just easier that way for everyone involved. What surprises me is that many of these people had no idea I was a sufferer. Well, that's simple, I perfected the art of hiding it but I found I had sympathy for those of whom had not yet mastered the art of camouflage.

Many depressives have had a lifetime of judgements and so do not want to judge others. I for one, do not wish to be seen as judgemental. We have all reached this point in our lives based on actions we had experienced. Who are we to judge others when we feel so little about ourselves? A depressive would always love you for who you really are, not how you want to be seen. I adore all of my friends but especially love my depressive friends because they are genuine and would do anything to protect others within their circle. That takes a special kind of person of which non-depressives can't appreciate.

From my own experiences, I have found that when talking to a depressive you don't have to say much. Listening is an art. Depressives don't want sound bites and certainly not sympathy. They just want to say things and not for you to speak but to listen – and of course know they are not going to be judged. Throughout my time with depression I have found that everyone thinks they are an expert and are keen to offer their advice (which is often wrong). I didn't need advice, I had a life time of that. We just want someone to listen and offer an alternative view – which is not advice. We just want to know you are there. Demands are not being made on anyone and there is no duress to make you stay. They just want to either listen or to be listened too. I had found that meeting other people with depression come from a range of backgrounds. Their journey to realisation had come from many sources and causes. As such people with depression are far more considerate of others than any other section of society. Our experiences are far and wide. I know that people find different ways of dealing with their suffering. As a result, I would never make direct suggestions to them as that would be inconsiderate. What works for me works for me and may not work for others. Therefore, I appreciate other people systems they have in place. If it works for them, then well done. A depressive would never intentionally hurt anyone. I know I have hurt people and this has become a heavy burden I carry. I have said "sorry" so many times and undoubtedly will continue to do so. Equally, I am always happy to welcome back into my arms those who hurt me – although I may remain cautious. I consider depressives as (generally) friendly. I know I try and appreciate the best in everyone. Equally, I try and offer the best I can to anyone. Is this a friendly characteristic? I hope so. But when I think of people I know with depression they would always stop to say "hello" and ask how I am. Even though I would always tell them that I am "okay". We say we are "okay" because we don't want to be a burden to others when we know they may have problems of their own. Yes this is being friendly, but it also overlaps into consideration.

This is something people with depression rarely recognise. I have and would openly talk about the decision to end it. Having survived these periods, I can now call myself (today) a survivor. When I made my mind up to go I was ready to end it. It was only circumstances or coincidences that stopped me.

It takes a strong personality to stop doing something that you have drive and conviction to do. So, any survivors out there I personally congratulate you. We have all made it this far and this is something people without depression would never be able to appreciate. Surviving in a hostile world is a daily struggle and getting through each day is far more than a simple achievement. It's an accomplishment. I had sat for about a week or so prior to writing this. I had tried to get a grip on who I am aiming it at. Am I aiming it at the depressive, the non-depressive or those of whom know a depressive? Well, on reflection, it doesn't matter. From the depressive point of view, I want to congratulate you for being a survivor and being the good person that you are. It is we who are in the exclusive club of which we didn't want people to know about. But I am proud of my association with other depressives and my illness. I think it made me into a good, caring man. And my associates are just lovely people – it's just that you don't know it yet. Or, perhaps like myself, refuse to accept it.

For those who care for a depressive I want you to recognise these qualities that your loved one has. Let them know it. If needs be get them to read this book. We know we can't be easy to live with and we know that. But I feel a depressive has a lot to offer . Its just that you need to be patient with us. I have found that many people just didn't know what to say when they come across someone with depression. Especially when it is a loved one or someone you consider to be close. I understand that people may say things with the best of intentions. But these can often be wrong.

My experiences have ranged from people saying nothing to being downright rude and offensive. For me the most offensive was either "pull yourself together" or (and this really used to make my blood boil) "get a grip". I found it better if people just said nothing. I just wanted someone to just sit there and to let me know they were nearby. 'Kind' words were not needed, because words didn't really ease what I was experiencing.

Studies show that mental health problems of all kinds, including depression, are caused by chemical and electrical imbalances in the brain. This means a depressed person's brain does not have the capacity to dwell on positive thoughts and feelings. Telling someone with depression to think their way out of it is a bit like telling an obese person to think themselves thin. It just doesn't work. Furthermore, a depressed person has probably spent most of their lives acting positive to keep other people happy. It has now got to the point whereby they are exhausted carrying out this fakery. And can now longer 'act' to keep you happy. Having spoken to other people about what they have experienced I compiled a brief list of some of the most stupid comments ever uttered to someone with depression. If the problems are being belittled it feels like a personal attack, and it may make the problem worse. People need to understand that victims have a different outlook on life and that your belittlement does not help to solve the problem. The victim's experiences are just as varied as everyone else's and may have had a different outcome previously. One of which you could not imagine (perhaps).

Medical treatment is necessary for most people struggling with depression. I have fully embraced medication and counselling to beat my depression. I have also come to accept it as an illness. Diabetes is an illness and you would expect a diabetic to take medication. So why can't a depressive be afforded the same dignity? Depression kills and needs to be recognised as a potentially fatal illness. Yes, it might pass but equally it might not. By saying "it would pass" is highlighting the person's ignorance of what it means to have depression. Alas, there is nothing dismissive about what it feels like to have such a heavy burden to carry.

I can understand why people say "Being depressed is better than ... ". I feel they are trying to put the illness into some form of perspective. However, it makes the sufferer feel as though you think they are making up their illness. Worse still, the sufferer may feel that their illness is irrelevant and small. Depression prevents normal thinking and so nothing has a true perspective which you balance with. Depression is not a condition of which people choose. Ideally depression wouldn't exist. But it does, and when it takes over it does not discriminate on how it grabs a hold. It suffocates and swallows its victim whole. There is nothing to compare it with.

"It's your own fault."

This was a favourite of my ex. She decided that her actions were based on my faults. Never tell a depressed person that they are struggling because of their own actions. Just like any other illness, I had no say or decision of when it would strike. One day I could be well and strong and the next the complete opposite. So outside factors didn't usually dictate how I felt. Therefore, it wasn't my fault, or for that matter anyone else's fault (this was certainly the case in my younger years). There needs to be more recognition from other people to acknowledge what a struggle it is to keep going. Certainly, never blame a sufferer for what they are feeling or try to point some form of blame. In an abusive relationship, this creates a power imbalance whereby the abuser deflects the blame for their actions onto the victim. "It's your fault" they may state "for being…" Therefore, beating the victim further down into the depression abyss. Someone with depression isn't just feeling down; they're experiencing a state of illness. Though considering the good things in life might help to emphasise the positive, it isn't a whole solution for someone with medical problems. I had spent hours pouring over old photographs recalling happy moments. I had tried again and again to see how lucky I am. Indeed, I am lucky. I have beautiful children and very good friends. I have a job people would love to do and I am reasonably healthy. So didn't you think I had counted my blessings? I have spent probably 40 years trying to pull myself out of depression and I was not very good at it. That is why I had sought further help and support.

"Don't feel sorry for yourself." This is a misunderstanding of where depression comes from. Clinical depression is different from getting the blues, and requires much more than a change in perspective to turn around. Depression cannot be shrugged off easily. We all have the blues at times but the two are in no way connected and cannot be treated the same. A person with depression knows when they have the blues and they also recognise when they are having a period of depression.

Although the phrase "I know how you feel." might seem helpful, saying you know how your depressed friend is feeling can actually be patronizing. My depression is not a temporary state as I had had it for years. Therefore, what I am feeling or experiencing could be vastly different to what you think I am feeling. It is appreciated what you are saying but it is wrong.

There is nothing wrong with trying to be supportive to someone with depression. In fact, I strongly advocate it. However, every case can be different. I strongly consider, that a little more thought is sometimes required before saying anything. I would also equally confirm that is sometimes okay to say nothing. As stated at the beginning of this chapter, just letting the person know that you are there is often enough in the fight against depression. A warm hand to hold or a friendly face to recognise would be enough. One day I took the step to tell a friend about what I had been through. I wanted him to know because I could see the signs that he was also suffering with depression. The difference between us was that I was more proficient at hiding it. He stated during the conversation that he had no idea that I had depression, but felt refreshed that I was able to share it and identify his plight too. I am able to say with great confidence that I have had depression for most of my life. Most people's teenage years are riddled with angst but I lived in a loveless home, I had accepted that I was adopted and evidence of depression was starting to emerge.

As I reached my 20s I was fully aware that there was a problem and started to seek some form of identification of what it was I was suffering. By the time I reached 30 I knew I was a sufferer. I adapted to my life and came to accept it. By the time I had reached mid 30s I was fully proficient at hiding it. I had learnt this because depression at this stage was seen as a weakness and there was no room for weakness in any parts of my life at that moment. As a result I had adapted and developed clever ways of hiding it from pretty much everyone around me. Unfortunately, this act stopped me from getting the professional help I needed at the time. In effect I had fooled myself into believing that my depression was not a problem and manageable. My depression went unseen and unrecognised. I was able to conceal my depression so well that I became conditioned to deal with my inner demons on a daily basis. This way my depression was not clearly visible to people who were not aware. By being able to do this I knew I had cracked the code of being able to hide my pains. I was not being deceitful, I was protecting myself and those I love. In effect, I intentionally made efforts to appear happy and upbeat. The perception that those with depression all have a dreary personality is false. My depression was more than just a mood. It was a way of life I had learnt to adapt to. I had learnt to create a happy persona that often required recycling old jokes and actions because I knew they worked at particular times. My depression was my pain and not anyone else's. I didn't want to bring anyone else down by exposing my true feelings. Depression for me felt like leprosy. I feared being rejected and cast aside. An outsider. Unloved and unclean. I had felt rejection at an early age due to my adoption and this was more deeply ingrained than I had given it credit for. I felt that if I had let someone in enough to see the depression, they would walk away. As a result, I can see now why I had had a series of failed relationships. It endorsed my need for secrecy, out of fear of rejection from those of whom I love. There was nothing more painful than to expose the ugliest layer of my personality that I wished to hide even from myself. During my lowest periods I knew how to avoid any unwanted attention. The use of humour was good, but I also used a tactic I called 'questioning'. I found that people often liked to talk about themselves. From this approach, I would ask an open question that required them to discuss their views and feelings on a subject. By doing this it required them to speak for longer than I needed to, hence I didn't have to talk or explain.

My relationship with medication was always a bit 'on and off'. I took them and then when I felt better, I stopped (foolish to do this). In-between these periods of medication I used to use activities that offered a routine. This gave me goals to reach by certain times of the day. It was often in the form of music, walks, and so on. If by 5 o'clock for example, I had made it to the time of day for my daily walk, then I was doing okay. I had always known that alcohol can be problematic for people with depression. As a result I became tea-total to avoid falling into its grasp. This was further validated by witnessing the effects of alcohol on people around me and ultimately my stepmother. I knew that caffeine was an upper and so was sugary foods. As a result, I favoured coffee over tea and could polish off a large amount of sweets quite easily.

I had spent most of my life trying to work it all out. Especially the meaning of life. Is it a pursuit of something, or are we to reach certain points in various stages of our lives? As a paramedic, I also witnessed a range of deaths. I quickly learnt which were more favourable ways to die over others. I feel I became an expert in death and its aftermath. As a result, even now whilst I feel okay, I have no fear of death. However, I must admit, following my treatments and medication I have given less time and thought to the latter. My goal in life was that I had a purpose. What I was needing to do was to find something that was worthwhile otherwise my life had been pointless. But for me I also needed reassurance that I was moving in the right direction (whatever that is or was). Recognising my depression also gave me a feeling of inadequacy. I felt inadequate compared to the people around me. Everyone was happier than I. Other people were better at their job than I and this compounded my feeling of being a failure even though I was fighting a battle to give my life a purpose. I felt I even failed when my best efforts were in place. As a result I was always trying to compensate in my life for the frailties that I had inside. Even now I am still striving and searching for more to validate my purpose in life. The reality of my life with depression is that I had been striving to find love and acceptance. This stemmed from trying to be accepted by my adopted family to the need to find my father. But the reality is that everyone strives for this requirement. It's human nature. My personal advice is to never turn away from a person who seems to be struggling. Love us, especially when it's difficult.

I once heard a quote from Stephen Fry who stated that

"I hate the fact that I had [depression]..... but I wouldn't want to live without it because it is a part of me that I had come to accept..."

What I want to say to my friend who I shared my secret with is this. I knew you had depression from the moment I first met you. How? Because you showed all the signs that I had perfected. As I had highlighted, it takes one to know one. Embrace it, it has made you the outstanding man that you are.

I was never really one to share my feelings or emotions with anyone and this became a problem within itself. I found it difficult to share what was going on and even more difficult to admit that I felt a failure and was a victim of my female partner. It was often found that I was justifying her actions and felt that in some way I deserved what I got. I was made to feel grateful that she was questioning everything I did or challenging my thoughts and feelings. During my relationship with my ex I felt as if I had a bag over my head. I could not see where I was going or what was happening and I just could not breath.

Following my encounter with the police I quickly learnt that everything I believed to be true, was clear nonsense. I was always led to believe that the police were there to protect us from harm. Yet when I needed their help they were far from helpful. As a result my long lack of trust was further cemented. I hated the world I was living in and hated what I knew to be true. Life became physically painful and it was a real effort to do the simplest of things like getting up or eating. It took a while to realise that the cause of my problems were no longer present in my life. Yet, I still had the habits of feeling that I needed to tell someone where I was or what I was doing. I had fear of going home, not knowing what to expect as I walked through the door and being verbally and emotionally abused. It also took a while to realise that her allegation of assault had no foundation or evidence and was based on sheer spite as she found out I intended to leave her. Of course, the events had and would change my perception of the world around me. I considered a new career. I was tempted to just disappear and start again somewhere else. I've considered so much but why should I run when I was the victim? Yet, I was suspended from work, I couldn't see my daughter and I had lost my home. Would this have happened if I had been female? I very much doubt it and the proof is in the status quo of my ex.

I would consider myself to be what's known as a 'blokey bloke' and as a result taking medication for me, was the equivalent of admitting there was a problem. My policy was not to take drugs unless it was a life or death situation. When I saw how medicine solved problems, I considered that;

- ≅ It was a sales ploy by the medicines manufacturers.
- ≅ They (the patient) should not have got themselves into that position in the first place.
- ≅ There must be other alternatives to medicines.
- ≅ The miracles of medications are often offset by side effects.
- ≅ Taking medication could be seen as a failure.
- ≅ You're not as strong as the people around you
- ≅ You would be judged.
- ≅ There is a stigma to taking medication (especially medications related to depression).

But when the choice was either dealing with the discomfort or taking medicine, I would always choose the discomfort. After all, it usually sorted itself out after a while anyway. I am aware that depression had played a major feature of my life and had, to a degree, shaped my personality. I didn't begrudge this as I am (today that is) reasonably happy with the way I've turned out. Of course, we all have our faults but I am happy to accept mine. As a paramedic, I often came across patients suffering some kind of physical trauma. It was both reasonable and morally right to administer some kind of pain relief, or a mixture of medications to maintain life. Yet, when it came to mental health it was somewhat different. This was partly due to the failures of the NHS to treat mental health on the same level as physical conditions. But it was also my male pride refusing to accept that I had a problem that could not cure itself. I must admit I've never really been a big fan of pills. My arm would need to be hanging off before I would even consider taking a paracetamol. It's not that I was being macho or anything. It's just that either I could not be bothered or thought they might not work. But I now want you to consider that there are benefits to taking medication. In my case Sertraline. Considering what I had been through and what I was experiencing I felt that I really needed some sort of support. After all, I had opened up to the idea of seeking counselling (which was a new experience) and so some form of "medication" may be beneficial. I sought treatment almost instantly following my release from the police back in May. My doctor initially gave me a low dose – just to see how I got on with them. I must admit it took a while to see any sort of improvement. Although there are other forms of medications available it is really is a case of trial and error to get the balance between any benefit and side effects. Initially my small dose of Sertraline seemed to be okay but, like I said, I had been given a low initial dosage. When I next visited my GP as a follow up and to see how I was getting on, I wasn't surprised when she suggested upping the dose. It is so difficult to consider how I would have been without them. But it's not a problem to see them as form of mental crutch. My view is that if I had broken a bone it would have been treated in a standard, recognised way. Okay, my head is broken, but I didn't see it as a problem to have medication to help me through this. After all, it was pride that had stopped me from getting things sorted in the first place.

During the early stages of me leaving the abusive relationship I decided to open up for the first time in my life and talk about what had happened at home. I opted not to stay silent anymore and talk about it. It was not easy to admit that I had been abused by my partner. The agony of sharing details related to sexual abuse was deeply shameful. I felt, and still feel that I would not be believed. To my surprise my manager was very understanding. As a result counselling was instantly offered. Throughout my life I had been wary of attending to such things but I felt that I had nothing left to loose by going ahead and see to what they had to offer. As you would expect, I had lost all faith and trust in any form of authority and so approached my first visit with some caution. Thoughts and feelings were shared and related topics discussed. It took about four weeks of two visits a week, to eventually be able to see things a little bit clearer. It had been a roller coaster of emotions and feelings. Suicide was not far from my thoughts as the system it felt, was clearly stacked against me. As stated, I was not allowed to see my daughter. I was suspended from work, and the social workers had not been doing their job properly by keeping me up to date. And as for the police, they were utterly useless

As requested I attended the police station following my 101 call. The police officers were utterly hopeless. In fact I had bought it to their attention that whilst I was there, not a single note had been taken. It was quite clearly a waste of everyone's time. Following my acceptance of dealing with depression and accepting that I was a victim of female abuse I researched (although not deeply) about why I felt so tired. I also wanted to know why I felt no emotion over things and was suffering with physical pains throughout my body.

It has been shown that chronic pain might not only be caused by physical injury but also by stress and emotional issues. In particular, people who had experienced trauma and suffer from Post Traumatic Stress Disorder (PTSD) are often at a higher risk to develop chronic pain. However, my mental pains had evolved over a short period of time. As previously stated I had been going through a period of tiredness and then I found myself suffering with physical pains. The only way to describe how I felt was to liken it to the pains following a heavy period in the gym or after a boot-camp. Not only was I still tired but I felt aches and pains in my joints, back, feet and suffered terrible headaches. These pains were prolonged and lasted for a long period of time. But let me be clear, I had not suffered any form of physical injury or had previously suffered with any similar symptoms. But I was sometimes finding that the pain would debilitate my ability to move with ease. But to make matters worse I had realised that it seemed to have increased my feelings of hopelessness, depression and anxiety. Prior to these pains I really thought I was doing well. A few months before this, I had locked myself away from people and sat in my room either reading or watching TV but again I was now finding that I was becoming introverted again. I had no time for other people and didn't really enjoy going out and about like I had previously. I had gone full circle. I felt I was getting better and then I found myself back to how I was. This 'merry-go-round' was exhausting in itself. I am familiar with the knowledge that emotional stress can lead to stomach pains and headaches. But I was wondering if my muscles were screaming out after a period of tension – was there a correlation? Had my muscles and joints become fatigued and so, as a result became inefficient?

Never in my life had I realised how wicked and cruel society can be to those who are finding things difficult. Perhaps my anxiety and stress had found a new focus at the abandonment I then felt by the people who should have helped conclude the events I had to endure. I think it may be reasonable to suggest that this was another form or branch of PTSD. I had this for a while and I had found a way of being able to manage it to a satisfactory point. However, I now consider that my cup had overflowed and it had all become too much. Peter Levine, an expert on trauma, explained that trauma happens;

"when our ability to respond to a perceived threat is in some way overwhelming."

Most researchers disagree on a precise definition of trauma, but do agree that a typical trauma response might include physiological and psychological symptoms such as numbing, hyperarousal, hypervigilance, nightmares, flashbacks, helplessness, and avoidance behaviour. I can accept all of these points. During and after the events I could now see that I fell into a 'survival mode' and so it may had been acceptable to consider that I was having difficulty to revert back to 'homoeostasis' of which seemed to distant to remember. This had seemed to create a vicious circle which was difficult to 'jump' from. I had actually found that I handled stressful situations so differently than before. I recently witnessed what would be considered a stressful situation (an accident on the motorway). As expected I felt nothing and had no consideration at all for the events as they unfolded. However, my physical and mental pains were making me feel as if I was being traumatized all over again, but in a different way. Perhaps I am not explaining this at all well. I just hope that you as the reader can understand what I am trying to say. I didn't feel stressed about stressful situations but I was getting stressed about how I had changed physically and mentally. Although people may not be aware of the lingering effect of a traumatic situation, or believe that the traumatic event had been put behind them, my body seemed to be clinging to unresolved issues. As my counselling sessions came to an end I actually felt as though I needed it more than ever before. I knew that I had laid my 'blokeyness' aside but I also recognized that my PTSD was rearing it's ugly head again. In fact, PTSD had become such a major part of my daily living I was wondering if I could include it on my CV as an occupation. When tiredness hit it was all I can think about. Nothing can get me to focus on anything else. I became tired and that is who I became, a man who was tired and needed sleep. I was not following any crazy schedules or working late shifts anymore. I was making a conscious effort to eat better. But I now discovered I could fall asleep should the opportunity have arisen. I awoke at a normal hour of the morning then found myself dropping off to sleep again after a short while.

I was aware that coffee and sweet foods can have an impact upon my sleeping patterns. As a result I cut out sugar from my drinks and I had reduced my coffee intake to about two cups a day. Of course, I had recently come out of a stressful situation but there were other stresses still going on. But nothing much had changed. I had started to feel better about myself but this was undoubtedly due to the medication and the coming to the end of my counselling. I was advised and undertook a blood test for something unrelated and nothing was highlighted. I had no change in my medication. So, what on earth was going on? I spoke to a medical friend about this and she drew an interesting comparison. She suggested that the psychological stresses that I had experienced – including the acquittal at court, may now be having a physical output. I was aware that I had been very near to breaking point and only kept it together because of the positive support I was receiving. But my physical health had clearly been side-lined. At the time I was getting more than the minimum requirements of sleep. I found that I was getting between 8-10 hours of sleep a night, then at least a few hours during the day. After a while I was starting to suffer with back pains and the odd leg cramps. My belly had returned and my skin was starting to look poor compared to how it used to be. So a lot of what was said made sense. But I didn't know what to do about it. I had been fortunate enough to have had time away and I was getting back into reading again (of which I had always enjoyed).

Following some simple research, I discovered that physical tiredness also brings about the following:

- ≅ Feeling drained mentally and physically – Literally everything involved an effort. As stated I could drop off to sleep whenever I got the opportunity.
- ≅ Inability to bounce back – This had been the case for a while. I realized that I had no emotions whatsoever. This had still not changed. I was not saying I am emotionally

void, it's just that I see a little more perspective on things and so didn't get so involved in things anymore.

≅ Headaches – These came and went but nothing blindingly bad.

≅ Joint pain – I had horrendous back pain. I had no idea what had caused it but it had been slow to disappear.

≅ Depression – Goes without saying.

≅ Poor short-term memory – I often had difficulty recalling what I had eaten yesterday but I could tell you in great detail events that happened years ago.

≅ Weight gain – My belly had come back. I worked hard to lose it a while ago but there it was, it was back.

Now, I know I was not being a hypochondriac and hoped that this would just go away, but following the recent events I didn't want to see my GP again. I was sure she must have been fed up of me at some stage.

Depression is often connected to problems with sleep. It can either be too much sleep (hypersomnia), or too little sleep (insomnia). There is also some debate about whether it can be the cause of weight gain and/or weight loss. My thoughts considered all of these factors and the benefits of medication, namely anti depressants and zopiclone. It had been estimated that more than 80 per cent of people suffering from depression had problems with their sleep (21), usually not getting enough . However, I had found that during my periods of depression I sleep more. This type of tiredness is like a constant state of exhaustion, which takes over your body from top to toe. It starts from the mental exhaustion from the daily battles you have inside your head. It affects your emotions, causing hypersensitivity and complete numbness and running the emotional gauntlet in between. Having to constantly explain or justify why you're tiredness was exhausting in itself. Being constantly tired made me feel weak and vulnerable. It made every decision harder to make and often meant not being able to think clearly or focus on the things you previously took for granted. I found that my sleep regime was dependent upon the events of the day and my general mood. There are, however, two major considerations that helped me sleep; Going to the gym had been beneficial for a number of reasons. Firstly, it offered a routine. I tended to go in the morning and then had the afternoon to 'get things done'. Secondly, it was highly recommended as a form of treatment as the body produces 'feel good chemicals' into the body following a good work out. Finally, it gave me an appetite when I left otherwise I probably wouldn't have bothered eating at all.

CHAPTER 10
Medication and 'mind-drives'

It took a while for my medication to work but this is a well-known consideration when taking anti-depressants. In my case I found that it took about four weeks and an increase in dosage for any measurable effect to be recognized. As previously stated, I found my sleeping pattern was very random. However, we now know that sleeping patterns of somebody with depression is very different to normal sleeping patterns:

- ≅ It takes much longer to get off to sleep
- ≅ The total sleep time is reduced
- ≅ There is little or no deep sleep
- ≅ REM sleep occurs earlier in the night

There were more frequent awakenings during the night, which lasted long enough for me to be aware of them. I often woke up early in the morning and couldn't get back to sleep, even if I was still feeling tired. Finding it difficult to sleep it can be extremely distressing. Fortunately, I found a number of things that helped me to improve my sleep. Below is some general advice for anybody who has difficulty getting to sleep.

- ≅ I found that getting into a routine with your sleep times helped. I got up at the same time each morning, even if I had not had a good night's sleep. I tried not to sleep during the day, and didn't go to bed early to try and get more
- ≅ I took some physical exercise during the day. This helped to make my body more tired in the evening and made it easier to get to sleep. Exercise is good for you physically, and there's also research that suggests that exercise can

have an antidepressant effect.

≅ Although I have stated that exercise is good for you try and avoid taking exercise in the two hours before bed. This is because exercise 'activates' the body, which can make it difficult to get off to sleep.

≅ Avoid watching disturbing or violent films prior to bedtime.

≅ Avoid drinking caffeine (tea, coffee, cola) in the evening after 6pm. Caffeine is a stimulant and can prevent sleep. Drink no more than four cups of tea, or of coffee, or cans of cola in a day. As previously stated, I reduced my coffee intake to just two a day.

≅ Drinking herbal teas or milky drinks such as Horlicks in the evening seem to offer some support towards sleep. Herbal teas didn't contain caffeine and milky drinks had been shown to be as good as sleeping tablets for many people. However, be aware that chocolate or cocoa milk drinks often contain caffeine.

≅ Avoid heavy meals in the two hours before bedtime. It can be extremely difficult to get off to sleep with a full stomach.

≅ Although I have been tea-total for many years, it is still useful to suggest avoiding alcohol in the evening. While alcohol is sedative, it is not a good idea to try to use it to sort out a sleep problem. This is because alcohol does not lead to normal restful sleep. In addition, alcohol causes you to pass increasing amounts of urine, which further disrupts sleep. Unfortunately, a significant number of people with depression develop an alcohol problem from using alcohol to help them sleep so trying to avoid alcohol intake is the better option if you can.

≅ You should associate your room with sleep: avoid having a TV or radio in your bedroom. For similar reasons do not check your mobile phone in bed or work on your laptop.

≅ Your bedroom should be warm and familiar with a comfortable bed and duvet, etc. Ideally, the room should be decorated in a relaxing way. This all helps in associating the room in your mind with restful sleep.

During my professional life I came across Zopiclone a number of times. I was aware that it was normally prescribed for insomnia but at the time I had never put sleeping problems and depression together. I did find that early on following my arrest I was subjected to regular flashbacks of events that happened during my relationship with my ex. Initially my GP was hesitant to prescribe zopiclone but we concluded that it was worth a try to help me get some form of sleep and rest. Zopiclone is usually prescribed for the short-term treatment of insomnia. Long-term use is not recommended, as tolerance and addiction is known to occur. I've been lucky with Zopiclone as I had managed to avoid some of the well-known side effects. These are listed as being dizziness, nausea and vomiting, headache, confusion and nightmares. However, be aware that just because they work for me doesn't necessarily mean they would be right for you.

Like myself, I discovered that a large number of depressed people experience overwhelming loss of energy. This can cause a person to stay home and avoid social interaction, and prevent a person from starting or finishing projects, maintaining previous interests, or exercising. The effects of diminished energy compound the effects of depression, when work, school, and family obligations are compromised. Also, lack of activity results in loss of muscle tone, muscle mass, and, eventually, bone mass. In turn, these effects lead to degeneration in physique, strength, and physical well-being. When depressed people lose the energy it takes to accomplish basic tasks, important needs such as eating are compromised. I had experienced this first hand. I had, like others lost my appetite. This in turn resulted in erratic eating habits and missed meals. The subsequent weight loss could result in nutritional deficiency and mental and physical sluggishness. I eventually realized that people with depression often have an increased appetite resulting in gain weight. These same people are usually the ones who oversleep. Problems sleeping are therefore, normal when it comes to dealing with depression. It does need to be managed otherwise it can create problems in other quarters and this may lead to an ever decreasing circle of despair and problems. I would like to suggest that when you are ready go and speak to your GP and have a go at trying out the gym.

When you sit and think about it, it's amazing how things can change so quickly. One day I was a family man and the next I was an enemy of the state and a not fit or anything. Equally so things can change within a few hours. One particular day I awoke early knowing I was going to see my counsellor. At this particular point in time I was pleased with my progress and equally keen to share my positive thoughts with her. As always, I arrived early and we discussed my feelings and how I was coping with daily experiences. I was proud of how I had changed over the last few days and started to feel ownership of myself and my thoughts for the first time in ages. As usual I had planned to go to the gym afterwards but here is where it all changed. I left my counsellor and sat in the car exhausted by talking and discussing. Perhaps I was not as advanced as I initially thought I was but I was okay with this. I knew it would be a long process and it was still early days. Instead of going to the gym I opted to drive to a coffee shop and pull myself together a little bit more. Whilst drinking coffee I contacted my daughter's mother asking if I could arrange a video call with my daughter. She replied after a while stating that she had social services coming around the following day and she would discuss it with them then. My god, even hardened murderers see their children, yet here I was, innocent of any crime (other than staying in an abusive relationship longer than I should have). This continual blocking cut deep and further enforced my anger at the injustice and heavy handedness of it all. If there is a domestic accusation you are indeed considered guilty until proven innocent. I would also point out that I had still not had any formal notification from social services about their actions. Well I returned to my friend's house and retired to bed. It was a place of safety for me. There was nothing wrong with this but I was starting to become aware that my recovery was taking longer than I initially gave myself credit for. My slow progress impeded my desire to go out and socialize with friends and work colleagues. Now when I say socialising with depression, I didn't mean going for a drink with your mate who happens to be called depression. It means leaving the house with an overshadowing feeling of guilt and pain.

Attempting to socialise when you can barely live with yourself is incredibly hard. Being able to put a smile on your face and tell everyone that everything is okay can be difficult or a normal part of your day. You've been doing it for so long that it becomes the norm. I found that not socialising or even going out was right for me at the early stages of my depression. I didn't want to go out. Mixing with other people – even complete strangers in supermarkets, felt personal and imposing. It's crazy to think it but I felt people were judging me without knowing what I was going through. In fact it became hard work to act 'normal'.

Part of my recovery came in slow steps and still is. On reflection I can see how it developed. I was encouraged to attend counselling which stimulated my need to get out of bed and leave the house. From there I was further encouraged to attend the gym. Now see this from my point, firstly, as I had previously stated, I was never one for talking (as I saw myself as a pillar of masculinity) and secondly, I was never one for the gym (not with my white chicken legs). But this created a routine that had been crucial to my recovery. Don't get me wrong, I went out occasionally between trips of routine. I might have had a coffee in a café but I was happy to sit in a corner and people watch (which is enjoyable in itself). But I felt this was something I should be doing as opposed to something I wanted to do. We all have different personas for different social situations and to overlap these can be both personal and encroaching. At work I was expected to be strong and supportive for other people – perhaps this was my own standard. But hiding my pains and difficulties became a normal act. At home and inwardly, I was a mess and I didn't want people who (I suspected) respected me for the characteristics I was willing to share publicly. Letting work colleagues see the other side of my character was a personal difficulty. Before all this happened, I had been invited out to a work mates leaving do. This had been planned for a while. Whilst with my ex I was often discouraged from going out with my work colleagues or socialising without her presence. I found it both hard and hurtful to think of excuses why I couldn't go whilst protecting my ex from her own stupidity and maintaining my socialising standards amongst my friends. But I was really looking forward to seeing my work mates after a reasonable period of time not seeing them. At least for a day or so prior to the leaving do I started to consider not going.

- ≅ I wouldn't be missed if I wasn't there
- ≅ I was too tired to attend
- ≅ It would feel awkward seeing people who would assume negative reasons for not being at work
- ≅ I felt a sense of shame about my depression

I was finally encouraged to go by close friends. It came as the 11th hour to pick myself up and break with the routine of not going out to the pub or out in the evening. I purposely arrived an hour later than the invitation time set. A few people were already there but what instantly struck me was how pleased those few people were to see me. The smiles felt genuine, but what is important to state is that no one asked or put pressure on me to say why I had not been around. I would stress that because of the shifts and work patterns of my job, it is not unusual to go for a period of time without crossing other people's paths. Of course, one or two people there knew why I was off but they made me comfortable, didn't judge and actually made me smile. I left earlier than everyone else but that was because I was tired. Socialising when suffering with depression is hard work and, I would admit, it left me shattered. From the outset I was not going to hide the fact that I was suffering with depression and PTSD. I was adamant that if anyone asked I was going to tell them. It transpired that many other people there had either been a sufferer previously or knew someone that was. This was refreshing and I felt it very supportive to think that other people were both okay with it and it almost seem normal to have such a condition. The following day I received a text from an ex boss who attended the social event. He stated that he was pleased to see me and was glad that I was there. It was nice that he took the time to send the message but it was also nice to consider that my presence was valued. Furthermore, breaking away from a controlling relationship still leaves scars of guilt when you do things beyond the norm. I initially felt twangs of guilt for going out alone and still considered asking for receipts for drinks.

Recovery is long and hard. But you must socialise with the people you care about as soon as you feel fit to do so. Furthermore, didn't be ashamed of depression. It's nothing to be ashamed of,. We should all feel proud that we have survived what is an extremely difficult time.. Whilst writing these pages and reflecting on events, I had discovered that I hate to use the word 'journey', it's just too cliché. What I had gone through is a list of experiences that had got me from A to B. For me this description of events is far better that calling it a 'journey'. I was re-reading through some of my recent pages and comments and I came across a comment that someone had sent about not being comfortable about going out. Together with this I also read an article about rebuilding a shattered life and not being able to go out.

Now, don't get me wrong but I was not claiming to be an expert on this matter but I can only reflect and share my own experiences.

I recall a conversation I once heard as a kid whilst travelling on a bus. During this said conversation, some girls were talking about the importance of dressing nicely (mainly when they went out) and this had stuck with me ever since. As a result, I once put this into practice the first time I went to buy a brand new car. I once walked into the show room purposely wearing jeans and a grey t-shirt. The result was that I was ignored. A week or so later I entered the same show room wearing a suit, shirt and tie. As a consequence, I had more people offering me assistance than I could shake a stick at. So what does this prove? Well, we have all heard the line 'clothes maketh the man'. This is so true. We are judged by what we wear or the accents we use. They draw a stereotype which may often be wrong but it is first impressions that count. I must admit that although I am aware of this pitfall I still do it. I'm not going to make any apology for it, as it is a form of unconscious self-defence. So how does this fit in with not feeling well? This was a direct question put to me once and I had to think long and hard about how I was going to answer this. Put simply, if you feel good you start to, well, feel better about yourself. Dressing nicely is the first step to building self-confidence because people do judge you. If you are treated with respect you tend to gain and give respect. To explain this better I had had many pajama days whereby I had not bothered to get dressed. As a result, the lazy attitude led to lazy actions. I probably didn't brush my teeth until 3pm that afternoon and undoubtedly, I probably ate rubbish that day resulting in me viewing that day as a lost day whereby nothing was achieved. I can consider that dressing well promotes a good first impression. When you wear an ensemble, you tend to carry yourself in a more confident way, because you know you look good, hence, you feel good. The way you dress is also a unique way of expressing yourself, and therefore allows people to get a sense of who you are. To hell with people who perhaps didn't understand your style or message. This is about you feeling yourself again. Appearances matter in real and fundamental ways that affect a person's daily life – from how they are greeted when meeting others for the first time to whether or not they'll be harassed whilst travelling. However, being all dressed up and having nowhere to go is not such a bad thing after all. The task of choosing an outfit with matching accessories can fill a good bit of time. But it goes back to that conversation I once heard on the bus as a kid. If you dress nicely, you feel nice. It's like slipping into a freshly made clean bed. We all know how good it feels but it is difficult to describe. But this is the same thing. Putting on a nicely pressed clean shirt feels more rewarding than putting on the t-shirt you found sitting at the bottom of the bed. Or wearing a suit that you had forgotten you had got (because it only comes out on certain occasions) because it makes you feel confident. One of the first pieces of advice I had found in self-help books is almost always something along the lines of "Get Your Personal Appearance Under Control!" It's good advice. People tend to perform better in life when they feel that they deserve to perform better. The automatic assumption that a well-dressed person should be treated with respect works when it's your reflection in the mirror, too. A few minutes spent spiffing yourself in the mirror before you leave home reinforces the idea that you deserve success and good treatment in your own mind. 'Just because' is no longer an option. The game has now moved to 'I am this and so I deserve this (in a positive fashion). Spend a day dressing nicely around your own home. I know of some women that would never want to be seen unless they are wearing make-up. Well each to their own but it's a good start. Having a standard is nothing to worry about or fear. It shows that you want to be seen a particular light and depression stops you having this desire. In effect, if you dress well you should also feel well (although this may take some time). Over many years I had heard women explain the feelings they get after a hairdo or having their nails done. I suppose I get the same feeling when my facial hair sits how I want it to or if my shoes match my trousers. As I see it once you start feeling good about yourself everything should follow. Such as dressing nicely and then having the courage to go for a walk around the block. Perhaps this could lead to dressing nicely and going into town for a coffee. Who knows where it could potentially lead to but you never see a well-dressed person and think 'victim'. I can say that for me this worked. Feeling nice is a pre-requisite to anything if you are on the road to recovery. Feeling and looking nice gives you a value that cannot be given but it is something that you find yourself building on. When you are deep in to your depression everything is difficult to do. As a result nothing gets done. This leads to a feeling of worthlessness and guilt.

Guilt is a feeling of regret or remorse. It could be a result over what you had or had not done in the past. Shame is thought to result from the feeling of being judged by those around you. These feelings can be normal. But when it comes to depression, these feelings can become magnified and distorted. In many cases depressive guilt and shame can become toxic and threaten our mental health and well being. During my research I came across an article that I wish to partially share. The article covers, with great clarity, how it feels to suffer when you don't want to.

I already had all these regrets of not doing anything, of thinking about the things I could have accomplished had I not convinced myself it wasn't worth it and just stayed in bed. The guilt is another physical being that holds me back. I feel bad for not being a "normal" person with a "normal" life. Instead, I just stare at the ceiling as the guilt eats away at me (22).

I had a mixture of feelings. I felt guilt for allowing the abuse in my relationship to have happened. A feeling of shame that I didn't stop it or share what was going on with other people. These feelings had left me exhausted and in the early stages I found I was treading water just to keep going.

CHAPTER 11
Suicide and aftermath

Having been open about a range of thoughts and feelings I was asked to explain how it feels when depression becomes too much to live with. How does the mind work when the person finally decides that all other options have failed? This is a massive step to take but I was going to put this into words to help them with their loss. This particular person had a relative who chose to end his life. As a result everyone related in one way or another were at a loss as to how they had failed to notice the signs. I had contemplated suicide on a number of occasions. Now don't judge me because I didn't want that. But I was telling you this because I want to tell you how 'ending it all' becomes a logical conclusion in a complicated mind. I want the reader to know how easy suicide can become. But, equally, I want those left behind to be able to work out the mind of that person who has gone.

There is never only one reason that people take their lives. Like our lives, things can be complicated or difficult, and therefore very few people talk about it once the decision has been made. These people didn't want to justify or explain their 'logical' conclusions. Especially when they run the risk of being talked out of it. The appeal of suicide is loss of consciousness, and thus the end of psychological pain being experienced. For suicidal people, that leaves only three ways to escape this painful self-awareness: drugs, sleep and death. And of these, only death, nature's great anesthesia, offers a permanent fix. During a conversation I had with someone several weeks ago, I went into great detail of it all. I didn't hold back. We discussed the planning, the build-up and then the act itself. What I wanted to emphasize was the fact that when the decision had finally been made a great feeling of relief becomes apparent. The verdict had been made and all other alternatives didn't fit the space in which everything fits. Nothing makes sense anymore other than the drive to finish with life. Even the grim, tedious details of organizing the act of suicide can offer a welcome reprieve. When preparing, the victim can finally cease to worry about the future, as there is no future. The past, too, had ceased to matter, for it is nearly ended and would no longer cause grief, worry, or anxiety. And the imminence of death may help focus the mind on the immediate present.

It is not at all apparent that those at risk of suicide are always aware that they are in fact suicidal, at least in the earliest stages. However, signs begin to manifest and show when the plans have been developed. Firstly, they may appear at ease. In fact, they may even seem jovial. They are happy with the decision that had been made and a conclusion to their miseries are now within reaching distance. Secondly, plans are made and things are given away. During my time as a paramedic I came across a number of victims who had spent the previous week or so tidying up the house or paying off debts. In some cases they may have given things away. But in every suicide I came into contact with, a letter was always found. One well-known "suicidologist," Edwin Shneidman, once wrote that, "Our best route to understanding suicide is not through the study of the structure of the brain, nor the study of social statistics, nor the study of mental diseases, but directly through the study of human emotions described in plain English, in the words of the suicidal person." (23) When I had read suicide notes I had often found that the deceased had tried to reach out after death or try to justify their actions. The notes can be simplistic but a great deal of thought had gone into these words (good or bad). But for them, these words are the most important they had ever committed to paper. And so, because of the rush or the path they had taken it can sometimes paint a picture of a confused and complicated mind.

From all of this one can conclude that a plan had been made. In my case I too had made a plan. But it is easy. It is easy for the victim at this stage because it is the right thing to do. There are no complications following death. Bills are paid. People have the things you wanted them to have and it is all done with ease. The mind had been made up and as the 'time' rushes towards the victim the relief is more and more tangible. In essence, any troubled mind had a feeling of clarity (probably for the first time in a long time) and everything makes sense because there is a final, logical conclusion. I cannot think of a single genuine suicide case whereby it had been done to spite anyone left behind. In fact, it is the opposite. A depressive feels like a burden to everyone around them. By ending it all would not only end the victims suffering, but they feel they would no longer be a problem to anyone else left behind. For the victim this planning is beneficial. It is better to do this than die suddenly with no plans or provisions made for the ones left behind. The victim would never understand the feeling of loss for those left behind. They only see their own conclusions and the control they now have over what is going to happen. You see this is the problem with mental illness – there is no control. It takes over and suicide gives ownership back to the victim. This may be the first time they have had control over themselves in a long time – and it feels good.

I am not claiming any of this makes sense. We are reading this with our own set values and understanding. But to the victim, their views and conclusions are equally valued in their own eyes. In fact the relatives who are left behind may scream it is illogical to do these things – but these are the patterns that suicidal people generally follow. In fact, you may be able to pinpoint the actions identified. If you do I hope it brings solace to know that they did it in a state of peace, of which they had not felt for a long time. In considering people's motivations for killing themselves, it is essential to recognize that most suicides are driven by a flash flood of strong emotions and feelings. It is not rational, philosophical thoughts in which the pros and cons are considered. The final act of suicide as an escape from themselves.

There you have it. I have shared it all in its gory details. I suspect for a few people it has been uncomfortable reading, but you have taken a glimpse into a mind that had been prepared to end it all on their terms. It's not nice for the victim or for those left behind but it is a reality. People will kill themselves for whatever reason but for the victim it all makes sense. Their pain is at an end and that is what they wanted. For me, I had learnt a lot. It's not about science because science hadn't stopped people killing themselves. I think it's all about perspective. It's how we see things. In a later section of this book I ask that by killing yourself it might be an own goal. I might have missed the best years to come. But for those in this situation that statement would never make sense.

There are many ways to die but suicide may be the most painful way for those left behind. I didn't want to write about the act of suicide itself but I want to talk about the aftermath for those following death by suicide. It is so easy to get access to details on suicide in all of its forms. But I want to look and consider what happens during the mourning processes of those friends and family members of a victim of suicide. Talking about suicide is not such a taboo subject anymore. Generations before us have had a range of views about the subject from avoidance and dismissiveness to openness and support. This change in approach may had led to it becoming de-criminalised. No country in Europe currently considers suicide or attempted suicide to be a crime. England and Wales decriminalized suicide via the Suicide Act 1961 and the Republic of Ireland in 1993. However, many Islamic countries still label it as a criminal offense. I once recall a relative saying, quite dismissively, that suicide was a 'coward's way out'. From the outset, I had difficulty squaring this concept. Much of my parent's views were based on their own generational experiences and understanding. It was also matched with their religious beliefs (I would say that I am a committed Agnostic now and have turned my back on formal religion). There are, in my view, a number of things to counter argue that suicide is a coward's way out. Firstly, how awful must a life be to consider that death is a better option than living? How hopeless must their plight be to consider that ending it there and then is the only option left following (presumably) a period of reflection? Secondly, there is nothing cowardly about causing self-pain and/or suicide. After all, we commit our lives to the avoidance of such things. I cringe at the thought of needles so anything greater can be quite distressing.

When I was a child a neighbour killed himself after the death of his wife. It became a morbid horror in the street that such a thing could happen in 'our neighborhood'. As I grew older I became more exposed to other people taking their own lives. Throughout, it was always a shock that people I knew could do such things. These people had showed no obvious signs which raised concern. This made it even more shocking when I had considered that I may have spoken to them a day (or a few days) prior to them dying unexpectedly. As time passed I gradually grew to accept that such things happen for a range of reasons and refused to condemn them for doing so. In fact with my growing history of depression, I came to understand and appreciate their reasons more. I too had considered taking my own life on numerous occasions. During my time working for the ambulance service self-harm and suicide became part of the job. People of all ages and backgrounds found ways of taking their own lives via a range of methods. Some peacefully and some traumatically. Generally, these people left a note of some form explaining their reasons or giving details about their funeral arrangements. However, what struck me time and again were their apologies to those left behind. In effect, all of these people had someone who would grieve for their loss.

I always had difficulty with the 'non-logical' (my own phrase) attempts of suicide. These people would take a very small dosage of medication then phone for an ambulance. Well do you want to die or not? It was usually following an argument with a partner and was mainly, although not exclusively, females. I recall attending a female in her 20's who was a 'non-logical' suicide attempt. She justified calling for an ambulance because she realised that she had booked a holiday with her 'girl-friends' and didn't want to let them down. Yes, I accept that it was a call for help. But it takes the focus from the real sufferers who needed our support. It could have saved a life. It's almost on a par with people who falsely claim rape as this diminished the value of true victims. Let's be clear. I am not condemning any victims of suicide. I have had suicidal thoughts on and off throughout my life. However, I had always found a reason to not commit the act or have obtained support just at the right time. But what I want to consider is the consequences felt by those left behind.

As stated, many suicide notes (and I've read a great many) try to explain their actions to their loved ones. Therefore, they do leave people behind. But it had always struck me that the processes of grieving is slightly different to any form of grief I had witnessed with different types of deaths (I suggest you look at Winstons Wish for an explanation of the five stages of grief - (24) These people go through the normal processes but experience an extra dynamic based on a lack of communication. Time and again I have heard relatives say things such as;

≅ Why couldn't they tell us…
≅ We failed to see the signs…

- ≅ If they had just told us…
- ≅ Why didn't we see it…
- ≅ And so on.

What I want you to consider is that grief is hard but the added burden of guilt or failure must be unbearable to those left behind.

Generally, there are four categories or causes of death. These are:

Natural Causes: Quite simply this is when the body ceases to function of its own accord. This also includes medical factors such as terminal illness, heart disease etc – this is generally referred to as death by natural causes.

Homicide: The taking of one human life by another human being by means of murder.

Accidental Death: This form of death can also be categorised as death by misadventure. This means that the victim had died by accident either whilst doing something they should not have been doing or by taking risks that would put them in mortal danger.

Suicide: The deliberate taking of one's own life. Suicide is neither accidental nor is it classified as death by misadventure.

I think the crucial differences for each cause of those left behind are;

Natural Causes: This is sometimes expected and planned for. The loved ones are allowed time to pre-grieve and make plans.

Homicide: Although unexpected, the victim was not responsible for their own deaths. Blame can be attributed easier and the loved ones loss can be aimed at another party.

Accidental Death: Again, this could be similar to homicide, whereby it was unexpected. Furthermore, there may also be a focus to lay the blame.

Suicide: There may be instant anger towards the deceased. This is not a characteristic of any other death as anger may follow much later. Furthermore, I have witnessed that this anger turns inward whereby, they blame themselves for the loss of a loved one. This is hard to witness. It is also difficult to convince them that they are not to blame, especially when they are adamant that they could have 'done more' to have stopped this happening. I had been aware that this form of guilt (and shame) often lasts for the rest of their lives.

Suicide is real. It happens and when it does there is no going back. The pain of living for these people had ended but it becomes a new pain for someone else. The burden of projecting my pain onto my loved ones is a heavy weight to consider. This consideration may have stopped me on a number of occasions.

PART 3
RELATIONSHIPS

CHAPTER 12
Different People

It is easy to refuse to accept the fact that the one you love does not love you anymore. We all build our relationships on a foundation of hopes, dreams and desires. Over time we have built a database of shared memories and happy moments. We also made promises that felt like realistic oaths of virtue at the time of saying them. When their love has ended you find yourself go back and forth between trying to accept what had happened and denying that it's true. You hope that something would change or it might be a phase. Another part of you feels the need to do something. You're not sure what, but you know you can't just sit there and do nothing. You may refuse to accept what is happening, or deny the events as they unfold. We have all experienced these feelings when you have either been given the news by your partner that they do not love you or you can see that it no longer exists for yourself. When it finally dawned on me that she no longer loved me I had to take a step back. I didn't want to try and work out her thoughts or mindset. Her actions had demonstrated what she was thinking anyway. I had now seen an ugly side to her that I didn't want to recognise in the person that I had once invested so much emotional value in.

There was no point tying to talk her around as any short term fix would result in her floating back to her new frame of mind. I realised that it would be a fallacy to attempt to get the person who didn't not want to be with me or respect me, to love me anymore. It would be a fraud as the true meaning of her feelings had now been made evident. I can now say that I didn't want someone who wasn't clever enough to see how valuable I was. Furthermore, I was no longer willing to be her emotional football or physical vent for her anger.

Following her final outburst, it was time to let her go completely. Her behaviour became unacceptable and I needed to regain my own dignity and respect. Especially after she had ripped it away so easily. It was time to think about everything I had known differently. I was finally happy to accept the breakup had happened. I had been walking around blind to the obvious things around me for so long. The fact that she had stopped loving me at a very early stage became evident. Perhaps, she would say that she did love me but her version of love was not what I had come to expect. It was based on abuse and ridicule that only fed her own ego and addressed her own insecurities. It took time for this to sink in. Only by leaving did I realise what my life had been like having lived in an unhappy home. Living with someone who didn't love me had taken up so much of my energy, physically, mentally and emotionally. I was left tired and drained and it was only now I accept that I couldn't have taken any more. I always tried try to change the situation. Eventually, I started to accept her unreasonable behaviour and justify her abuse in the hope that she would change or accept that she was acting wrongly. I wanted to stop my feelings of sadness, betrayal and rejection. But, when I decided to let go of my feelings for her, the reality of what had been going on began to surface. I now accept that I was a victim of her viciousness but refused to identify it when we lived together. Unreasonably, I tried to think of ways to try and win her affection. Stupidly, to gain any morsels of love or respect from her, I developed lists in my head of what I could do. I decided that I could compromise my values to meet her unacceptability even further than what I had already. Her abuse had set the goals too high for any sane person to meet, but I just didn't see it at the time because I loved her. I thought I would be willing to do anything, for her to love me like how I loved her. But now I can see that the abuser would take this as a signal to continue to abuse. By giving away my own freedoms of thoughts and liberties, it played straight into her hands and she continued to kick the emotional shit out of me. The emotional, financial and psychological abuse eventually developed into sexual, thus, physical abuse. And I allowed it to happen, because I thought that this was what was needed to win her love.

I want you to consider this, forget about changing for someone else, especially if they are not willing to meet you half way. Stop bargaining for what you should have without bribes. And never change your whole life just so someone who doesn't appreciate you and your worth to love you. Forget it! If this person does not value you and all that you are then there is only one outcome that makes sense: walk away and be yourself.

My relationship with my ex became a learning experience. I had learnt that there are parts of me that indeed may need some improvement. But it is me who had identified these areas of my personality, not her. I had also learnt that my self-worth far outweighs what she was willing to invest into the relationship. I am so glad that it is now over.

For the first time in a very long time, I have been able to focus on me, and who I am. I can also see who I want to be. Not what she was trying to shape with her manipulation and abuse. I had learnt from this mistake and can now see a little bit more clearly. When I realised the relationship was failing and that the love was only one way it was a hit to my self-esteem. It was a realisation that stung. How could I have been so stupid to have allowed things to have gone that far? When the time came, it was the right time to go. It was also the right time to stop the damaging self-assessments that I had replayed day in and day out whilst living with her. It is important to stop hurting yourself with questions about what is wrong with you. You have tried and invested commitment (and everything else) to try and breathe life into something that is actually dead anyway. If they cannot be bothered then neither should you be.

The term 'Narcissist' originated from Greek mythology, where the young Narcissus fell in love with his own image reflected in a pool of water. Living with a narcissist or an abuser is difficult to identify until you look at it with hindsight. Their manipulation and cunning is their expertise and, therefore, becomes their profession. Narcissists only care about themselves and who stop at nothing to get exactly what they want. As a result, they would always place their own needs, desires, and emotions above anyone else's, including ours. Furthermore when making decisions they won't think twice about using people for their own advantage. They constantly pursue personal power and success which is why they're so manipulative, deceitful, and bad to be around Reading around the subject of narcissism there appears to be 7 ways in which narcissists manipulate and use others to their own advantage: They find a way to play the victim. Narcissists constantly play mind games and pretend to be a victim. This way they get more attention and pity from others when they lead them to believe they are sick, in trouble, or need help. When you feel sorry for them you're more likely want to help them out, and that's exactly what they want. They also use this tactic as a way to justify or excuse their terrible behaviour. Also, by turning your focus away from all the negative, deceitful things they've done, they make you less guarded and therefore more open to even more manipulation by the abuser. My ex felt it was necessary to constantly be in contact with my family, even after I had left. Unfortunately, my relationship with my father took a nose dive. However, on the flip side a more positive relationship was built with my son.

They justify the use of aggression and intimidation. One thing that all narcissists use is scare tactics. They employ everything from subtle, underhand threats to overt physical violence in order to bully others into giving in and bending to their will. More often than not the intimidation is psychological and emotional in nature. They might keep you from seeing family and friends or always put you down and verbally assault you because it makes them feel dominant and in control. My ex often threatened to have me disposed of with the help of her ex (who incidentally she tried to have arrest for assaulting her, but it was never proved) – do you see a pattern here? They excel at downplaying your accomplishments. When you first meet a narcissist they often hide their true colours. They build you up with positive comments just so they can tear you down later. When that happens it's as if a switch gets suddenly flipped and all of those kind words go out the door. Once you feel devalued you find that you end up working twice as hard to regain their favour and please them. They are experts at being able to blame you into thinking everything is your fault. They blame you for all of their bad behaviour along with all of the trouble and repercussions it brings with it. No matter what the facts or situation may be, it's inevitably your fault.

I constantly found that I was apologising for things that I had either never said or done. As a result, and over time, I used to think that perhaps it was my fault. She tried to make me feel grateful for her help in identifying where my faults were. After all, she was quick to identify that I was a poor father and she had had better relationships previously.

Do you find that they only ever talk about themselves? They have nothing good to say about anything else and can drone on endlessly about themselves and their own over inflated achievements. Throughout my relationship with my ex she often reminded me at how she could get any man eating out of her hand and often gloated about her achievements with members of the opposite sex. She made it quite clear that her blonde hair and blue eyes could help her get away with anything.

They make great use of a tool called 'Triangulation'. This is when a narcissist, you, and one other person are all involved in a triangular mind game. The other person is brought in by the narcissist after they have been led to believe that you are in the wrong or the problem. Basically, by pitting you and a third party against each other the heat is taken off the narcissist, as is any blame, and they get off scot-free. The other person would also stand up for and support them and this feeds right into their 'needs to be liked' persona and perceived as right all the time. This was my ex's favourite tool in the art of abuse. She was very clever at using her daughters against me. She had previously brought them up to be anti-man following the split from their father. Her daughters re-enforced the silent treatments and manipulations that went on at home. In effect, it could be argued that this was abuse of her daughters as they were not allowed to have their own thoughts or opinions. Furthermore, her charms had worked on my father. As previously stated, my relationship with my father had, in effect, come to an end because of her lies and manipulation. However, it must be said that I feel my father had a weak character anyway and his history shows he was always swayed by a skirt.. Unfortunately, they will never change. Once a narcissist, always a narcissist. They would continue to act shallow, manipulate, and be deceitful. Their issues are deep rooted and ingrained within their personalities. Even after you've removed them from your life, they would simply move on to their next unsuspecting victim and start ruining their life too.

As is often said, hindsight is a wonderful thing. It is wrong to blame yourself for the position that you found yourself in. This is important because their long shadow must come to an end. You were the victim, not them. Remember to keep a record of everything that had happened or is happening – this is invaluable.

The decision to end a relationship, especially when children are involved, is one of the most difficult decisions you can make. But is it right to stay? Unfortunately, breakups tend to bring out the worst in people. If you grieve then so must your children. Following the decision to end a relationship you have to now deal with the fact that you no longer have a partner. However, the children have lost a parent. As a result, they may blame themselves for what has happened, they may withdraw and become introverted, and they may also become aggressive. Grief is the normal emotional response after the end of the relationship. Everyone grieves in different ways. Children, like adults, may grieve inconsistently, seeming fine one day, only to be very upset and depressed the next.

The children may:

- Blame themselves for the breakup
- Exhibit aggressive or withdrawn behaviour
- Have regular nightmares or difficulty sleeping – they may want to sleep with you
- Show out-of-character behaviour, such as temper tantrums
- Start to have difficulties with school work
- Be more fearful than usual
- Cover up hurt through indifferent or cold behaviour
- Have physical complaints, such as headaches
- Blame the parent they are spending most of time with
- Worry excessively, particularly about family members who are upset
- Regress to an earlier stage of development – for example, thumb sucking or bedwetting.

Breaking up is an emotionally difficult time. It can be fair to assume that you can be so wrapped up with your own pain that you are unable to support your child in theirs. Your child may also need professional support and counselling. Much of this advice would depend upon the age of your child. After trawling the internet a great deal of advice is as follows;

- If possible, both parents should explain the breakup to

the child, particularly when breaking the news.
- ≅ Reassure your child that the breakup is not their fault in any way and that both parents still love them.
- ≅ Allow your child to ask as many questions as they want.
- ≅ Answer truthfully and honestly. It is OKAY to be upset.
- ≅ Use age-appropriate language.
- ≅ As the child matures, you can explain the separation in more sophisticated ways.
- ≅ Be prepared to explain the separation to the child again and again.

Whether you're the victim of domestic abuse, or you and your partner simply didn't love one another anymore, staying together for the kids is not a healthy decision. Don't criticise the other parent. This is important whether the children live with you or not. The children may feel pressured to disapprove of the other parent in order to secure your ongoing affection. Each parent may have grievances or complaints about the other. It is important that the children do not become involved in these grievances, as this adds further distress for the children. The children may still love them and deserves an untainted relationship with your ex. Don't criticise the other parent and never use your children to 'spy' on your ex-partner. Always consider, what is your relationship the type your children would model for their own? Whatever kind of relationship you have, is how the children will consider normal. This may become the foundation of their own future relationships, romantic or otherwise.

The behaviour that has been displayed in the home would set a precedence for how your children would behave as adults. They learn what it means to be in a 'romantic' relationships, how to be a husband or wife and how to effectively (or ineffectively) deal with conflict within that relationship. When you stay in an unhappy relationship you're showing them that your happiness and your self-worth are not important things. You're teaching them that it's not as important to love yourself as it is to love other people.

Following the break up with my ex she used her children (although they were my stepchildren) against me. They had a sense of loyalty to her which she used to the fullest. The children were encouraged to either give me the 'silent treatment' or to treat me in a negative way – which they were encouraged to do. This, I would argue was a form of abuse to the children. They were encouraged to not only disrespect another person but it would ultimately shape their interpretations of a mature adult relationship.

I was never allowed to give my point of view to them as they had been tainted by her version of events. They were only encouraged to hear one side. This had also been enforced by their relationship with their natural father for whom they had no respect. It bothers me further that due to the fact that they were all girls the negative views of men would be perpetuated for generations to come. My door would always be open to the stepchildren and I do have fond memories of them. But I realise the relationship with them is (possibly) destroyed due to her mother's lies and manipulation. When I reflect on it she often took the view that the more people she had on her side the more right she was, and using the children proves this (triangulation). This was typical of her manipulative ways and it would have been foolish to consider it any other way Ultimately, unhappy parents tend to raise unhappy children. And unhealthy relationships that "stay together for the kids" when the relationship is destructive tend to produce children who have unhealthy relationships as adults.

I consider (and I am prepared to accept if I am wrong), but it's not necessarily the break up that determines whether or not your kids would be okay, but rather how each adult behaves during and after the break up. The reality is this; all of the nice things have gone. In fact they probably stopped ages ago and it is only now that you realise this. You have probably lived in hope that things would work out and everything would be fine. But the truth is, things are going to be pretty difficult for a while. If any of you are going through the same thing, I promise that it's not the end of the world.

CHAPTER 13
After the breakup

It's easy to just want to watch TV all day after a difficult breakup. But don't forget that for you to feel better, you have to move on with your life. Start with small goals first. This is a great time to keep your mind occupied with productive things. Below are some things you can do to help yourself cope and heal. I've tried and tested these for myself and they do help. But you must realise that you need to work at your own pace and not that set by others.

It is important to have time to grieve. You may feel that what had happened is the "worst possible thing that can ever happen." You may feel that this is an accurate description of how you feel right now. It's really like all the butterflies died and you feel like you're being stabbed over and over again and there's nothing you can do to stop it. I felt I was confused and in denial at what she had done to me. It felt like there was this hole inside of me that was never going to be filled again. I couldn't believe that the person who once told me things like "I love you" and "Don't ever leave me". She was now the same person telling me she "wishes I was dead" or "I would destroy you at the earliest opportunity". I was left feeling weak and broken. I could not eat properly and I had to resort to sleeping pills just to get some sleep. Sleeping was often plagued by nightmares and flashbacks of what went on behind closed doors. Every little thing seemed to remind me of her from songs to smells and so on. If you find yourself in the same situation, know that it's okay to feel the pain. It is inevitable, unavoidable and necessary. No one's stopping you and it's better to do so than repress (especially if you are a male – we are well known for this), because you might end up exploding one day and the implications would be much worse. Don't ever rush things and let the time pass. You'll eventually get exhausted and run out of tears before you even realize it.

My greatest mistake was that I let it consume me for far longer than it should have. I consider that it is okay to feel the hurt and bitterness, but you have to remember to pick yourself up every time. Don't let it get the better of you.

I found that writing everything down and attending the gym helped me to recover (possibly quicker than doing nothing about it).

It's not your fault, so stop blaming yourself. You had offered them every opportunity to change their ways but their hatred was so deeply ingrained there was nothing more you could do than protect yourself from them. There's no use dwelling over the things you could have or should have done to save it. If you continually fought to keep it alive, then you should be proud of yourself. But equally proud that you have now found the strength to walk away. Bear in mind that if the other person isn't willing to compromise or work it out anymore then there's no point in staying. Following recent discussions with various people who found the courage to leave they are still struggling with 'what ifs'. Let me be clear, rose tinted glasses are fake. They show you falsehoods. I strongly advise that it is best to cut all sorts of contact with them after the breakup. She was the source of all my difficulties and once I had left I wanted to be as far away as possible from her. You must never text them, call them or even stalk them online. She had now become a stranger and would she be willing or able to answers the questions which you feel you are entitled to? I doubt it. She would never admit what she had done was wrong. Why should she when she was able to convince everyone that I was at fault and so continue the fakery.

There are various stages of guilt. There would come a point when anger and hatred would replace what was once pain, and it would leave you exhausted. You would wonder how vile and inhumane they had become. You would be thinking "How could she do this?" Don't let the anger get the best of you. A lot of people who've gone through breakups say that one day you'll wake up and just not care anymore. Wouldn't it be nice to just feel nothing for the person rather than hate for a long time? Remember: the opposite of love is not hate as hate is an emotion, but apathy. I know it's always easier said than done, but there's always a silver lining in every grey cloud. The breakup will ultimately be a blessing in disguise. The fact remains that you cannot make someone love you who doesn't. It just won't happen or work anyway.

Make time for those who love you unconditionally. Join more organizations, focus on your goals, and make new plans for the future. I had found new enjoyment by visiting the library or walking around a supermarket. It sounds simple but that's all I wanted, the simple things. I havr reflected back on all the things that I used to enjoy doing prior to meeting my ex and I intended to start doing them again. Your ex who just broke you clearly wasn't the best. You deserve stability; someone who won't ever take it out on you when things get difficult. You deserve decency at all times. Everyone should to be treated right. We are owed respect and compassion; otherwise it isn't love at all. I can now see that the abuse in my relationship arose over time. Perhaps it stemmed from her insecurities. Therefore, I found it easy to compensate for her behaviour, even when she was being abusive. Most people, even abusive people, have some good qualities and I continued to try and remember her for those assets. Yet the bad ended up over-shadowing the good which eventually became her recognized personality. I tried to understand her changing frame of mind. As a result I put up with her explosions, poor behaviour and abuse. I eventually found that I was compromising my own self-respect and dignity to justify and excuse her lack of. You can have compassion for someone's flaws but you should not accept being overwhelmed by abuse or fear. I found that I lived in a defensive, fearful state. I could not speak my mind and did anything to avoid conflict, even apologising for things I had not said or done. As a result I found that I was living in a constant state of dread and a deep sense of insecurity. Despite feeling guilt, fear, or feeling like a failure, you must remind yourself that leaving an abusive person is an act of self-protection and self-respect. I can say this now, but when I reflect on what happened, I knew it was wrong. I tried to stay in the relationship for the relationships sake, but it was dead long ago. Recording events and feelings must be done to remind yourself how things can easily spiral out of your control and as a piece of evidence when things turn really nasty. I have often read and re-read my notes and comments about what was going on at the time. I can now reflect on times of difficulty and how it made me feel at the time. I suppose I can now say I find it difficult to recognize who I was then but I was who I was living in an environment that I didn't recognize was toxic at the time. Whilst making notes for this book I had discovered something new about myself. I had become very observant about other people. It initially started when I was looking for inspiration for things to write about. I was surprised at how easy it became. Firstly, I had discovered that I really enjoy writing. This is certainly a journey of self-discovery and finding who I really am. I really like this new me that freedom has now allowed to flourish. Secondly, I had found that I have been able to develop ideas based on what is either around me or from what I overhear in conversations.

It appears that relationship breakdowns are common. And just about everywhere we look there is evidence of such a phenomenon. During periods of observations I had come across a number of people who had suffered humiliation following a break up. My break-up was simple (although traumatic) compared to others I had met or come across. I left the property and that was it. I had met people whose partners had left and then posted their break-up all over social media such as Social media for example. These posts had included direct hostility with venomous phrases that were fully intended for everyone to see. In some cases photographs of themselves with their new bit of 'whatever' was plastered all over the place. I personally think there should be more dignity in separations, especially if children are involved, but I appear (and I hope that I am wrong) to be in a minority.

When I've looked at why people attempt to humiliate others three factors seem to dominate my train of thought.

1 – They hate themselves

I've put this at the top of the list because it seems the most prevalent. It seems that those who had left their partner for someone else seemed to feel guilty for what they had done. So, to deflect their guilt they try and project their guilt on to the one they've left behind. For example, I've heard it suggested that 'they made me have an affair and so they must blame themselves for what had happened'. This is evidence of weak characteristics of which we will read about in bullying personalities. They are heavily burdened with their own guilt and fail to apologise for their own failings. They become surrounded by their own self-importance and so cannot consider the views of anyone else. Especially the ones they are hurting.

Following conversations with victims of humiliation, they had also said that their ex's still tried to maintain a level of control with regards to basic needs. To explain this further, one person told me that her ex suggested that she had the house – this was a payoff for his guilt of having an affair. It appears that he thought he knew what was best for her and still tried to offset his guilt by 'allowing' her to have certain things – like her own house. The humiliator maintains that they know what is best for you and are more than happy to tell the whole world what they had let you have on their behalf. But what about telling everyone the full story? Well it won't happen because they want the upper hand of playing the victim and survivalist of the failed relationship. They just cannot carry the true burden of their own self-hate.

2 – They want to be you

The humiliator envies you for keeping it together when all was lost. They admire your strength over their weaknesses and so try and make themselves look stronger. They can only do this by bringing you down to their level and hope that you would react in a similar way. Why should you expect them to behave with any integrity when they didn't during the relationship? The fact is they are riddled with the good things you had together and fail to acknowledge that you had some input into those good times. All you can probably recall is the dying few months or moments when it all fell apart. If you're not happy then why should they be – and this is why happy pictures of them in their new relationships are a complete fallacy.

3 – They see you as a threat.

You know the truth about their abusive behaviour or indiscretions and fear that you would expose them for what they are to their friends and family. As a result they would post 'over happy' pictures of themselves implying that they are happier without you. This behaviour is to make the victim feel that it was their fault and wonder why they are so good to the new person in their life. They also intend to make friends and family think it was your fault and not theirs. After all; look how happy they are with their new 'bit'. It further adds to their illusions that all the bad things they said about you must be true. You know this is 'bullshit' and what is more, so do they.

Although I can state that I had not been a victim of humiliation following the break up (I cut all ties including social media and phone calls), my ex did make contact with my family to try and justify her behaviour. This was mainly to imply to my family that she was the victim and her life had been a misery. Again, time after time I had suggested the importance of keeping records to disprove anything my ex had suggested. Since the breakup I have had ample opportunity to fire accusations and statements back at her. But I've not. And this has made me the better person. I used to think that the hurt coming from name calling was a measurement of weakness and people need to get over it. But as I saw things that people have done to each other, I began to understand that I was wrong. If the one left behind finds they are a target it is really only because of one or more of the above mentioned three reasons. The tormentors are playing the bully. I would argue with a great level of conviction, that when they see someone go through something humiliating, they find it funny because they're not on the receiving end for a change. I am aware that it is easy for me to say, but by not rising to it they have no ammunition to fire with. I refused to feed her ego and let her drown in her own self-indulgence. I think that in most cases, the humiliator would stop trying to hurt you when they no longer can. When it appears that it no longer hurts you it would no longer be rewarding for them. A key feature of Narcissists behaviours is that they are motivated by other people's pain. They enjoy it. It makes them feel powerful to be able to cause pain in someone's life, especially when they had figured out what they are. Therefore, your humiliator is a Narcissist and they need to be dealt with accordingly. You are only being humiliated because there's something wrong with them. Not with you. If your friends cannot see the truth and the good in you then they are not friends and not worth keeping. Your family is a different matter but blood does not have to be thicker than water. Your self-worth is more valuable than the air these idiots deserve.

As part of my bail conditions I was not allowed to return to my home address. I am also not allowed to contact either my ex or her daughter. That's okay to be honest as I was happy to be out of the situation now. However, I recently found out that she had been in contact with my family. She seems to be under the impression that the more people that offer her some form of sympathy would validate her actions against me. She had attempted to get my son to testify against me (he told her where to go) and she had been in contact with my father. I must stress that I am deeply disappointed with my father. At no point had he tried to call me to ask me how I was. It is clear that he had taken what she had said as gospel. My counsellor has since suggested that he may have thought 'he was in with a chance' with her. She would have loved that.

CHAPTER 14
Parents

I had two fathers. A natural father and an adoptive father. I will at some point talk about my adoptive father in greater details later in this chapter. But for these following few pages I want to discuss my natural father.

It took forty years to find my father after some extensive research and investigations. I wanted to find him because he was a part of me that I didn't know much about. As a child, I only ever saw one photograph of him and it wasn't the greatest of pictures. It was taken from a distance and his hair covered most of his face anyway. The photograph had discoloured over time and was curling at the edges. But it was all I had, and all kinds of thoughts and metaphors sprouted from this hazy image.

I had contacted the Salvation Army in my late 20s and they replied by stating they could not help me because I had been adopted. Although this was a backwards step it still didn't put me off. At times I would find him only to discover that he had moved many years previously. It was frustrating but it gave me the realisation that I was on the right track. It was difficult to shape a view on fatherhood other than what I had experienced from my adoptive father. My adopted father was a very straight minded, middle class Englishman. For years I had considered him to be the most intelligent man who ever lived. However, as time developed I noticed more and more flaws within his character and so I became more drawn to the mystery man who was a shadowy figure in a distant memory. I know all teenagers do this (I was sure mine did too) but I started to create a character based on what I desired from a father. I had this romantic image of him being something phenomenal who would be intelligent, energetic and be considerate to others. There was nothing to base this image on as I had had no contact with my mother for many years, and she was, to say the least a very bitter and angry woman. I felt that I was intelligent enough to make my own mind up and not base opinions on what other people thought. Everyone was entitled to make impressions for themselves – and that included my absent father. Equally, I wanted to be forgiving of any faults he may have had.

I first made contact with my father in April 2012 after finding him via his publisher (he is an author). We chatted on the phone for several days lasting an hour or so with each call. We discussed who we were and what we had done with our lives. Our conversations found common denominators such as our love of history and the arts and how we had often thought of each other. I met my father in May of 2012. Our first meeting went well. I met my brother and step mother who were characters themselves. My brother was very (shall I say) 'earthy'. He was very much in touch with the natural things around him and didn't really take much care of his appearance. My stepmother was a short thin woman whose body had paid a very heavy price for excessive drinking – it eventually killed her, but not without warning. My father was a short man with a pot belly. He was loud and confident in his views and opinions. In some ways I considered him to be old fashioned. He worked and none of his wives had (yes that's right he had been married a further two times after my mother). I liked the confidence he displayed. It was refreshing as we held long intelligent conversations over a range of subjects. He also exhibited a level of pride in his 'boys' that was warmfelt and kind. Following these early meeting I decided to reclaim my birth name and became double-barrelled. It was nice. I had a name reflecting my bloodline and a name reflecting my upbringing.

However, after a couple of years things started to become apparent. It initially started with my brother mentioning that he was a difficult man to deal with if you disagreed with anything he said. I had seen it for myself, but dismissed it. If for example, you disagreed with his view on politics he would just repeat what he said previously – but louder. He had a strange view of women too.

I was sure he loved his wives but was not what I would consider in love with them. He had a need to be needed and this was evident with his choice of wives. This sense of charity seemed to feed his ego. Yet, I was still willing to forgive these character flaws as he was my father. I found my father a little bit creepy around my ex-partner. I would cringe with the way he may have stood too close to them or the things he would say under the guise of a 'joke'. He was often inappropriate. I would not only apologise for his actions and comments but I would warn people of his mannerisms prior to him arriving. Yet, I still forgave him.

I had a realisation a few months ago about who he really was. Following the break up with my abusive ex, it transpired that both he and her had been having a series of telephone conversations. At no point had my father made any effort to contact me to ask for my version of events. He had been utterly taken in by what she wanted people to know. In fact there had been no contact for so long I called him on my birthday as I had not heard anything from him (as time progressed it was always me making the contact). He was pathetic. He had an opinion and wanted me to hear it. Of course it was one-sided and wrong. I finished the conversation with the fact that he had not made any effort at all to find out the truth or my side of the story. I've not heard from him since.

During my counselling sessions, my childhood was touched upon. I explained the actions of my father and how disappointed I was with him. There and then, my counsellor hit the nail on the head. She suggested that he may have thought he was in with a chance with her – she played the maiden in distress and he always wanted to be the knight in shining armour. He was available following the death of his wife to alcohol. Furthermore, she would love the idea of having any man, especially my father, eating out of her hand. I had read many stories and comments about abusive and toxic parents. My father was not abusive to me but he was/is a poor father. My brother had very little to do with him and now neither do I. I offered a golden opportunity to build a good father and son relationship. Instead he opted for the power of persuasion by my ex without gathering the facts. I want people to know that blood is not thicker than water in the metaphorical sense. If I think about it now, I wouldn't have had him as a friend so perhaps I expected too much as a son. I consider that I forgave too much because I saw what I wanted to see. I had 40 years without him and I can have another 40 years without him. There is enough disappointment in life without encouraging it.

I was woken up by the rain tapping against the window one morning. I didn't really have much planned to do that particular day so I intended to sleep in for a while longer than normal. But, as stated this wasn't the case. As I could hear the rain it dawned on me that I didn't like rain. Don't get me wrong, it would never stop me going out – unless it was torrential. But I find it uncomfortable getting wet and it's just an all-round hindrance. Furthermore, it leaves me with the dilemma of what to wear. If I wrap up it would, undoubtable get warm later. But where did this dislike of rain come from? I was never actively instructed to dislike rain. It just developed. After all, where does the dislike of spiders come from? We are lucky here in England as we have very few venomous creatures to avoid. So, the English fear of spiders is clearly irrational. But this brings me straight to the question – where do we acquire such feelings and thoughts? If you recall, I earlier went into some detail about my relationship with my natural father. He had absolutely no input into my upbringing. As a child and a young adult, he was a shadow. It was only later when I reached 40 that my thoughts became flesh and I had finally found him. We had a few similarities as we both liked history and the arts. We were also within the medical profession. But on reflection that was pretty much it. I drew the line at his outdated views of the roles of women. We were poles apart politically. I was quiet and he was loud. He just loved attention. Especially female attention. He took advantage and I was happy to supply. But my views and personality must have been shaped somehow by someone. Whilst realising that the rain made almost rhythmical patterns it dawned on me that I was stuck in the question of nature verses nurture. There are indeed parts of me that are unidentifiable. I just didn't know where these features come from. But there are others I can directly attribute to key figures in my life. And this is where I want to reach now. I want to talk about my adopted father.

My adopted father was a good man. He had acquired a lot of his father's traits. Both were well-spoken and gentle. My grandfather (for ease I would address him as so) always wore a cardigan regardless of the weather and this gave him an endearing character. When he laughed his shoulders would rise and fall – and what was nice, was that he did this often.

Days spent with my grandfather always seemed sunny and I utterly adored him. He would hold my hand and I would smile, so any opportunity to spend time with him was always welcome. I never met his wife as she died two years before I was born, but I know he missed her. I know this because he told me. He had a black and white photograph of her in a frame on the mantelpiece. She was also beautiful. Typical of her time with her hair in a fashionable bob. I also knew that he talked to the picture because I heard him one morning. This made him seem vulnerable yet loveable in equal measure. He smoked because he lived in a time when it was expected and fashionable. He loved classical music but enjoyed sharing my tapes (remember them?). Musically, I introduced him to the Pet Shop Boys and he introduced me to Puccini. Food wise, I introduced him to prawn cocktail crisps and he introduced me to chocolate limes. I still love those sweets. But he treated me as an equal which was lacking at home. He passed away in 1988 after finally admitting he had cancer. He had known for a while but didn't want to make a fuss. Not making a fuss finally killed him. But this was typical of him. He would allow me to watch my programmes when he wanted to watch the news or we would eat chocolate instead of salad. I never really recovered losing him. He was really loved by me. As a result, I gave my son his middle name as homage when he was born. It was such a shame that the two never met.

My adopted father had acquired his father's best features. He was middle class in ideals and nature. Soft and caring. During my formative years I had considered him to be the most intelligent man ever to have lived. He could explain mathematical problems to me of which I struggled with at school. He could make a sideboard out of an old wardrobe. Furthermore, he tried to see the good in everyone. And that was the problem.

My adopted mother (and I didn't want to go into much detail about her here) was the complete opposite. Where she screamed he just spoke, where she beat he just shook his head. In reality, I just cannot see how they ever got together. He was middle class in character, yet she was spit and saw dust, working class. I had often considered that I took the beatings for him. Which was wrong.

Many years after I had stood up to her and the beatings had stopped, she was admitted into hospital for a stomach problem. It was nothing major but it required her to be admitted for a few days. It was during this time that he spoke to me in-depth. I recall us walking through the park on the way to the shops and it was during this walk that he revealed that she was a troubled woman. It took me by surprise, because I had never expected to hear this from his mouth. Furthermore, it had cemented my view of her after all. From this point, I knew a mother's love was not what I had come to accept. It was also a time when it dawned on me that he was not as intelligent as I had considered him to be. He could have stopped the physical chastisements by her hand. Why had he not stepped up to the mark and supported me during the difficult times of my identity struggles? But he didn't. Why? Well that's simple, he was too nice to have done any of that. He just wanted the quiet life. I suppose we would call it 'hen-pecked' today. But he was out of his depth with what to do. He had in effect, put his head in the sand to deny any of it. And here lay the similarities. His father had done it before him (cancer) and I had done it with my depression and abuse. It is only now that I realise this. I had acquired his character. I also wanted the quiet life. This was not a dreadful thing to have. I would rather be like him than her. But my character dictated my future. I could fight if I had to (adopted mother characteristic) which protected me from being bullied at school. But my failure to admit problems came from him.

A few years ago, I took the step to directly highlight my adopted mother's failures. I identified that comfort and care had been restricted and rationed. Furthermore, I wanted her to know that her treatment of me over their child had been unequal and harsh. I really wanted her to admit it and to try and help me build bridges with her. But her response didn't come as a surprise. She rejected my claims and dismissed any further comments I had to make. She just failed to identify or admit any failure on her part. Yet she made it clear that I should forever be in her debt and it was my duty to identify this. Unfortunately, my adopted father was present and as expected he said nothing. He neither defended me or her. And that didn't come as a surprise either. A week or so later my adopted father came to my house. We sat alone in the living room whilst he drank tea. I knew this was his good-bye. We spoke about things that had bothered me and he calmly listened and considered what I had said. Ultimately though, he had to conclude that she was his wife and that he could not be seen to side with anyone but her. I accepted this as I knew from the moment he arrived at my door that this would have been the case. I never saw either of them ever again. To give her up meant I had to lose him too. It was, alas, a price that I had to pay.

There are many things I disliked about my adopted father. He was weak and never really spoke his mind. The opportunity to stop the physical punishments were missed by him. Chances to treat the children equally had also passed by. Yet, I hope that I have the best of him. I hope that I am sensitive when its needed. It would be great if my children thought I was intelligent. His loyalty was obvious. He was just a nice man – simple. If this is the case (I was sure people would be quick to tell me otherwise), then parts of the nurture debate are true. I made a positive decision to not be like my adopted mother, and to date I didn't think I am. But I want to care and love and I want to hide from the horrors of life. And that was who he was.

We all have something in common. We either look at ourselves in the mirror when we wash or dress. Or if we can't stand the way we look, then we can witness our own reflection in passing windows. But, we all build up a picture of ourselves based on how we are described or recognised by others. These views can become so deeply ingrained that they are shaped into facts about how the rest of the world sees us. Furthermore, it also measures our own self-worth and how we see ourselves. Self-esteem is a close relation of depression and anxiety. Yet, all of their causes can have different origins. For the following few pages I want to consider and discuss how self-esteem is created and how it creates the people we are. I want to discuss how it draws us into a range of problems based on our decisions and how we value who we are. Generally, people with low self-esteem are at risk, of not fulfilling their true potential. In later pages, I draw an important comparison with a girl I knew from school. I discussed how, due her experience of being bullied it had an impact on her adult decisions. She believed what she had been told by others during the period of bullying and concluded that they must have been right. Her self-opinion was low and therefore, her self-esteem was poor. The relationship between low self-esteem and depression is linked by having to hide your true feelings. Earlier in this book, I explained how people with depression have learnt to develop self-protection techniques. People with low self-esteem may consider that the choices they have made have been based on poor judgement. But how can it be? Poor outcomes could be based on what you think you are worth.

Everyone deserves a loving family. In my case my adopted family were pretending to be the perfect example. My adopted father had a regular and reasonably well-paid job. My adopted mother played the perfect housewife. The house was always clean and well maintained. To top it all, this church going family were also seen as charitable by taking in a child (me) through adoption. It played into their hands of respectability of which (my adopted mother mainly) played a full part.

I grew to accept poor treatment from my family and partners. My childhood was plagued with inconsistencies and questionable parenting abilities. I was made to feel grateful for the smallest offerings of parenting responsibilities from people who should have known better. As you may recall I was adopted at an early age and I was made to consider that my adopted parents had done me a great favour. Therefore, I had to earn any form of love or acceptance. To further compound the issue, I was always compared to the wonderment of their natural daughter. I had been adopted because they thought they couldn't have children – a year after the adoption my adopted mother became pregnant. By being compared to their daughter I always played second best but was set up to fail because their artificial standards were set too high for the young child that I was. My low self-esteem carried on into my adulthood. Only now I can consider, and perhaps realise, that it had interfered with my ability to lead a fulfilling, healthy life. I consider that I had never really reached what would have been my full potential. Although I have attended University, it was only as an adult. I was never encouraged to apply for Grammer School, or congratulated for the smallest of achievements at school. I also consider that my low self-esteem shaped my poor self-worth and set the foundations for depression. Physical punishment was the norm when it came to chastisement. I recall being kept off school due to the obvious bruising on my body. Yet I liked to go to school because I was safe from the harm I suffered at home. My adopted mother (who did most of the discipline) failed to recognise where she was going wrong. And so, all the excessive punishment I received was valid in her eyes. From her point of view, I was a naughty child. As a young adult, I raised this contradiction with her but yet she still failed to acknowledge her shortcomings. As a result, I gave in and walked away. I have not spoken to them since. These exposures left me with a feeling of inferiority. It was almost like a 'Cinderella' effect, whereby the sister had it all and I was worth nothing. This poor self-value created poor self-esteem as a growing adult leading into full adulthood.

A smack or a slap was the usual chastisement for me as a child (I cannot ever recall their daughter getting punished in any form). I was made to feel that I had deserved this action and so I needed to address the ills of my own ways. In effect I was forced to be grateful that my adopted parents had acknowledged the problems before I got deeper into trouble. But it was wrong. The punishment was excessive and it was unequal within a sibling relationship. I took the slap, their daughter was put onto a pedestal. Without doubt I became drawn to a certain kind of partner. Let me be clear here, not all my partners have been abusive. But by being abused by a partner was, in my eyes, an acceptable form of love. If I was with someone who wasn't abusive, I questioned their love for me because it was abnormal (in my eyes). I carry a lot of guilt for past choices. I had a lot of guilt for getting things wrong as I grew up. As a father, I could have done a lot better. Whilst working, I could have worked those extra few hours. Having suffered with depression, I could have made it stop earlier and saved myself from years of negativity. I now see this as I write these words down. But to justify doing nothing, what could I have done? As a child, I would have been seen as ungrateful for the charity I had received. I could have tackled my depression years ago, but I didn't recognise that I had it until I was much older. Wanting to tackle my low self-esteem was impossible because I knew nothing else about my personality. And so the cycle continued. When you get used to feeling, thinking and talking about yourself in a particular way, it becomes a habit. The only example I can give is like riding a bicycle. When you learn how to ride one it becomes a second habit and you do it without thinking. I am adamant that thoughts and feelings actually work in the same way. As I had so often been made to feel worthless or inferior that it became a part of me. I came to accept second best because that was all I was worth and so I came to accept abuse in a relationship because another alternative was difficult to recognise.

When I accepted that I had depression I knew that I needed to get some help and support. However, I was equally combative because I wanted to deny that I had a problem – I was being a blokey bloke. Now at the age of 45 I hold no such convictions. I have found writing to be more therapeutic than I would have initially gave it credit for. It had been a revelation. I had forced myself to answer the questions that I had held back for all of my life. Following my open revelations about what had happened – especially the abusive relationship. I have been afforded some of the best help I could have ever imagined. It's okay to accept it all. But it is even better to share my thoughts with others. It's almost like having a big family that I never knew existed. I do have low self-esteem, but I can deal with that as much as I acknowledge that I have depression. It won't instantly heal itself but it can be managed – slowly, but it will.

PART IV
AFTER EFFECTS

CHAPTER 15
Making sense of it all

I've quickly learnt that I don't like sitting there, doing nothing. I tend to find that my mind wanders and reflects on past events and present outcomes. I've learnt that my personality requires me to keep busy. Having a routine makes me get up and get things done. Initially it was suggested to me to join a gym. It was a good idea, and as it helps my mental health I was also hoping that it would help eradicate my belly. I've found that I have become somewhat competitive with myself. Over the last few weeks I've increased my times on each machine and raised the difficulty level. It's kept my mind focused whilst I am there but it has also given me a sense of achievement. I must admit that I had some initial reservations about the type of people who would be there. Would they all be "body beautiful" laughing at me with my belly and skinny pale legs. But no. There were all sorts. Some old, some young, some large and some small. It appears on observation, that there is some form of etiquette whereby you didn't talk to anyone (unless you know them and came with them) and you don't do eye contact – which suits me. You just get on with your task and you're left alone, which is just ideal for people like us. On reflection, I wasn't the worst there but equally I wasn't the best. I had found that filling my day with something was an essential thing to stop negative thoughts and feelings. This does, I must stress, go hand in hand with my medication and counselling. I cannot rely on these things alone but together, they were a big step to take but a good one.

Not being believed is one thing, but having to retell the events over and over again to get people to listen to you involves reliving the events you had tried to bury. And I just didn't know which is the worst. For me, telling and retelling the catalogue of events felt like a constant kick in the head. I had had to bat off the quizzical expression and the occasional uplifted eyebrow. I eventually wondered if my story was too much to be believed and started to consider that my comments were hollow and my hopes of being believed unrealistic. The real challenge of not being believed is how big the price would be. It took all of my courage to try and take my self-respect back and fight against the abuse. It was a dreadful step to reveal the shame of being both abused by my partner but also to reveal a lifelong condition of depression. I had spent all my life hiding the depression from everyone, and revealing it broke my life long conventions. To add to this exposure, I also admitted that I, a fully grown adult male, had been abused by my female partner. Shame on me, this was not supposed to happen. But to admit all that was only half the problem. The other half was not only being disbelieved but to try to get support from quarters I had expected more from.

I am sure that my ex knew she was doing wrong. Not just once, but every time she let the abuse happen. This was why, during her nice periods, she used so many words to convince me that I had asked for it. And I initially believed her words. I had the awareness that the way I was living was wrong, it took a whirlwind of thoughts to make a plan of action. I was sure I would be believed, I had to be because I was telling the truth. People had to be able to see that? Even the police. It's strange how people still see physical abuse as "real" abuse and mental/emotional abuse as, a case of 'get over it'. Both types of abuse are horrible and utterly unacceptable. The scar on my hand from a burn is healing. But words never heal, they never seem to want to leave me. And the deeper hurts have never been forgotten. I can't remember the first time I felt the sharp pain of a cane on the back of my legs from my adopted mother. But I can vividly recall the moment she pointed her finger at me, saying that I was "worthless and would amount to nothing". After a while, when it is physical pain you learn to 'harden up' as you know how it feels when you know it's coming. But words are unpredictable and knock you off your balance when you least expect it. I had equally forgotten the first time my ex punched me in the ribs saying it was a joke. But I can now recognise that she had had a life time of inflicting misery on everyone she met. The only difference was that I wanted to fight back. And my arsenal included the weapon of honesty. Her weapon was one of denial.

The need for acceptance is like an addictive drug. You need

more to feed the habit of desire. The need to be desired by others. And to be loved by someone who seems to be making it difficult. I needed all this from both my ex and my adopted mother because I needed convincing that I had a value in somebody's eyes (if not my own). All of this led to a disbelief of my own place in this world. As a result, I believed the untruths to accommodate my own beliefs of right from wrong. As a result, if I couldn't believe myself, who would believe me when I called out for help? Sometimes when I used to speak to my counsellor, I wondered if she questioned the validity of what I had to say. She appeared honest and kind (and still does), but when I left I often asked myself if she believed me because she had to rather than wanted to. I didn't blame her. It's a natural reaction to have a question of doubt. It's a defensive mechanism I suppose. Even more so when it is a male who is talking about being abused by his female partner. Society still has a problem with this concept. Things changed when I took the time to talk about the history of my events. She implied that she did have a pre-conceived 'story' in her head about the events. Now I had clarified things a little she seemed to have a better grasp of where I was coming from. At that moment, I felt believed. It gave a sense of relief. It felt like a breath of fresh air when I knew I was being believed. However, it was naturally short lived. Like the addictive drug I needed to feed my validation. I wanted more people to believe me now the 'cat was out of the bag'. I wanted to share the fact that I was now convinced that what had happened was wrong and I needed to convince others around me.

At the heart of my denial was a core belief system. Mothers should love their children. Fathers should support their children. And partners should 'love and cherish.' It flies in the face of what I now know to be true. It is wrong that a Mother has no empathy for her children. It's beyond comprehension that a father believes the worst about his children. And it is crushing that a partner would degrade the very person they vowed to "love." It just appears to be all wrong. It couldn't possibly have happened. But, it did. My abusers knew it flew in the face of what was morally right and each of them used words to convince me that I deserved it, or I had asked for it. Their justifications were the flip-side of my expectations of right from wrong.   If I had not believed their actions to be wrong, then I wouldn't have been in denial. I still fear not being believed. All the courage I had summoned to leave myself exposed and vulnerable to other peoples' picking had been life changing. I had held everything I value up high for other people to value or disregard as they see fit. And this is hard. All my 'dirty little secrets' had been forced out of me and it is difficult to cleanse, even more so when people are willing to walk all over it in the name of belief. I had spoken after years of saying nothing. I just want to be heard. Not judged or disrespected. Just heard.

When you sit back and think about it, it's amazing that humans have any forms of relationships at all. We are all different, requiring different needs and requirements. Our desires change over time and it's a lot to expect that another person can appreciate these changes as you would theirs. I am fully aware that I am not the same man I was ten years ago and I very much expect to be different again in another ten. I am certainly not the same person I was a year ago. Relationships come in all forms. We all have parents and we all have friends. These are relationships and they give us things like support, advice and contact. It is a two-way street. Obviously, relationships are fluid and they change over time. So why can we not accept it with romantic relationships? And here is where I want to focus – I want to consider how we get over a romantic relationship, especially if it is a long term one. Relationships can still 'own' us long after they're over. I find it difficult to understand that the person who was the major part of your life at one stage, you find yourself crossing the road to avoid them the next. That person eventually becomes nothing more than a memory – good or bad. This will take time, but can you recall an ex from 10 or 20 years ago?

Breakdowns are now more difficult than ever. I love the convenience of mobile phones where a text can be so easy to write (who writes letters these days anyway?). Or the ability to look up old friends on social media. It's all so easy and disposable. We can do these things instantly without much effort or physical input. But for some it means that their ex is just a click away. I wonder how many of you have looked your ex up on Social media and looked at their pictures? Let's be honest, we have all done so. Old photographs could be thrown away but electronic media owns everything we share and there is no way of disposing of these items easily. But don't be fooled. These people are not as happy as the picture suggests. An ex can be as easily blocked as it is to contact them. I would never message my ex as I would not want her to have the feeling of accomplishment over me. She is blocked and will remain so. However, there comes a time when we need to accept that what's done is done and begin to look forward to what might be coming next. Following my break-up, I found a world of opportunity and self-discovery. I can now see that my break-up has had a positive outcome, but it wasn't that way to begin with. I am at the other end of it all now and can look back on it to see it for what it was. The reality is that if it had not ended then it would have ended at some point. Although, I am prepared to accept that not everyone has this luxury. Like the complications of human nature, break-ups can equally be complex. What is important to acknowledge at this stage is that I now realise you cannot get someone who never loved you, to start loving you now. It just won't happen. I found that my emotions were identical to those I had experienced following a bereavement. I experienced; denial, anger, emptiness, and sadness and they came in quick succession. I even felt betrayed and emotionally robbed, especially as I had invested my hope of a bright future with that one person. The emotional 'bank account' had been raided and I had been left with nothing. I have had this discussion with various people from various backgrounds about break-ups. Alas, there is no definitive answer on the correct actions to take. Some suggested that people need to just 'snap out of it' or to 'get online' and find another one. The truth is, how someone responds to the end of a relationship is different for each of us: there's no right or wrong way to do it.

The important thing, from my point of view, is that you give yourself the time and support you need to feel better. I suggest being selfish and start falling in love with yourself again. My relationship beat me down and so I am building myself up to be better, stronger and most importantly, wiser. I found that the hardest thing to let go of was my anger. I was furious that I had let her do those things to me but I was equally furious that I had allowed it to happen in the first place. My anger moved its focus from her to myself. I eventually recognised that I had pity for her as she was never going to change, whereas, I was changing. I felt so disappointed with myself. Wrongly, I had considered that I was intelligent and could work things out, but I failed to see the abuse until it became impossible to change. I was ultimately, disappointed with myself and this added to the shame of the breakdown.

I must admit, I am still playing the 'blame game' – I am endlessly questioning who did what, what could have been done differently and so on. But I didn't see a problem with this. I have been able to do an autopsy on a relationship that was dead long ago. I can now see what went wrong and how it died. A word of warning though, if you are not careful you can tend to go in circles and eventually draw no valuable conclusions. I can confirm that the end of the relationship for me was eventually a liberating experience. It meant I was no longer fighting to try and obtain a dream from a nightmare. I felt I no longer had to justify her negative behaviour and abuse. There was no longer any need to feel fear on a daily basis. For me this new-found sense of freedom eventually (not instantly I must admit) came with a rush of positive emotions. I rediscovered lost loves such as reading and writing. I even went to the ballet, of which I was never allowed to do when living under her regime. Funnily enough, I didn't have a clue what was going on – but I really enjoyed it. But that's not the point – I was able to do it without obtaining authorization first.

By now, if you have been reading this book from the beginning, you will appreciate that I have been on a journey of self-discovery. I have attempted to establish the meaning of happiness and to share it. My journey has enabled me to self-reflect on events and actions that were previously out of my control. And how they shaped me as a person I didn't want to be. I did these things for another persons' happiness and not my own. Please allow yourself to be selfish. I want to suggest that self-appreciation is a liberating experience following an abusive relationship. Having eventually left the abusive relationship I found that struggles began in other areas. PTSD (Post Traumatic Stress Disorder) became a daily (and nightly) problem. For me this didn't make any sense, here I was now free of any form of abuse - although I was still struggling with depression. Yet I was experiencing all manner of 'flashbacks'. Furthermore, there was no initial trigger or understanding why they were happening. The worst was waking up following a bad dream thinking that she was in the room with me.

Having to admit to being a male victim of domestic abuse (especially sexual assault) was extremely difficult. Perhaps these episodes of PTSD was a way of venting this frustration against a world of whom I considered did not care – this was enforced and endorsed by the police who failed to react or support me in my complaints of abuse. Enduring any length of abuse whether physical, emotional, sexual or psychological would leave some form of mark. Some domestic violence survivors, like myself, would suffer with PTSD. Suffering these emotions does not indicate any form of weakness. I have had to deal with my PTSD which had made me relive my ordeal through flashbacks and nightmares that had interfered with my ability to function normally on a daily basis. This had often left me tired or uninterested in doing daily activities. Further research on the subject directed me to other symptoms. These can also include;

- Intrusive memories of the abuse – this can come following certain songs or smells or even being in certain places at certain times. There are no strict rules to this – it can just happen anywhere at any time.
- Loss of interest in other people and the outside world – I found that I isolated myself from friends and was happy to stay indoors.
- Insomnia
- Agitation – I found that I would often jump at the slightest movement by other people
- Depression – Goes without saying
- Overwhelming feelings of sadness, fear, despair, guilt or self-hatred. I regularly questioned my own self-worth. If I could allow one person to do these things to me what was my true worth?
- Physical pain that migrates throughout the body. I had experienced headaches and joint pains.
- An inability to imagine a positive future.

Following research I found that these symptoms can last for at least a month and can occur either directly after the trauma, or be delayed, beginning six months, a year or 20 years after the abuse had ended. Everyone recovers at their own pace. As a minimum you should be seeking help and support from your doctor. In my case, after I had left the abusive home I had to move to temporary accommodation. As a result I registered with the local GP there. I must stress that from the outset they were fantastic. My new doctor took the time to listen to events and the subsequent aftershocks. I was prescribed medication for both my depression and my sleep problems which I had found to be a great help. My work supplied and paid for counselling sessions. Initially, I was cautious about sharing my thoughts and experiences with a complete stranger but my counsellor allowed me to work at my own pace. I sometimes wondered if the effects of abuse would ever go away. Yes, I am still jumpy at times and I still experience thoughts following certain triggers but I recognise these now and can prepare myself for this. I have not fully recovered but I sense a certain amount of freedom from PTSD. There was a time when I stayed silent about the abuse but a part of my recovery was to share what happened either with friends or by writing it down (hence this book), medication, counselling and a slow recognition of my own self-worth.

Whilst out in town one Saturday afternoon I discovered the taste of individuality and freedom. This was a big step to take. To many people reading this my revelation may be an anticlimax. But on that Saturday I bought some burgundy coloured trousers. So why is this such a big step? Well firstly, whilst looking I had a feeling of guilt that I was buying something for myself. It was unusual not to ask permission to purchase an item for myself. Although I had earned good money, buying things for myself required a series of steps prior to have agreement handed to me. Secondly, as stated, my new trousers were burgundy. I was always expected to wear more sombre colours that fitted with her perception of what I was allowed to wear. Yes, I had a feeling of guilt whilst eventually wearing them. But equally I thought 'well done me'. I was wearing something I had picked myself This was empowering. I didn't have someone looking over my shoulder giving a list of reasons why her decisions far outweighed my own. It was a colour I would never have dreamt of wearing a matter of weeks previously. I was so used to wearing what she liked. Burgundy trousers would had been considered rebellious against her conservative choices for me. She thought she was right and right she had to be. She may have been right but her ability to take away my power of choice was wrong.

I never asked her why she chose what I wore or purchased. It became a slow 'take over' process whereby (if I recall) I would ask her opinion on what I was wearing. It eventually became an assumption that this was her responsibility to ensure I dressed to her requirements. As a result it became a position where I was not allowed to decide unless she chose for me. Now don't get me wrong, I think I dress well. Quite dapper in fact, but it was only on the day of the purchase of the burgundy trousers that I realised it was another area of my life she had had control over. This area of the recovery process was actually a good period of rediscovering myself and who I am. Her control over me limited my personal freedom and freedom of choice There's a fine line between expressing an opinion and requiring a person to act or do certain things. Telling the difference between an opinion and abusive behaviour might seem easy, but it can be difficult to interpret.

Following my moves to rebuild my life after eventually leaving, I opted to apply for different jobs. A new start in everything was what I required. Following the completion of various application forms I was invited to a number of interviews. One interview that I had attended went surprisingly well, although I knew I probably wouldn't get it. As always during my counselling sessions, we discussed a range of things. Some going over old ground and some thought provoking discussions. However, we also discussed thoughts and feelings and considered my views on events and the future. I've decided that, by nature I had a pessimistic view to life. Just look at the above paragraph again. You can see the negativity following the good interview statement. When I think about it I have always had a 'half empty' view of life. I think it is the fail safe for a great number of people. If we prepare for the worst then we are ready for it when it happens. Anything positive is, therefore, a bonus. It must be a psychological safety net for so many people. There is nothing wrong with being safety conscious in the crazy world we now find ourselves living in. But pessimism is not such a bad thing really. My counsellor gave a brilliant analogy. She stated that it is a good defense mechanism. "If the caveman" she said "had not had an element of caution then the human race might have been wiped out". I further endorsed this by mentioning that the Dodo became extinct (partly) because it had no fear of humans – laughably I now consider that the Dodo was not stupid, it was just an optimist.

I could have started this book by saying that it would have been an utter waste of time writing it. Nobody would read it and if they did I would only get negative comments. I would then probably cry into my coffee and go to bed. Undoubtedly, I would be pelted with rotten vegetables as I head out to the shops. But it hasn't happened – ever. Even after taking the first steps into the world of writing where I was at my most vulnerable. As time had developed during my writing, I have been more and more open and honest. I have left myself exposed to criticism and perhaps even ridicule. But no, it hasn't happened. I've not been looking for it because that kind of 'thing' finds you. I was sure people do have a negative view about what I have said, but I had probably, unconsciously, dismissed it. It doesn't mean that what I say, write or do is correct. It just means that my 'defensive pessimism' had worn off a little bit and I am now delighted to call myself a 'writer'. So, why do we read works by authors who are profoundly pessimistic? And what sense are we to make of their work in our ordinary, hopefully not uncheerful lives?

I am lucky enough to have written two books. This one of which I consider to be deep and meaningful. I hope people heed my words or value my advice and perhaps act upon it. My other book is a play based on two hapless teenage boys who get lost on the moors. It is a comedy poke at life that I hope entertains. It had 'throw away' comments that I hope people giggle at then move on to their next activity or scene. Two very opposite characteristics that feed off each other amazingly well. But not all pessimists have the same fondness for my kind of comedy which is perfectly okay. In both books, I cater for those that want to read them. Not for people who dismiss them. Modern society as a whole, tends to lean towards a sort of institutional pessimism. Soap operas are based upon negative situations and 'bust ups' in the local pub, people sleeping behind the backs of other people and so on. Yet we see this as a form of entertainment. We watch people being banished to remote islands to watch them fail in their endeavours. People are put into a locked house and we watch them argue and fall out. Yet we are encouraged to believe happiness is at least potentially available for all as the 'dramas' fade into another story. But when we look at life we can see that it is filled with misery and pain and if we managed to escape these, boredom would lie in wait at every corner. In effect, we have embraced the evil side of life. The 'baddy' in action films always get the nice car, nice clothes and is the best character to play. In general, playing the baddy is always the most sought after by actors around the world. There would be no story without one. The news headlines always tell us negative stories. Occasionally a happy story comes along about a dog who can talk or something, yet we still watch the news – sometimes four times a day. Why? Well perhaps we like to know that other people lives are worse than ours. When I think about it we always moan about the negative person in the office or down the pub. I had found myself avoiding these people on a number of occasions. I may have crossed the road or dived into a shop before I was spotted. But think of the alternative. The over-happy type of person, instantly in your face. This type of person is even worse to endure. We leave that kind of person to present children's TV (where they belong). So being a pessimist is not such a bad thing after all. Yes, I suppose I am a pessimist but it could be worse. But by saying that am I now an optimist?

CHAPTER 16
Feeling no emotion – Court case

I spoke to my counsellor one morning about having no feelings or emotions. I found that she was right when she suggested that I didn't need to go out looking for an emotion or a reason to be emotional, it would just come. But I was still left feeling void of anything. I was looking forward to what the future had to offer and what it may bring but I felt like I was just treading water at that moment, so not actually going anywhere. In fact, at that moment, I just felt just a little bit lost. I had changed a few things over those past few months. I know I used to bang on about the benefits of going to the gym, but I had stopped going and I didn't actually miss it. I started to read a lot more than I had a few months previously which showed that my concentration was returning. But

I was hoping that a change in routine may have offered me another perspective – but it hadn't. Surely this couldn't be right?

The day of the court appearance finally arrived. And as expected although I had dreaded this particular day I equally wanted it over. I don't want to talk about each 'nut and bolt' of the hearing. But it went my way. I won and all the truths came out. It took me a while for the fact of being acquitted to eventually set in. I consider that my reservations were mainly because I had been waiting for it to hit home a little more than it had. When the judge delivered her deliberation I actually felt nothing. Nothing at all. In response to her verdict I just said, "thank you". I only said this because I had to give some kind of response. But even then I didn't think I meant what I said. I know it's a cliché when I say this but it was a 'hollow victory.' Her lies were exposed like a pebble being thrown into a pond. The ripples continually echoed exposing more and more untruths throughout the hearing. What did upset me was that she got her daughter to testify and also lie on her behalf. My solicitor stated that he felt awkward exposing a 17 year old as a liar. I would never have used my children (regardless of age) to stand in a witness box and testify. The poor child was utterly humiliated.

I arrived at the court early (I always arrive early for appointments) and waited around for a while. I met my solicitor who talked me through the case and what he planned to do. It all seemed logical to me. However, the trial was supposed to start at 9am but was delayed until 3pm. The waiting was hard work. Almost on a level of psychological torture. I never wanted to go to court in the first place. I just wanted the relationship to be over at the earliest opportunity. It was just events that took hold and it had spiralled to the present situation that I found myself in. So being in court was a horrible event to say the least. By delaying it I just wanted it to be over with even more. By the time I was called into the court room I literally ran because I wanted the whole thing to be over with. The only analogy I can give is how it must feel to be on death row. The agony of waiting must be worse than the act of execution itself. I had got to the point that regardless of the outcome I just wanted it to be over with. The hearing was like a verbal tennis match. Vile things were said (on both sides) by the lawyers. Yet there were also times of humour which seemed out of place within the formality of the court room. Glances were passed too and thrown when lies were exposed and contradictions made. Evidence was supplied on a number of factors. Whilst I sat there listening to it all I was hurt by the personal attacks made but equally relieved to have supplied the evidence required to dismiss much of what had been said. I sometimes heard myself giving a sigh at the relief that I had recorded such events of which benefited my case. The whole hearing was a theatrical experience. There was, as stated, elements of humour and dark scenes of which any human would wince at hearing. But overall, it was a tragedy of Shakespearian proportions. There were character assassinations, repercussions and finally the murder of the old life. The only thing missing was the make-up and the applause at the end of each scene. When I left the court, I can honestly say I felt nothing. I stopped for a while standing still, just to make sure that the feelings I was experiencing were indelible. Importantly, I didn't want to forget this feeling. I knew I wanted to be able to recall this moment and that's why I wanted to take a second to try and take it all in. But, like I said, I actually felt nothing. I didn't feel victorious although I should have let the euphoria take hold. But I didn't. In fact I couldn't even feel the sun on my face or the breeze wafting past me. I was just aware that my feet were following the usual pattern of walking just to get me away from where I had spent the last few hours. That seemed more natural than any emotional feeling that I was not experiencing. When I eventually made it home, I just watched TV. I thought I was concentrating on the events on TV as they unfolded. But I wasn't. It was a soap opera which I never follow anyway. I just felt nothing, not even hunger. Nothing at all. And this was my concern – at what point would I feel anything and when it came how would I deal with it? The only thing I can identify as an emotion was that I felt tired about two days later. That was it. Nothing more. I was still waiting patiently for something to happen.

But I can now reflect. Lessons have been learnt. I've discovered a lot about myself and how things work and develop. The value of keeping records is certainly worth mentioning. Keeping calm when the court room actors point fingers and make accusations. Dismissing lies and forgiving. I didn't hold any negative feelings for anyone. Only pity. I pity the ex for her mental disadvantages and lack of humanity. I also pity her daughter for being put through it all and her solicitor for fighting an un-winnable case. Well that should be it. It was all done and over with in the formal sense. I was aware that I still have a new path to walk which is exciting. Time and again I had said to a number of people that I am not the same person I was last year. To that effect, I am not the same person I was at the time of the wrongful arrest. But I suppose I am more than okay with that. The new path which I now tread still needs to deal with older demons that need to be shaken. Or, and this is why I had been wary – I still think there are new challenges to come. My numbness about what happened after the court room experience cannot be maintained. The anesthetic would wear off at some point I am sure. I just want to be ready and prepared for when the awakening happens.

About two weeks after my acquittal I managed to speak to someone from work. I expressed to them how let down I felt by the lack of support I was given other than the counselling from work. It's as if the mantra of not being seen equates to not being a problem that exists. In fact, as you are aware, I had spent the last few days looking for alternative employment. I didn't think I wanted to return to an industry that really doesn't care for its staff, regardless of what they claim.

I think feeling lost reflects a lack of purpose. I finally know what I want but I'm still not really sure how to go about it. I didn't want to be a paramedic anymore, that's for sure. I would love to write for a living but it's full of potholes and would never pay enough to meet the bills. I had found a great relief in writing letters of complaint about certain individuals whom I had recently had the misfortune of coming into contact with. These individuals had the audacity to claim to be professional. However, I discovered, whilst gathering evidence to put forward and to support my complaint that one of these said people had been acting illegally. So, I suppose, at that moment, I had become the new Poirot of Gloucestershire.

Following my victory in the courtroom I decided to treat myself. So, I went out and bought a new car. I suppose I could justify it as my old one was due for renewal anyway. It's just that it is far grander than my old one. But even now when I look at it parked on the drive I can safely say I think I deserve it. I had been through one of the worst experiences of my life with little support from those who should have offered it. I now know who my friends are and where my loyalties now rest. But this car is a 'well-done you' message to myself. And, like I said, I didn't feel bad about it.

Probably about three months after the acquittal, I babysat for my grandson whilst my son took his partner away. It was lovely. Really lovely. He is such a happy baby. We sat and watched TV whilst he was awake and I found myself singing to him. His little face lit up when I sang and so I continued. I felt a bit guilty really that I had not seen him as much as I could have the previous months. But it was nice to have the time to reflect and enjoy the moments I had with him. I suppose this was the only time I've had any form of emotion or feeling. I was proud to change his nappy and make his bottles. I enjoyed feeding him and watching him happily drink his milk. It was just a nice period of time that went far too quickly. I'm not writing this to spout any kind of philosophy or deep and meaningful thoughts. I am writing this to get some kind of grip or understanding about what was going on. I was not looking for an emotion yet, even after all of this time, I still felt absolutely nothing. I was not angry, although I was somewhat disappointed with a few people. I was not sad. In fact it's the dead opposite, I was looking forward to things changing. I was not even bored as I had so much to do. I was just a little bit lost as to how to feel. Surely by now, I thought, I should have had some form of daily structure?

Chapter 17
Aftermath

I recall as a child often waking in the night after a nightmare. After all of these years I cannot recall the exact nature of these dreams but I can remember waking in my bed crying. After a while they must have subdued as there had been many years between my childhood night terrors and what I had experienced recently. It does not necessarily mean that by not being able to recall the dreams that they did not happen. Sometimes I had awoken with a feeling that things were not right. This is often in the dead of night when there was no reason to either be awake or any reason to have been awoken following the dream. However, sometimes I could recall the visions and they did seem to have had a relevance to what had been going on. Many of the nightmares had been based on things that had either happened recently or from events I experienced many years ago. There seemed to be no logic to their visitations as time, when it comes to dreams, did not appear to be linier.

The problem with night terrors is the feeling of vulnerability. From the dreams, I can recall experiencing a feeling of helplessness within the horrors I was experiencing. These horrors could be based on recent experiences or a time that I would rather forget. As stated it had no logic and time had no relevance to the dreams. In some dreams I was a child again, or an adult fighting in Iraq or Afghanistan. I was also aware that some of the dreams were events related to the abuse I had experienced several months before. However, I had also experienced dreams that are somewhat out of the box. For example, one night I dreamt that I was a soldier during the first world war. The environment was real. I found myself fighting Germans in a deep muddy trench where puddles splashed onto my uniform. The faces of those soldiers I was killing were real with uniforms and facial features. However, during the fighting I spotted my ex in an enemy's uniform trying to kill me. The strangest thing was that I was unable to fight her off. I was utterly defenseless against her attacks. I am aware that all manner of interpretations can be made with regards to this specific dream. But when it effects your health interpretation have very little importance other than you wanting them to stop. Now, I am aware that this may sound very strange but I think it reminded me of my vulnerability whilst I was with her. For heaven's sake, I was able to fight off a number of heavily armed and experienced combatants yet I was helpless when I was in her line of fire. There is a vast range of other experiences I can give. But I found that the common denominator was based upon the wickedness I had experienced at the hands of my abusive ex.

Waking became a relief and an escape from the reality of that moment. Yet, I am able to recall the dreams much better than when I experienced them many years ago. I had often awoken completely disorientated and the confusion was compounded because the reality of the dream did not match up to the room in which I awoke in. To explain this better, the reality of being in the trench was tangible. I could feel the mud under my feet. The smell of blood, sweat and explosives were also real. The physical effort of fighting could be felt in my muscles (I was still experiencing physical pains on a daily basis at this point) and the sounds were loud and unmissable. But when I awoke, the complete opposite was the reality. The room was in darkness and my safety felt assured. Yet it woke me up with a jolt of which was difficult to grasp when I was not sure of which reality I found myself in.

It's silly really, but as an adult I can distinguish the difference between the dream world and reality. Yet the fact remains that whilst curled up in the safety of a new home, warm in bed, we are perhaps all vulnerable to things out of our control. And I feel this is where the terror lies. There is no escape because we have no control over our dreams. In the waking world if I feel unsafe or uncomfortable I have the option to either get up and leave or address my concerns directly. However, we don't have that luxury in a dream. We are carried by uncontrollable forces into undesirable circumstances. And that is not nice at all.

After leaving the forces many years ago I also had similar experiences that were evident but slowly faded away. However, those recent dreams now seemed to have overlapped what I felt I had recovered from before. These restless nights obviously had an impact upon my day time pursuits. I became constantly tired and craved a decent night's sleep. Yet my sleep was often either broken by the night terrors or the physical pains I felt with my PTSD. It's no surprise, therefore, that abuse victims and people with depression feel so tired and ill all the time. There is, in effect, no escape from both a living nightmare and those of which invade our thoughts during the night. I mentioned these dreams to my GP when I saw her next. She directly attributed them to the PTSD I was experiencing. What was extra worrying was the fact that she informed me that it may take a while to recover from the situation I now found myself in. It was only complete exhaustion that allowed me to get some sleep but this was often hard to predict as it sometimes happened during the day.

Let me make this clear. I am not religious. I was brought up as a Methodist but gradually turned my back on formal religion as I grew older. There are many reasons for this but far too many to include within these pages. However, not being religious does not make me a bad person. Far from it. I was more at peace than most of the religious people I knew. However, a matter of fact dawned on me when I attended a funeral. I always enter a funeral with an open mind. When it comes to religion I have a level of respect for people who can have a belief in something that has questionable 'facts'. I am not having a 'pop' at religion. As I see it, it offers relief and support to those who require it. That must, therefore, be a good thing. Anyway, one vein I had found with most religions is its attempt to 'forgive'. This is a massive request to ask of most people. Especially people who have been hurt or are hurting right now.

From my own perspective, I had experienced hatred (I've possibly been hated too). But I had found my hate turn to resentment then pity, and finally apathy. But why is forgiveness not the answer to all the hurt and pain we feel? I know (deep, deep down) that is probably the best thing to do. But I didn't think 'forgiveness is the 'be all – end all' to the pain of abuse. I had tried so hard to forgive my ex for the things she had said and done. I refused to excuse the reasons for her behaviour as she is responsible, as an adult, for those actions. And ultimately the consequences, to both herself and I. I just felt at that moment, a sense of pity. Pity because she had no idea what she had done, the problems that this had caused and the damage it had done. Furthermore, I felt pity for her as she would one day wonder why she is alone. She cannot depend on her looks for ever. They fade. But real beauty is based on character and personality. And hers, ladies and gentlemen was ugly. I feel pity for all of those things within her and yet is what to become of her. Yet I still find it hard to forgive. I have seen it said in many self-help books that forgiveness can lead to:

- ≅ Healthier relationships
- ≅ Greater spiritual and psychological well-being
- ≅ Less anxiety, stress and hostility
- ≅ Lower blood pressure
- ≅ Fewer symptoms of depression

- ≅ Stronger immune system
- ≅ Improved heart health
- ≅ Higher self-esteem

Yet, she was the cause of all these problems. I have been proud of my physical health in general. I have never attended hospital although I do have a history of depression. I've never even had a filling. But the abuse I suffered left me with a greater level of anxiety, a greater level of depression and PTSD. And little, if any self-esteem. Yet I still felt pity for her, because I know I would get better. Her life was based on denial and bitterness. Her problems cannot be treated with medication alone. So I don't need to forgive. I just have pity for her.

I had literally found tons of literature stating that forgiveness can improve your mental and physical health. It also focuses on the idea of easing anxiety and depression. Letting go of a grudge, it seems, may be up there with exercising and getting enough sleep as one of the best things you can do for yourself. But I believe that refusing to forgive is a healthy frame of mind that protects you against further damage. It further stops you from being someone else's 'door mat'. What's wrong with that? From my point of view, nothing. I am more than happy to promote self-protection. I think it is wrong and a fallacy to suggest to anyone that they cannot move on without forgiveness. To even suggest that this is the only way out of unhappiness is a cruel suggestion, especially when no one else has walked in your shoes. Let's make it clear, it's not anybody's place to tell you when to forgive or not. It is your decision when, and only when, the time is right. Whether that is today, next year or never, then so be it.

I had found that wanting to move away from the damage and hurt (isn't that what we are all trying to do?), does not require you to say "I forgive you". You can get the same relief and escape from your pains by taking a new approach to these problems. Previously, my approach usually meant rolling over and accepting her poisons. However, my new approach involved; counselling, medication, keeping a journal and so on. I had not forgiven, yet here I was feeling pretty good. I think this is mainly down to the fact that it wasn't me at fault, it was all her. What is there to forgive when she would never change anyway. Forgiveness for her would be an utter waste of time. I had no anger, just pity for a lost soul. A soul who thinks it's okay to abuse in all of it ugly forms. There is enough pressure on people like us already to try and rebuild our lives without the added pressure of not forgiving. Especially to those who abused. And by the people who have no idea. Undoubtedly, I will probably get a long line of people criticising what I have just said. And I consider that to be perfectly fine. We are all entitled to our opinions and this is mine (I make no apology for it). But from my point of view if I forgave her she would not see the damage she had done because I had seemed to forgive so easily. I want her to know she had done wrong. Deep down I want her to stop for her own well-being. That does not require forgiveness. It requires pity. But, I firmly believe that I should not be carrying the burden of not forgiving. No one can point the finger at me and condemn me for feeling pain and distress caused by others. After all, would our abusers condemn us for standing up for ourselves. Mine didn't condemn, she just dug herself in even deeper and I walked away. Therefore, I have no reason to forgive someone who continues to damage everything around her and will continue to do so. Again, I just pity her.

I am not a psychiatrist, and although I work in the medical profession I mainly work in trauma. I had realised that the power of the mind far outweighs physical strength in so many ways. There are various views about how much of the brain is actually being used at any one time, and these theories are still under discussion and investigation. I had spent many nights lying awake not being able to sleep because my mind was bouncing with thoughts or ideas. I had also had days when I had recalled past events either from decades ago or more recently, which sometimes triggered feelings of self-doubt or utter sadness. Although on the flip side it is just as easy to recall happier moments which brought feelings of warmth and contentment.

It can be considered that our trains of thought can be built on habits. For example, every one of us can attach a memory to a certain song (either good or bad). Or we may recall when we first had a certain meal. For me, I can recall walking along the River Avon in Evesham every time I consume a chocolate lime for example. This is a positive recall. However, I can now associate a certain song with being punched in the back, or a fragrance being attached to a specific human. I once joined a slimming club many years ago. It was utter agony. Throughout my period of membership, I was constantly recalling how lovely chocolate tasted, or how lovely KFC chicken actually smelt on an empty stomach. In fact, I failed at being a vegetarian because my will power over a bacon sandwich was just not strong enough. But is it fair to argue or consider that people who slim, or people who try to refrain from smoking suffer the same torments as someone who has just left an abusive relationship. Are we drawn to the evils because we are used to it and we are only addicted because our minds crave the routine of which we are now used to? Many years ago, I went on a course, I really cannot recall what it was about, but one thing really stuck in my head, and I am going to share it with you now. The host said to us all "whatever you do, I plead with you not to think of a red balloon". Well yes you guessed it, everyone, including myself thought of a red balloon. I don't know the science behind it, perhaps it was a suggestive thought, but the power that individual had over my free thoughts was phenomenal. So, to put this into perspective; when you try to avoid certain foods because of a diet – all you can think about is that food. If you are trying to forget an ex, they instantly spring to mind. When you try and forget why you flinch every time a certain word is mentioned you are flashed back to a specific event.

No longer would I be held to ransom by the actions of an ex. I had moved on but she still accommodates an area of my mind. I was fighting depression, but my life had so many associations attached to such events. I had tried to stop but when I do I often find my mind wonders back to those moments. Perhaps my brain is seeking safety in a place it recognises. If this is the case it's an uncomfortable state to live in. One day whilst in the kitchen making coffee, I heard a song on the radio. Instantly, I recalled an uncomfortable memory about my ex. My mouth went dry and I could feel my heart race. It was if my abusive ex was present in the same room. I instantly felt vulnerable. To be honest with you, I felt quite scared by my lack of strength even after all this time. It was an unreasonable feeling that I was experiencing at that moment. I knew she wasn't there. In fact I knew she was miles away. But the power of my thoughts was shocking. It had lost utter control of my physical self. It was at this moment that I tried something new. The song was playing but I refused to switch the radio off. So, I picked up the dog and hugged her. I would hope to think that the next time I hear that specific song I would now associate it with hugging the dog as opposed to blocking a punch. Even now as I write this I am recalling lifted the dog and holding her like a small child. That is surely a better memory to associate that specific song with. It would be impossible to wipe clean your whole life. We are after all, a product of past events. I remember when my son was younger and he did something which required a stern word. Instantly, I recalled being told the same thing by my own parents – or did I just sound like my (adopted) mother at that specific moment? I remember as a teenager in the 1980's I could recall any phone number. Being able to dial the numbers like how a secretary types, with speed and not looking at the keyboard. I think back then, I could recall probably about seven or eight numbers instantly. In fact if you gave me the first few numbers of a specific telephone number I could probably still continue the rest. 0121 475…., 0121 443….. But we don't need to remember numbers anymore. Modern phones only require you to remember the name of the person you are about to call.

But modern life and its instruments almost reinforces negative memories. When I flick through my 'Pictures' file, I come across a range of photographs that were taken many years ago. Instantly, my mind is flashed back to that moment of capture. This is also the case with things such as social media, for example. I had read many comments that people had written statements saying things like 'they had looked up an ex on Social media'. Why? The pictures are fake in so far as they captured a moment of staged smiles. But your memories are real. They are an ex for a reason. No-one (that I know of) had stayed in a toxic relationship because they liked their abusers 'smile' – which is all you see in a photograph. If you look at those specific pictures, try and recall them kicking the shit out of you or of them screaming in your face. Remember your mind is suggesting something. I would like to suggest, if you can recall, a red balloon. Ironically, I am not asking you to stop reading the pages within this book in case it makes the reader recall negative events or thoughts. I have embarked on writing these pages because I want to share my experiences and offer an alternative to what you are experiencing. It might even be that you are reading this book and saying "yes, I've had that too, I was, therefore, not alone". But I want to offer a glimmer of hope. Perhaps the ability to think differently was an indication that I was recovering. Perhaps I was at that moment getting better. I hope so. My depression took away my best years and my ex tried to smash the remaining. I didn't want to lose any more. Is that an unreasonable thing to ask for?

I would like the opportunity to continue to write. And I want to continue with my experiment of disassociation. It's about time I tried to break the cycle, I hope it works. But I would love to hear from anyone else that tries this approach and to see if it works. Perhaps I might be on to something here and if it makes anyone rich, remember you heard it here first!!

I don't know whether it's just me but sometimes I might hear something and it sits with me for a while until either something else replaces it within my thought bank or I investigate it further. I was awake one night watching TV in bed when I observed a programme discussing the state of the present legal system in the UK. One particular guest stated; "if we have responsibilities, then we must have the right". For me this was like a light bulb moment. These two words 'rights' and 'responsibilities' should have an obvious connection. They should be united in their meanings. But they have not been allowed to be. They have had a divorce forced upon them with both parties unwilling to separate. The word 'rights' has, and is, often misused and often taken for granted. A dictionary definition of rights states;

right/rʌɪt/

noun

plural noun: rights

that which is morally correct, just, or honourable.

"she doesn't understand the difference between right and wrong"

synonyms: goodness, rightness, righteousness, virtue, virtuousness, integrity, rectitude, uprightness, principle, propriety, morality, truth, truthfulness, honesty, honour, honourableness, justice, justness, fairness, equity, equitableness, impartiality; More lawfulness, legality

"the difference between right and wrong"

antonyms: wrong

a moral or legal entitlement to have or do something.

"she had every right to be angry"
synonyms: entitlement, prerogative, privilege, advantage, due,
birthright, liberty, authority, authorization, power, licence,
permission, dispensation, leave, consent, warrant, charter,
franchise, sanction, exemption, immunity, indemnity;

There is significant disagreement about what is meant precisely by the term 'rights'. It has been used by different groups and thinkers for different purposes, over different periods of time. Very often with different and sometimes opposing definitions. The precise definition of this principle, beyond having something to do with normative rules of some sort or another, is controversial.

Natural rights are rights which are deemed to be 'natural' in the sense of not being artificial or not man-made. In effect these are rights deriving from human nature or from the edicts of a god. For example, it has been argued that humans have a natural right to life. These are, in my view, moral rights or absolute rights that no state can dictate to or interfere with. In contrast, legal rights, are based on a society's customs, laws and statutes. An example of a legal right is the right to vote. Citizenship, itself, is often considered as the basis for having legal rights. Legal rights are sometimes called civil rights or statutory rights and are culturally and politically relative since they depend on a specific common framework to have meaning. Throughout time thinkers have seen rights in only one sense while others accept that both senses have a measure of validity. There has been considerable debate about these senses throughout history. For example, Jeremy Bentham (15 February 1748 – 6 June 1832) believed that legal rights were at the heart of rights, and he denied the existence of natural rights. Thomas Aquinas (1225 – 1274), however, argued that rights claimed by positive law but not grounded in natural law were not properly rights at all, but only a facade or pretense of rights. As I see it, therefore, the general populace is still shrouded in confusion when they discuss 'their rights'. Time and again I have heard people state it is their right to wear whatever they want or to do whatever they wish. But this may be contrary to the rights of others who may see this as offensive or just downright wrong. For example, I disagree with blood sports of any kind – it is my right to have this view – but it would be wrong for me to force my opinions on others who disagree. It is the role of law for this to change if it is to be considered as an absolute wrong. And I would like to think that a majority of the human population would take and accept this stance. My argument is also supported by the concept of the 'Human Rights Act 1998'. Indeed, the very title claims to the right of humans but it is only reinforced by manmade laws contained in the European Convention on Human Rights. Which in turn is not a natural right at all but man-made decisions. What also bothers me about this title is the presumption by the majority of people is that they consider that they are free to do what ever they want under the protection of this said act. I wonder how many people who scream about 'their human rights' have actually read the document? I consider not many have.

I like the word responsibility. It has a feeling of 'duty' or 'liability' about it. Put simply, it is my responsibility as a father to clothe, feed and educate my children. I also have a responsibility to drive my car without recklessness or dangerously. Of course, these responsibilities are enshrined in law (Tort) but that is to protect those with whom I come into contact and not to protect myself. In essence, and I hope you agree, having 'responsibility' is to hold a duty or obligation. The dictionary definition holds that;

"...the state or fact of being responsible, answerable, or accountable for something within one's power, control, or management."

In an ideal world I would love each and every one of us to know with some certainty that our rights and responsibilities are equal and firmly married. But, alas, they are not. For those of whom govern, having these two concepts together would fly in the face of state control. And so the myth has been able to perpetuate. As a father I know about my responsibilities (as previously stated) but the law does not protect my right as a father to equal access to the children. I can give so many examples where this is so. Yet, I am expected to carry out my duty (responsibility) without the protection of the law. There is just an assumption and assumption is not a protection in law.

But let me look at this a little further. The average man is allowed to live freely within his home. But his partner abuses him. He has the right to leave but cannot expect the protection he requires as of his assumed right. And why is this? Well it now transpires that the police and the CPS will not protect your right to equality in the law because your rights are compromised by their inefficiency, corruption and selectiveness of evidence to prove the truth. Yes, the abused man has a responsibility to not hit back or counter assault; but he does not have the right to equal protection from wrongful arrest or to be protected equally. There is no equality in law, there is no equality in refuge and there is no equality to the rights to our children. Yet we must always maintain our responsibilities. I am happy to uphold my responsibilities. It offers a sense of duty and protection. This concept of responsibility also protects me in my daily existence. But alas, it doesn't protect me from an abusive partner because I don't hold the right to protection. It is just assumed it is there until I need it. And for so many it isn't there. It just doesn't exist.

For those who have followed my writing you will have probably noticed a bit of a shift in my focus. As I write this I am satisfied that from the outset I knew this blog would become organic and grow. At the beginning I talked about what happened to me and this flowed into anger directed at my abusive ex. From my perception I consider that I got over her a while ago, but my new focus is the corruption and failings of a system that not only failed me (and many others) but also protected the abuser. As I have stated numerous times before she had a history of abuse and was, time after time, able to get away with it. But, even with her history she is still protected by what she knows to be a failing in the system to protect victims. Thus, promote abuse within the home. The rhetoric of protecting victims does not stand up to simple scrutiny.

We have known from reading recent news articles that time and again both the police and CPS have failed to disclose evidence and facts. Therefore, how is the right to liberty and equality guaranteed in a so called civilised society, when this simple belief is chosen to be ignored? In essence, rights and responsibilities translate as, it is our responsibility to do what is perceived as being decent and respectable, yet we cannot expect the right of protection regardless of how it is flowered up to desperate victim.

PART V
COMPLAINTS

CHAPTER 18
Police & Social Services

After a long period of reflection and consideration, I eventually took the initiative to make a formal complaint to the Independent Police Complaints Commission (IPCC). Initially I was going to leave it all alone, lick my wounds and move on. But I finally decided to address what I saw as an injustice. This injustice had made me so angry and consumed so much energy that my disappointment was almost nuclear. Firstly, I researched the background to my complaint on line and discovered that there is a clause called 'Direction and Control'. As my complaint is not about a specific officer, but is about their lack of ability to recognise a male victim of abuse this option seems to fit the complaint better. They physically and purposely chose to ignore hard evidence given to them and failed to recognise the signs when shown to them. They utterly failed in their duty to protect and serve the community they claim to represent and protect. Although the form was fairly easy to find (https://www.ipcc.gov.uk/complaints), the form was pretty unremarkable. There was very little specific space to write what my complaint was about so I wrote down everything in the boxes that I had available. I pity the poor person who had to process what I had written but it was cathartic to pound the keys on the keyboard expressing my frustration at the lack of 'policemanship' and the experience of prejudice based on my gender. My motive for the complaint was complaint was six fold. Firstly, I wanted to highlight the utter lack of interest in my allegations against her. No officer had or had ever asked about my considerations or experience both before, during or after the event. Secondly, they failed to follow up any evidence that I had supplied to them. How on earth can their actions therefore be considered unbiased? Thirdly, it appears that they went for the easier option of harassing the male rather than getting their hands dirty on the truth of the matter – the female was the abuser with a history of abuse towards men. Her allegations had no grounding or evidence but they still attempted to pursue a prosecution. Fourthly, when I spoke to an officer about my allegations he did not take a single note. I advised him that I was aware that he had not written anything and he became clearly embarrassed that I had noted this. Fifthly, the police's action (or inaction) nearly cost me my job and reputation. Although I would never expect a real apology about this, they had to realise the consequence of their actions when they opt to pick and choose whatever evidence they want, regardless of the dubious nature of it. And finally, following my acquittal there had been no explanation why it was allowed to go that far when even my abuser's solicitor indicated it was a hopeless case. This must have cost the taxpayer thousands, when from the outset, there was no case to answer.

Following my acquittal it had played on my mind that she had been allowed to do this unhindered. Not only to myself but to her other ex-partners also. I had always had the belief that as an adult you should be held responsible for your actions. Yet, it appears that this is not the case if the police can either not be bothered or see it as being too complicated to deal with. The evidence based on the police actions seems to indicate that if a male is involved in any form of domestic abuse, he must therefore, be guilty, regardless of any counter evidence that is supplied. This philosophy is wrong and although I doubted that anything would come of my complaint, I felt I needed to say something. I had previously said that it is a shame people didn't come with a label. But it appears they do. If you are a male and found guilty then you are put on what is known as 'Claire's Register'. Although, in essence I don't have a problem with this, it appears to be heavily weighted against men. This whole experience had signaled that this is the case. She made a false allegation and had not had to answer for her crimes. It is people like this who need to be put on a register so men can be protected from her. Isn't this the same principle behind women who make false rape allegations. The male always appears to be named before any allegations are disproved and so it seems to continue. Of course, let's get real. My complaint, like everything I have done since, would fall on deaf ears and be talked about behind closed doors. The reality of getting any proper closure to this was very unlikely. The talk of justice would no doubt be mentioned but would never bear fruit. I am not being naïve but I do think some sort of record needs to made about an individual who continually makes false allegations. Following my decision to move my approach to one of complaining I received a phone call shortly afterwards. I spoke to a gentleman who took the time to listen to my points and clarify certain details. The conversation took a number of approaches. I discussed in great detail my concerns about the unfair and biased approaches the police took with regards to my case. I stressed that the police had failed to investigate the allegations I had made and how they had chosen to pick and choose what evidence they wanted. In effect, I argued that they only chose to consider any evidence that would secure my wrongful conviction. I also commented that their officers took a gender specific approach. They instantly assumed that the male was guilty to what had been claimed. Furthermore, they chose to ignore the accounts I had gathered of which were supported by my managers, the health service and previous solicitors involvements. I was instantly surprised by his response of agreement and this had sort of set a precedent amongst other complaints I had subsequently made. The investigator stated that I had a valid complaint and that investigations would be made against two officers. One of the officers was the arresting officer (who was female) and the second was the officer who took no notes during my complaint meeting after my arrest. He further stated that the first officer had acted with questionable professionalism and the second appeared under-experienced. However, he agreed that he would need time to investigate my complaint fully of which I agreed was fair and reasonable. One major feature of the phone call was that he said I now had a case to have my ex arrested on the grounds of assault, sexual assault and theft. However, he stood his ground to state that he would give me time to give it some consideration and to offer me a period of recovery following my recent events.

Following my acquittal, I found that it had become a hollow victory. It appeared to me that many of the organisations assumed guilt before the case had been heard and so had put in place things in readiness for my guilt. Yet when I was found not guilty they literally had no idea what to do. In fact many of them where literally out of their depth and so were quick to distance themselves from many of the decision makers.

I had raised two separate complaints about two individual social workers of whom I had argued had acted both unprofessionally and above and beyond their scope of practice. Luckily for me social workers and paramedics are responsible to the same governing body and so I had ready access to codes of practice and what is expected. This was critical in my case whereby I had raised my complaints. From previous experiences when dealing with official organisations I had found that they tended to close ranks and stick together. However, when I was able to identify key points of concerns against professional practice expectations, it became evident that many of the managers were quick to distance themselves from those specific individuals.

The first social worker I will discuss tripped over his own arrogance and attempted to call my bluff. After a long period of time this said social worker only made contact with me when I informed his receptionist that I had employed a solicitor to take this specific social worker to court to obtain answers for his actions. It was only then that he called. The telephone conversation I had with him was dreadful. He initially called me a liar stating that I was a wicked evil and dangerous man. Of course I can state that this is not the case. But what bothered me was that he had made this statement prior to my court case and so based his assumptions by the story of one person – and we all now know what a liar she was. Following this initial 'combative' conversation, I questioned the quality of his record keeping. His dates did not match up with my own (time after time I had stressed the importance of keeping a record). When I directly challenged his incapacity to do his job properly he became aggressive and even said "how dare I challenge him when he is a social worker". Well, this was like a red rag to a bull. I informed him that I would be making two complaints. One to his direct manager and the other to the HCPC. In response he told me to 'go ahead' and that he 'didn't care.' Now, why would a supposed professional give a false name if they were adamant that they had acted correctly? And here is where the questionable professionalism gained its crown. When I asked for his name he gave me a false name!!! I eventually made contact with his manager who was extremely apologetic and listened to my issues and concerns. She was without doubt the polar opposite of what I had experienced to date. I received a letter about two weeks after the telephone call informing me that the said social worker had been sacked and I was invited to a meeting to discuss my concerns directly.

I attended the meeting shortly afterwards, and to their credit they (there were two) admitted that there had been failings and incompetence on their part. Like I have previously said, it was evident that they wanted to distance themselves as far as possible from their ex-work colleague. I do on reflection, think they were more fearful about what further potential problems I could raise such as suing and/or going to the papers. I am sure that would be their biggest fear at that point. They admitted that they (or at least the sacked social worker) had acted unprofessionally, and with an obvious bias against me. They also accepted that their time frame was unacceptable. It all came as a bit of a shock really. I had never expected a government department to be so instantly apologetic as this department had been.

My second meeting was held on the afternoon of the same day. I had some concerns that if there was going to be a closed shop attitude it would have come from these people. I arrived usually nice and early to be ready for my meeting and from the outset I was treated with politeness and courtesy. Perhaps my reputation had gone before me. This meeting was slightly more defensive on their part. I had raised a complaint about a social worker that had directly said to my managers that I was "a dangerous individual of whom members of staff and the general public should fear". I directly challenged this on a number of points

1. You cannot go around saying things like that without evidence
2. He was making a direct attack upon my character without substantive evidence. My careers to date would not have tolerated such features. I am not only a member of the HCPC who hold very strict guidelines but I am also a member of the General Teaching Council. Being both a paramedic and a qualified teacher would mean that no employer would allow such a violent person to be in those professions.
3. It could have created problems with relationships of

friends and family. Luckily enough everyone knew my true characteristics – but that was not the point.

4. It is illegal to say such things.
5. He was difficult to get hold of via phone or email to question his reasonings for such comments – in fact to date I have still not heard from him.
6. He had no grounding to say such things prior to a court case (therefore presuming guilt) and I do not and have not ever held a criminal record.
7. It is highly unprofessional
8. It shows that this individual goes around throwing his weight and not expecting to answer for it.

To a degree I can see why his manager was defensive towards his colleague. From the outset I had stated the importance of presumption of innocence prior to proven guilt. And he rightfully took this approach waiting for me to disprove his views. It is just a shame that they didn't offer this same level of courtesy to their clients/victims. The meeting was challenging. He argued that his employee had acted in the best interest of which, to a degree, I agreed with. But when I mentioned key legal points of libel law and professional standards expected via the HCPC his manager calmed down somewhat. In effect, the manager now realised he could not defend the indefensible. It came as no surprise to know that there had been a number of complaints made against this said social worker. It further came as no surprise that the said social worker was absent due to 'sickness'. Now you can call me cynical but I do find this to be a little 'convenient'? It was later in the evening that I had a phone call from the manager in the second meeting. He stated that my complaint would be upheld and that considerations would be made with regards to this social workers' future career (as soon as he returns to work after a bout of convenient illness). He expressed his apologies and stated that there was clearly a training need amongst his staff. I must stress that I was not only happy and surprised by his call, but I was pleased to see that he had considered my points and accepted a level of responsibility.

Again, when I had proved my point it showed how quickly they wanted to distance themselves from the corrupt individuals within their employment. I should mention at this stage that I thought I was going to be ignored and further slighted (based on actions and events to date). I knew it was going to be a challenge to question the behaviour of two police officers and two social workers. After all, they had the backing of whoever and whatever and here was I. Just me, myself and a bottled up feeling of injustice and rage. What I had discovered is that when you have evidence Goliath crumbles to become a specific individual. Just little people who cannot hide behind the massive wall of formal protection. When I had proven that these individuals acted beyond their remit and possibly even illegally their bosses were so quick to hang them out to dry and distance themselves from what could be potentially devastating. I was sure I could sue and I know the papers would love this kind of story. But nobody is beyond the law and is answerable for their actions and this is the point I wanted to raise via my formal complaints.

I often stay up late watching documentaries on TV. However, one night it dawned on me that this could have been so much worse. I want to consider a time when the death penalty was in force. Would the officials have challenged the police and social workers like I did? I had now experienced how officials can lie or seek a 'truth' that fits within their assumptions of guilt and almost get away with it- unchallenged. How many other innocent people had gone through this to be faced with a wall of false and malicious officialdom to be found guilty (or even swung from a rope). We know it had happened with cases such as Timothy Evans who hung for a crime he never committed in the face of dubious evidence. Alas it appears that little had changed especially when we consider the more recent case of Liam Allan (I will go into more detail later). I am glad that certain individuals have now become answerable. They created a whirlwind of which I found myself in the middle of. But luckily for me I was able to grab hold of it and tame it. The big machines of officialdom are actually small individual cogs when you look closely. They do indeed get knocked down to size when formally challenged . The Nuremburg Trials did not accept the defense of 'following orders'. But when individuals act with a 'god given right' it needs to be challenged. And I had. One had been sacked, one may yet to be sacked. A whole department is going to be trained and updated with regards to what they can and cannot do. Two police officers were also under investigation. Why? Because they all fear bad publicity and paying out financial damages. Furthermore, the cause of all this will also need to face her own whirlwind. Without her none of this would have happened. She had got away with it before and arrogantly assumed that she is getting away with it again. I was just waiting for the police update to direct them to arrest my ex for the abuse she subjected me to. However, the big advantage I have is that I had good solid evidence and I had spoken the truth.

After a week or so following my meetings with social services I received my second apology letter today. Their letter was long winded and a little bit (what I would consider to be) wet. But it contained what I wanted. Firstly, an apology and secondly that my complaints had been upheld. It was during the weekend after receipt of the said letters that I took a step back and looked at it from a different angle. Yes, I had been treated badly by two different county council social workers departments. But I considered two points. Firstly, how can one person be so unlucky to have dealt with two different departments to be handled by two failing social workers? Secondly, if I am only one person to have found these faults how rife must mismanagement and unprofessionalism actually be within official governmental departments? But how many other people, throughout the world, who had found themselves in my situation had also (unknowingly) had to deal with corruption, lies and unprofessionalism without redress? How many other lives had been damaged without the knowledge of challenging such decisions? Perhaps we will never know. I was sure no government departments would keep statistics on such matters. But if I was only one, and this is my first experience, it must be more widespread than any of us can imagine.

Many of us will know that if we have responsible jobs we are constantly subjected to scrutiny and assessments. In some cases, we may even be responsible to a governing body. But surely how can two different social workers in two different councils get it so wrong? Is it them or should their departments be answerable as a whole. Furthermore, could I also suggest that a higher authority go an inspect their previous cases because I can state with some authority that I bet I was not the only one to have felt the roughness of their so called justice. During my first meeting with

Warwickshire County Council, I stated that to them people are just a number or a file on a shelf. But this couldn't be further from the truth. Each case is a human being suffering in some way that feels lost or forgotten due to the inhumanity of it all. And this is an important point. As we all live and breathe, we are all different to each other and so some formulas may not work on each and every case. Each name is a person, each complaint has a story to tell and each case needs to be looked at beyond its face value. I was never given the decency of this expectation at all. I still feel more could be done. I know many people would be glad that it was 'all over' and perhaps roll over and be glad it's all concluded with. Yet I feel each and every one of us had a duty to fight against any form of injustice. If I had not said, "this is wrong" these corrupt social workers would continue to go about their business unhindered and wrong. How many more lives could they have ruined? It could be yours next. I was not prepared to let this go. How can it be that one day you are seen as a pillar of society with no criminal record to becoming the devil incarnate and a dangerous man the next? Well, we know it all stemmed from one person's lies. She would of course be dealt with appropriately because I would make it my business to make sure it is done correctly. Like myself, we all have a duty to work to our greatest abilities or to be a better person. But alas, I have found that many in authority don't seem to carry this philosophy and I find this a dangerous precedent. A real turning point was when it was said to me; "how dare I challenge him when he is a social worker". What kind of explanation is that? Don't we put down dogs because they bite – after all that's what dog do.

Perhaps things will change. We can complain to higher authorities pushing our complaints further. But this should never be the case in the first place as things should be dealt with correctly from the outset. But unfortunately, I must suggest that this would never be the case because these individuals do indeed hide behind official walls. Believing themselves to be untouchable. Okay, one social worker had been sacked but it doesn't stop him from getting another social worker's job somewhere else. No doubt, he would still go home to his comfortable home and family. His only regret would be the fact that he was caught out (but I still bet that he has no regrets on what he did). The other is off sick. I still find this very convenient. The longer he is off the less chance they have to question him about his conduct. I doubt he would get sacked and eventually, as he looks through his rear-view mirror on life, I would just be a mere shadow. Yet these individuals have been mountains in my life. I don't think I will ever forget the damage they have caused all in the name of them thinking (?) they were doing the right thing at the time. Even though I had proven that to be both wrong and illegal.

CHAPTER 19
"Corruption is the abuse of power"

If you recall in my previous chapters following my acquittal, I raised a number of complaints to various establishments. One of these complaints was to the police raising my concerns about unfair treatment and their heavy handedness and blinkered views when it came to male victims of domestic abuse. A short time after my formal complaint, I was invited by the police to attend their station and put my account across about what had happened to me. Following the interview I felt comfortable (if not elated) that for once I was being listened to. During the interview I provided evidence based on statements, texts and emails I had received from my ex and independent diary accounts of when I had reported the assaults I had endured. My statement to the police totalled about eight or nine pages and I was happy to sign each page confirming that what I said was true, accurate and I was would be willing to attend court to state the facts as and when required. The police officer taking the statement stated that she was satisfied that there was enough evidence to prosecute my ex. I must admit that on the morning of the police meeting I was slightly reluctant to go ahead with this because I know the pain of being arrested and questioned under caution. Yet I knew I was telling the truth. Furthermore, as you may recall, she had a history of such actions and saw it as her right to create problems for men when she knew the relationship was over. She had her previous ex arrested and charged for the same things as I and on each occasion the cases were thrown out at court. Therefore, with this history I felt it was justified to go ahead and push for a prosecution.

However, after a month of investigations I received a phone

call from the police to say that after consideration they were not going to follow the case up any further. It is fair to say I was livid. I stated that I had given them hard and irrefutable evidence that included statements from other people and professional agencies. I also informed the police officer that the police were all unjustifiably over me following her fake and malicious 999 call. Furthermore, she had also supplied dubious evidence which the court had dismissed due to its lack of credence and validity. This police officer (an inspector) was not only dismissive but clearly ignorant of the facts as I put them and the evidence that proved I was right.

But let's consider this further for a moment. Let's look at the facts as they now appear. Firstly, I had reported my assaults to my work organisation that kept dates and comprehensive details about the assaults and threats I had received by my ex. Secondly, I had kept text and emails from my ex highlighting what kind of assaults she was prepared to carry out upon me. And finally, I had independent witness statements from people who knew me and were aware of what I was enduring. Furthermore, one of the witnesses also knew my ex and what she was like. Each statement supported my view and accounts. But here is the 'rub' which I now consider as fact. The final response from the police now indicated and proves why men didn't bother reporting abuse to the police. I opened up about events and actions that no-one should ever endure in a relationship. I stated facts that were uncomfortable and I had each statement tested for validity. Yet they ultimately failed to do anything and chose to remain ignorant of any wrong doing. It now appears evident that the police are blinkered and biased when it comes to domestic abuse. They failed me and had now continued to do so.

I would stress now, if you are a male in an abusive relationship and you manage to get out (or for that matter have to remain in the family home) don't bother calling the police. All you would do is create un-needed stress and upset. You would be left bereft at the level of ignorance and unreasonableness by the police. Let me remind you, this happens here and now within a democratic society that claims to be civilized, and yet the abuse is allowed to go on in so many places right under the noses of the police and the authorities. Unfortunately, we men have little, if any, protection under the law to combat domestic abuse.

I have learnt that I absolutely love writing. I also pride myself on writing fair and unbiased opinions. However, what I am about to write won't be unbiased. It will however, be honest and open based on my experiences and knowledge. undoubtedly, I will get some form of critism for what I have written but I want to be convinced that I am wrong. I want my faith restored in the system. But it would take a lot of convincing I'm afraid.

I was brought up to respect the hierarchy of society, its laws and customs. I knew where I stood and I knew my place within my community. As an honest hard-working citizen, I came to expect and assume that the police would protect myself and my loved ones in our hours of need. I looked up to these officers thanking them for their self-sacrifices in the name of law and order. But it transpires I was fed on lies and propaganda. Yet, time and time again I had witnessed and read a continual list of police failures. I recall my great grandmother telling me a story about police corruption during the first world war. She would recount how they profited from black market deals and would expect to be able to sit in the back of her shop on rainy days (whilst they hung their coats up outside). And that is without discussing pimping and theft. I would often dismiss her stories as random ramblings from an old lady. Although, much of what she told me had become reflected in my own experiences of the police service.

Let's be clear, I would never want to be a policeman, mainly because I didn't consider myself to be arrogant and holier than thou. Yet they have made a rod for their own backs and deserve a lot of the criticism they appear to get. Because for police officers in this country, corruption has become routine. Imagine that the police increasingly used their powers to crack down not on criminals but on anyone who dares to speak out against them. Well they do, not in a banana republic, but here in England. It is not that power corrupts. In a modern society power is needed to protect the rights of individuals. Yet, it is that power which attracts the corrupted. The very idea of joining the police service must require a certain lack of empathy, because by definition, the police cannot produce anything, only act upon a claim. All the police can do is coerce, jump to unsubstantiated conclusions, and use force to achieve its ends. Does that sound like something a 'good person' wants to do? Some of this was revealed in a little-noticed report by HM Inspectorate of Constabulary (25), which went on to deliver some even more shocking news. Nearly half of 17,200 officers and staff surveyed said that if they discovered corruption among their colleagues and chose to report it, they didn't believe their evidence would be treated in confidence and would fear 'adverse consequences'. This appalling lack of protection for whistle-blowers — often amounting to persecution — has become commonplace throughout the public services and creates a climate in which dishonesty and malpractice flourish. The second report, compiled by the Serious Organised Crime Agency (26), bears this out. It says there has been a sharp increase over the past five years in the number of police officers dealing heroin, cocaine and amphetamines and an equally startling rise in the number of officers abusing their power 'for sexual gratification' — in other words bullying or cajoling suspects, witnesses and even victims into having sex with them.

I recall a policeman moving into the house next to mine a few years ago. He came around to introduce himself (god knows why because it's not something I would do). He said two things. Firstly he stated, "Hello my name is....", instantly followed by "...and I am a policeman". Well what the hell did he expect me to do about that? Perhaps fall to my knees and sing his praises? I would never state to my neighbours on first introduction that I am a paramedic. It's irrelevant and not needed. Ironically, the local burglary rate went up (including a break in of his own shed and had his bike stolen). I could not believe how much this man loved himself. Furthermore, he would invite his (uniformed) friends around often playing loud music until the late hours of the evening. He saw himself as the law and often considered himself to be above it. He would swagger around the estate putting John Wayne to shame with his macho walking techniques. I was once burgled and as expected I called the police (this was a different house). The police eventually turned up a day later and half-heartedly took a statement. What an utter waste of time. Nobody was ever brought to book and I don't even recall them taking fingerprints. However, foolishly I still held them in high regard. As you are probably now aware my faith was utterly broken when I attempted to report my ex for assault and abuse. As I should have expected they did absolutely nothing. In fact when I arrived at the police station for a booked appointment I had to remind the young officer that he had not taken a single note. He was only embarrassed because he thought I hadn't noticed.

On the 3 August 2017, an article was printed in 'The Telegraph' highlighting the police's utter failure when it comes to domestic abuse towards the men (24). It states…

"…Police forces insist they are making great strides in tackling the problem with the number of women convicted of domestic abuse quadrupling in the last decade from 806 in 2004/05 to 3,735 in 2013/14."

But the problem remains still largely hidden and campaigners insisting much more needs to be done to encourage victims to come forward and have the confidence to report an offence. One male victim who took part in the study, but did not want to be named described how he had been arrested on three separate occasions following false allegations by his wife. He said:

"In the latest incident I made the initial complaint to police as my wife assaulted me. But when they arrived, they showed little concern and instead arrested me because my wife made a counter allegation….I certainly feel that more compassion and empathy needs to be shown towards male victims of domestic violence."

Time and again, following research and investigations I had found that the police do not operate to protect the law or its victims but only seem to operate a policy of the 'easy option'. It is easier for them to blame a male victim than a female perpetrator. And this is wrong. Morally and professionally.

I recall driving to work one morning and spotting a policeman having some difficulty with a suspect. Thinking I was doing my public duty by helping the officer involved I stepped in. Today, I would never take such an undertaking. I would view it that the policeman was either unjustifiably throwing his weight around and became unstuck. Or, like every other police officer I know he was corrupt. My son had always disliked the police and I never really knew why. Recently when I asked him his reasons he stated that "the police are driven by targets and not crime fighting". I must admit he is right and I have spent my whole life being wrong with regards to trusting and believing in the police. I struggled to argue an alternative view, because I did not believe in an alternative argument to his view.

I want to be like so many other male victims of domestic abuse, and to be treated with the respect we deserve and not be re-traumatized by the police's failure to do what they should be expected to do. If they can't see fit to offer a prosecution against my ex then I want reassurance what happened to me will never ever happen again. But I fear each individual police officer I have met lacks the comprehension to understand my request.

Let's be clear, this book is not about men being the only victims. Domestic abuse is a real factor in the world we live in. What does concern me is that victims are not being afforded the decency and respect they should require from the representatives of the law of whom we are expected to respect. The facts and actions I have witnessed, however, do not merit respect from me. The police had constantly failed me and I have had enough of not being able to talk about it.

CHAPTER 20
Who are policing the police?

Following my previous chapter highlighting the continued failure of the police, I received a letter from the CPS (Crown Prosecution Service) to whom I had also raised concerns. The contents of their letter was, to be fair, very educational and informative. Within the said letter it stated that the police and CPS operate on a policy (or frame work) called 'The Full Code Test'. Obviously, I then 'googled' the said phrase and considered the content of the said framework. I spent some time reflecting on how it measured up with my experiences. It was to be fair, enlightening, but it further showed that they had not only operated unfairly in my case but they had also failed to consider the steps towards a reasonable arrest. The specific page I used was; https://www.cps.gov.uk/publications/code_for_crown_prosecutors/codetest.html As a result of these useful findings I then sent a response to the CPS letter of which I had received. Below is the response I sent to their complaints officer of whom offered me the insight to how the CPS and police work when considering a potential prosecution. For obvious reasons I have hidden the names of specific people. Furthermore, the sections in **bold** are directly lifted from the CPS 'Full Code Test'. My responses are written in *italics*.

Dear Mrs XX

Thank you for your letter dated 12th December 2017.

I have of course, noted the contents. I am without doubt deeply disappointed with your response and as such I would like you to reconsider based on what I wish to highlight.

As with your letter I too would like to break down my response into two parts, namely 'that I was arrested and charged although there was no evidence' and 'the CPS did not want to pursue a prosecution against my ex'.

As a result of your letter I too researched your policy of the 'Full Code Test' and as a result it appears to give me greater strength and emphasis to push my complaint to you further.

As you know there appears to be 2 sections that you have to consider (I don't intend to teach you to suck eggs – but I feel it is a relevant point to raise).

Firstly, if we consider The Evidential Stage it states;

≅ **Prosecutors must be satisfied that there is sufficient evidence to provide a realistic prospect of conviction against each suspect on each charge. They must consider what the defence case may be, and how it is likely to affect the prospects of conviction....**

The only evidence that my ex supplied was a statement by her daughter (hardly impartial) who clearly stated in her statement that she was not in the room when the supposed assault took place. Furthermore, there was no photographic evidence or any other forms of evidence to support my ex's claim. Furthermore, the supposed incident happened several weeks previously to her malicious 999 call to the police.

Hence, I will highlight the fact that there was insufficient evidence to satisfy any prospect of a conviction.

≅ **The finding that there is a realistic prospect of conviction is based on the prosecutor's objective assessment of the evidence, including the impact of any defence, and any other information that the suspect has put forward or on which he or she might rely. It means that an objective, impartial and reasonable jury or bench of magistrates or judge hearing a case alone, properly directed and acting in accordance with the law, is more likely than not to convict the defendant of the charge alleged. This is a different test from the one that the criminal courts themselves must apply. A court may only convict if it is sure that the defendant is guilty.**

It appeared following my questioning that at no point was my defence ever taken into consideration (I will of course go into greater detail of within the second section of this letter).

As stated the whole case rested on a weak statement from a biased witnessed who actually didn't witness anything. I am sure that you are aware this is far from satisfactory to consider any form of a successful prosecution.

With this being the only form of evidence, it was clear that an objective and impartial and reasonable magistrate would not convict – there is clearly a lack of evidence. As a point of note, this was also stated by the magistrates summing up at the end of the hearing.

In effect there was nothing to contribute or support a view of beyond reasonable doubt.

≅ **When deciding whether there is sufficient evidence to prosecute, prosecutors should ask themselves the following:**

Can the evidence be used in court?

Prosecutors should consider whether there is any question over the admissibility of certain evidence. In doing so, prosecutors should assess:

...the likelihood of that evidence being held as inadmissible by the court;

I appreciate that as this was the only evidence she had thus the magistrates had nothing else to consider

…the importance of that evidence in relation to the evidence as a whole.

As stated this was the only piece of evidence of which the magistrates had available to consider

≅ **Is the evidence reliable?**

Prosecutors should consider whether there are any reasons to question the reliability of the evidence, including its accuracy or integrity.

The evidence has questionable quality. It was written by her 17-year-old daughter who obviously wished to support her mother, thus was biased and lacked integrity. Furthermore, she also stated that she was not in the room when the supposed incident happened.

This was the only piece of evidence available so could not be supported by any other form of evidence. Furthermore, the incident supposedly happened several weeks before the 999 call to the police. I could not recall what I was doing on that suggested date let alone claim to have assaulted her. It all seems very convenient on her behalf to suggest such a date. Hence, based on The Full Code of which you operate, her claim and evidence does not stand up to reliability, accuracy and integrity.

≅ *Is the evidence credible?*

Prosecutors should consider whether there are any reasons to doubt the credibility of the evidence.

I think I have proven this beyond reasonable doubt.

Next, I would like to consider The Public Interest Stage.

As you are aware this is a large section to cover so I will be as brief as I can highlighting failures at this stage.

≅ **In every case where there is sufficient evidence to justify a prosecution, prosecutors must go on to consider whether a prosecution is required in the public interest.**

I struggle to identify any area of protecting the public interest in this case.

I have a good standing within the community and have a history of good character. To support this fact the occupations that I have held and still hold would require me to be of good character. I served as an Officer in the RAF, I am a fully qualified teacher and a paramedic.

≅ **Prosecutors should consider each of the following questions:**

How serious is the offence committed?

The more serious the offence, the more likely it is that a prosecution is required.

According to her statement I had supposedly spat at my ex. Well if this had happened I am sure she would have photographed it to support her claim (but there were no photographs as the event had never actually happened). I assume the idea of claiming to have spat at her would mean that there were no long-lasting bruises to call upon – it's all very convenient. Furthermore, I would like to suggest that the act of spitting is not really putting the public to any form of risk of further harm or damage.

≅ **What is the level of culpability of the suspect?**

Culpability is likely to be determined by the suspect's level of involvement; the extent to which the offending was premeditated and/or planned; whether they have previous criminal convictions and/or out-of-court disposals and any offending whilst on bail; or whilst subject to a court order; whether the offending was or is likely to be continued, repeated or escalated; and the suspect's age or maturity (see paragraph d) below for suspects under 18).

As stated I have no criminal record, I am of good character and my careers endorse this fact. Furthermore, I can argue that every human being is also capable of spitting, hence it's an irrelevant argument.

≅ **The cost to the CPS prosecution service and the wider criminal justice system, especially where it could be regarded as excessive when weighed against any likely penalty (Prosecutors should not decide the public interest on the basis of this factor alone. It is essential that regard is also given to the public interest factors identified when considering the other questions in paragraphs 12 a) to g), but cost is a relevant factor when making an overall assessment of the public interest).**

I dread to think of the costs of this case. When no true and scrutable evidence was really supplied and was not really held in the interests of the public.

This now brings me to the second part of this letter.

I currently have a complaint on-going against Inspector XXXXXX. The complaint is to question why he has not pursued an arrest of my ex based on your principles of prosecution.

Following my acquittal, I raised a complaint to West Mercia Police stating that my complaint of domestic abuse had not been considered or investigated. The reply I had from Inspector XXXXXX was far from satisfactory and did not stand up to scrutiny. Unfortunately, the complaint is still within the processing stages.

However, based on your principles I would like to highlight why I consider to have a justifiable case for prosecution as opposed to the case you had upon myself.

Firstly, if we consider The Evidential Stage;

≅ **Prosecutors must be satisfied that there is sufficient evidence to provide a realistic prospect of conviction against each suspect on each charge. They must consider what the defence case may be, and how it is likely to affect the prospects of conviction. A case which does not pass the evidential stage must not proceed, no matter how serious or sensitive it may be.**

At the time of my arrest I informed the police officer that I held diaries, emails and texts, witness statements and evidence from my work (XXXXX XXXXX Ambulance Service) highlighting the history of abuse I had endured at the hands of my ex-partner. At no point has this ever been called upon or requested. In effect I am able to supply evidence from a range of individual and professional witnesses.

I am sure that with my evidence it would be more likely to secure a prosecution than the case you had against me.

≅ **The finding that there is a realistic prospect of conviction is based on the prosecutor's objective assessment of the evidence, including the impact of any defence, and any other information that the suspect has put forward or on which he or she might rely. It means that an objective, impartial and reasonable jury or**

bench of magistrates or judge hearing a case alone, properly directed and acting in accordance with the law, is more likely than not to convict the defendant of the charge alleged. This is a different test from the one that the criminal courts themselves must apply. A court may only convict if it is sure that the defendant is guilty.

I would consider that based on the same principles you applied to my case you would find enough evidence to pursue a prosecution against my ex. As stated I have a range of statements from independent people to prove I was a victim of her abuse and other evidence of which could be supplied.

≅ **When deciding whether there is sufficient evidence to prosecute, prosecutors should ask themselves the following:**

Can the evidence be used in court?

Prosecutors should consider whether there is any question over the admissibility of certain evidence. In doing so, prosecutors should assess:

the likelihood of that evidence being held as inadmissible by the court...

My evidence would be due to its range and depth

...the importance of that evidence in relation to the evidence as a whole.

I have far greater evidence than that used against me.

Is the evidence reliable?

Prosecutors should consider whether there are any reasons to question the reliability of the evidence, including its accuracy or integrity.

I have medical evidence as could be supplied by my GP. I also hold evidence from my employer (XXXXXX XXXX Ambulance Service) of whom I would argue would be independent and high with integrity. I also hold statements from a range of people from all manner of backgrounds that were aware of the abuse my ex subjected me to.

Is the evidence credible?

Prosecutors should consider whether there are any reasons to doubt the credibility of the evidence.

It is credible (see my answer above). It has been supplied from independent people with a range of views and history of my case. I would now like to consider The Public Interest Stage

≅ **In every case where there is sufficient evidence to justify a prosecution, prosecutors must go on to consider whether a prosecution is required in the public interest.**

This for me is an area of concern. I learnt that she has a history of abusing her partners. She had previously sought prosecutions against two of her exs for a range of various reasons. Furthermore, and this is my major concern, she works with young children at a local primary school. To put this into perspective, if I knew the past history and temperament of this member of staff I would not allow my children to attend such a school. I don't think this is an unreasonable approach as the evidence I have is beyond reasonable doubt.

≅ **It is quite possible that one public interest factor alone may outweigh a number of other factors which tend in the opposite direction. Although there may be public interest factors tending against prosecution in a particular case, prosecutors should consider whether nonetheless a prosecution should go ahead and those factors put to the court for consideration when sentence is passed.**

Prosecutors should consider each of the following questions:

How serious is the offence committed?

The more serious the offence, the more likely it is that a prosecution is required.

When deciding the level of seriousness of the offence committed, prosecutors should include amongst the factors for consideration the suspect's culpability and the harm to the victim by asking themselves the questions at b) and c).

This clause raises a number of options.

Firstly, are you able to prosecute based on wasting everyone's time on a none winnable case based on false evidence?

Secondly, my ex has a track record of abuse against me and other men. Surely this must be within the realms of public interest?

Thirdly, I hold evidence of abuse against myself.

Fourthly, I always assumed it was illegal to request a witness to lie on their behalf and under oath. As in this case where she got her daughter to make a false allegation to support her mother's statement.

≅ **What is the level of culpability of the suspect?**

Culpability is likely to be determined by the suspect's level of involvement; the extent to which the offending was premeditated and/or planned; whether they have previous criminal convictions and/or out-of-court disposals and any offending whilst on bail; or whilst subject to a court order; whether the offending was or is likely to be continued, repeated or escalated; and the suspect's age or maturity (see paragraph d) below for suspects under 18).

Prosecutors should also have regard when considering culpability as to whether the suspect is, or was at the time of the offence, suffering from any significant mental or physical ill health as in some circumstances this may mean that it is less likely that a prosecution is required. However, prosecutors will also need to consider how serious the offence was, whether it is likely to be repeated and the need to safeguard the public or those providing care to such persons.

I would consider that she had planned the 999 call for some time. Especially when she claimed to have been a victim several weeks before the call. Also some thought and consideration would have gone into the thought of what she wanted to claim.

As stated she has a track record of making these allegations (which have always been dismissed). Hence I consider her actions to be premeditated and planned against myself. With this operation alone I would argue that she is still considered to be a risk to all males who come into contact with her.

≅ **What are the circumstances of and the harm caused to the victim?**

The circumstances of the victim are highly relevant. The greater the vulnerability of the victim, the more likely it is that a prosecution is required. This includes where a position of trust or authority exists between the suspect and victim.

Due to what I had experienced I now suffer with PTSD, anxiety and depression. Furthermore, I have been diagnosed with diabetes of which my GP and diabetic nurse directly contribute to the stresses I have recently endured by my ex, the arrest and the subsequent pursuit of some form of equal justice. To-date, I have still not returned to work.

This has also re-enforced the view that male victims of domestic abuse are ignored by the authorities and as a result don't bother to report such crimes. I would, therefore, assume that this is a case that is essential to the protection of the public.

≅ **Prosecutors must also have regard to whether the offence was motivated by any form of discrimination against the victim's ethnic or national origin, gender, disability, age, religion or belief, sexual orientation or gender identity; or the suspect demonstrated hostility towards the victim based on any of those characteristics. The presence of any such motivation or hostility will mean that it is more likely that prosecution is required.**

Based on my ex's history and the way she has brought her daughters up, it would appear that she is a man hater. She has openly talked about how all men are 'bastards'. Thus she is specifically motivated against males. This is further enforced by her track record of trying to prosecute other men.

≅ **In deciding whether a prosecution is required in the public interest, prosecutors should take into account the views expressed by the victim about the impact that the offence has had. In appropriate cases, this may also include the views of the victim's family.**

As previously stated, I now suffer with PTSD, anxiety and depression of which my GP directly contribute to the stresses I have recently endured by my ex, the arrest and the subsequent pursuit of some form of equal justice. To-date, I have still not returned to work.

This has also re-enforced the view that male victims of domestic abuse are ignored by the authorities and as a result don't bother to report such crimes. I would, therefore, assume that this is a case that is essential to the protection of the public.

My confidence with the police and the legal system has now developed into a view of total distrust and failure. The one and only time I had ever requested help from the police they failed me on a number of occasions. Furthermore, there are no viable male refuges of which I could have moved to.

≅ **What is the impact on the community?**

The greater the impact of the offending on the community, the more likely it is that a prosecution is required. In considering this question, prosecutors should have regard to how community is an inclusive term and is not restricted to communities defined by location.

As stated she has targeted males to make false accusations and has manipulated her own daughters to hold men in low esteem.

I hope that these points raised will help you to reconsider my original complaint. Although I am aware that you have no powers over the police I am sure you can see (by your own measurements) that I was treated unfairly and heavy-handedly. I also include the CPS within that specific claim.

I trust that you will look again at my complaint.

I look forward to hearing from you again in due course.

The present system of investigations and prosecutions by both the police and the Crown Prosecution Service is more than regrettable, it's absolutely atrocious. It is only now the dam has burst that there is a flood of questions and accusations aimed at the fitness of our legal system. I very much doubt that the excuse of funding cuts would be a valid reason for these recent failings but I firmly believe that it is the mindset of both the police and the CPS that if they have a "victim", that victim needs justice and the only way to obtain that is to secure a conviction. This train of thought is also found within social services approach to accusations and claims but also within the health service when a victim is seeking medical help after an alleged assault, whether sexual or not.

It is evident that believing the victim now trumps 'objective and thorough' investigations. In effect it appears that there is no requirement for an investigation if they feel that the victim is being honest. Any educated person will know the dangers of judging people of stereotypes. My complaints have been focused on this very point. Time and again I have highlighted and identified when the police and the CPS have cherry picked the evidence put before them. This has also been confirmed by my solicitor (he wishes to remain nameless) when he stated that the CPS and the police have been put under 'unjustifiable pressure' to obtain convictions that come under certain headings. These, namely being sexual assaults/rapes and domestic abuse. As a result, there has been no impetus to investigate every claim objectively as our legal system is now operating like a sales room aiming to hit targets by whatever means and at whatever cost.

With regards to my writing in a later chapter about the Liam Allen's case it appears that the investigating officer had not read all of the 40,000 messages proving his innocence. But after greater scrutiny by someone who is not a police officer it was proved that there was no crime. Liam Allen should never have been charged in the first place. From the very beginning of his arrest 3 years previously Liam Allen had told the police that there was evidence held on a mobile phone to prove his innocence. It was finally investigated by the barristers dealing with the case that it was proven that Liam Allen was an innocent man, when, if the police had reviewed them properly, no charges would ever have been brought in the first place. Therefore, If the lawyers had accepted what the police had told them, Liam Allen would have served 12 years wrongfully behind bars and life on a sex offenders register. But to an untrained eye, I can only draw one sickening conclusion, and it is that there will be undoubtably individuals who've had trials where material wasn't willfully or knowingly, disclosed.

The Director of Public Prosecutions; Alison Saunders who has pushed hard the concept of 'victim centred' prosecutions seems to be (so far) untouchable. Time and again she has been accused of inflating rape conviction figures. It also transpires that this individual is also responsible for the catastrophe befallen crimes related to domestic abuse. The only comment she has made with - regards to this shambles is to make an apology to Liam Allan – but what about the potentially 100s of other victims of her indiscretions and erroneous policies? One cannot help but notice that these crimes are female victim focused and therefore, would not seek to help male victims of such crimes. As a result, Ms Saunders should do the honourable thing and resign from her position as all credibility for her and what she represents is now questionable. Is it not enough that innocent men have had their lives destroyed on the basis of spurious claims later rejected in court. Or worse, innocent men have been found guilty because there has been little interest to pursue the truth. As I have previously stated "The highest mode of corruption is the abuse of power." This 'victim-centred justice' now entrenched within the British legal justice system — has resulted in either unfair convictions or the life-long shame of being publicly accused of rape, despite an acquittal. This fact is further compounded by the re-opening of questionable convictions and/or the acquittal of so many so called 'criminals'.

From my perspective I have supplied a vast array of evidence to the police. Yet, it has been clear to me and others involved in my case that these documents, texts and statements have been dismissed by the police without real considerations from the outset (and this consideration just gets better as you will need to read on to hear what the CPS had to say about this). Of course, this fact of recklessness has been handed to the IPCC to review. It has also compounded the fact that a female focus has been adopted because they based their whole prosecution attempts on one statement from her daughter that was not even in the room when the supposed assault had happened.

If you take the time to research what it is a police officer supposedly does you can find a range of explanations. To put it simply, police officers should maintain law and order: protect members of the public and their property; and prevent, detect and (and this is my point) investigate crime. Whilst investigating the Police Code of Practice, I found a very good example held within the West Midlands and Cleveland Constabulary Codes of Practice (of which are in bold below)
(http://www.clevelandpf.org.uk/regulations/discipline.pdf)
(http://www.westmidlands-pcc.gov.uk/media/185119/code-of-conduct-for-pcc-dpcc-board-members.pdf)
Within the said documents I found some key points;
• Honesty and integrity
It is of paramount importance that the public has faith in the honesty and integrity of police officers. Officers should therefore be open and truthful in their dealings; avoid being improperly beholden to any person or institution; and discharge their duties

with integrity.

• Fairness and impartiality

I have discovered that the police had not handed my evidence to the CPS as they claimed to have had no knowledge of my counter claim or evidence against my ex. Therefore, my initial complaint to the CPS of lack of consideration for counter evidence made no sense to them. This is counter to the CPS code of practice called the 'Full Code Test' when it states in sections 4.2 and 4.5; 4.2 In most cases, prosecutors should only decide whether to prosecute after the investigation has been completed and after all the available evidence has been reviewed... 4.5 The finding that there is a realistic prospect of conviction is based on the prosecutor's objective assessment of the evidence, including the impact of any defence, and any other information that the suspect has put forward or on which he or she might rely. It means that an objective, impartial and reasonable jury or bench of magistrates or judge hearing a case alone, properly directed and acting in accordance with the law, is more likely than not to convict the defendant of the charge alleged. This is a different test from the one that the criminal courts themselves must apply. A court may only convict if it is sure that the defendant is guilty. Police officers have a particular responsibility to act with fairness and impartiality in all their dealings with the public and their colleagues. There has been no fairness or impartiality when the attempted prosecution is 'victim focused'. As stated, when all the evidence had been supplied it was cherry picked to fit their presumptions. Hence the CPS did not have the full facts to hand.

The West Midlands Police Code of Practice, also states

• OBJECTIVITY

Holders of public office must act and take decisions impartially, fairly and on merit, using the best evidence and without discrimination or bias.

As stated it has now transpired that the CPS had not seen my evidence supplied to the police by myself. This does not meet the police standard of impartiality, fairness and merit. Furthermore, there is no evidence from the police actions that the best evidence was used without discrimination or bias Most professionals (I would like to include myself in this category) work to the expected standard. In fact, many professionals I have met often exceed the minimum but get no extra thanks for this. Many of these people know what is expected but do that little bit extra to secure a greater level of satisfaction for the people of whom they are serving. I am a member of two professional bodies. Firstly, I am a member of the General Teaching Council (GTC) and the Health Care Professions Council (HCPC). If we take a look at the GTC Standards of Practice for example. Within its constitution it clearly states;

The GTC could make the decision to remove from their register or restrict any teacher who had 'compromised the public confidence of the profession' or who had put 'the safety and welfare of children at risk'

In fact, this is a common feature with the HCPC, The Nursing & Midwives Council (NMC), Chartered Institute of Management Accountants (CIMA), even The British and International Golf Greenkeepers Association (BIGGA). In fact, the list is endless for any occupation claiming to be both legitimate and professional. But, as stated, they all profess to hold the principle of 'public confidence' with high esteem. If I look at the discipline policies of both teachers and health professionals (it is easier for me as I have a good working knowledge of both of these professions) there is a process. At the first stage one would be interviewed by a superior (usually within the same profession) and then it can be referred to the governing body who are not necessarily within the professions frame work. This gives an air of comfort as it implies a sense of independence or at least a relative distance from senior managers of whom the individual maybe in conflict with. Yet, if I analyse my complaints to the police there have been two. I have ultimately been referred to the IPCC (Independent Police Complaints Commission). Yet, even at this higher level I have found it is the police policing the police (it has only gone higher because I have raised my issue with a senior police officer following a revelation from the CPS). In my eyes this would be like seeking a reference for a child minders job from Josef Fritzl. How on earth is this independent, fair or truly objective? In effect, it is the police policing the police of which I now consider to be of questionable quality. If I recall, the question of honesty with regards to the police (specifically West Midland Police) was raised in 1989. The

West Midlands Serious Crime Squad was a police unit which operated from 1974 to 1989. It was disbanded after an investigation into allegations against some of its officers of incompetence and abuses of power unearthed serious questions about the credibility of such a unit. Several resulting miscarriages of justice were later overturned on appeal, including the cases of George Glen Lewis, Keith Twitchell the Birmingham Six and on 17 October 2014, Martin Foran who had been wrongly convicted in 1978 for four counts of robbery. As of January 2017, a total of 64 appellants had their convictions involving the squad overturned. I can also recall my great grandmother telling me a story about police corruption during the first world war. She would recount how they profited from black market deals and would expect to be able to sit in the back of her shop on rainy days (whilst they hung their coats up outside). And that is without discussing pimping and theft. Okay, fair enough, one may argue that principles and codes of practice were not in operation during this period but I'm afraid to announce that the apple never falls far from the tree. And again, as previously stated; "The highest mode of corruption is the abuse of power." This whole system raises a five-fold concern. With the publicly known failings of the present system it will affect the whole of society.

- Criminals – I still stand by the fact that it is better to let off a true criminal rather than send one innocent person to prison. This is a view held that, the truth will eventually come out and the criminal will face justice at some point. However, with the new-found doubt of the integrity of our present legal system, an element of doubt will cloud the principle of 'proof beyond reasonable doubt'. Hence prosecutions may indeed drop thus allowing criminals to walk our streets unhindered by the chance of a real prosecution.

- Jury - The role of the jury is described as that of a finder of fact, while the judge is seen as having the sole responsibility of interpreting the appropriate law and instructing the jury accordingly. The jury determines the truth or falsity of factual allegations and concentrates on a verdict on whether a criminal defendant is guilty or not. But how can a jury be able to decipher the facts of a case when the conduct of the police and CPS be questioned from the outset? It had been assumed that the legal system was incorruptible, honorable and moral. But to allow the principle of cherry picking evidence over shadows that assumption.

≅ Public perception – the principle of law is the back bone of a decent and civil society. Alas, public perception of the police and the CPS will be shattered by the recent revelations. Both the public and the law are dependent upon each other for their own survival. Yet, if one side is seen as not playing by the rules then the rules can be broken on both sides of the fence. And this is a worrying concept to comprehend.

≅ Victims – from a male point of view there seems little benefit of reporting a crime. The evidence I supplied did not fit into the category of which the police and CPS seem to operate in. Being a white, male heterosexual they perceived that I could not therefore, be perceived as a victim. Thus, my points and facts were given no more consideration than being filed away. From a female point of view, a victim may now fear not being believed.

≅ Holding the Trump card – having said all of this I am now pleased to consider that the 'Trump-card' that has been used against men for so long will now be nearing its end. As you may recall, when I told my ex I was leaving she used the female victim card and got what she wanted. If the police and CPS really do start to investigate themselves more forensically then this victim centred approach my now have the life blood squeezed out of it. Thank god for that. These liars can no longer depend upon the law to sow their seeds of unwarranted and unfettered destruction.

I would argue that it is now time that anonymity for defendants accused of sex crimes unless proven guilty should be re-introduced. Perhaps it is also fair to suggest that that two police officers should be assigned to every case — one to investigate the complainant's account and another to investigate the defendant to ensure objectivity, and a senior officer or a member of the CPS to then review all the evidence.

I suppose all of these revelations have come at a good time for me. I have stated my claims of dismissal by the authorities and these recent news stories have proved my case. From this I have been told that an inspector will be questioned about his justifications with regards to my case - both my wrongful arrest and the dismissal of my counter evidence. Furthermore, the CPS will now get the chance to actually see what I supplied to the police in the first place.

CHAPTER 21
Is it more than a coincidence?

I recently said to somebody that I believe I have learnt more after leaving school than whilst I was there. I can now equally say that I have learnt more about the 'system' after having the shit kicked out of me by it. I assume I can state that you, the reader, will now know that I am highly critical of the police and the legal system when it comes to the status and protection of male domestic abuse victims. I suppose I can also suggest that it also fails our sister victims too.

To recap, I have had to deal with the police, social services and recently the Crown Prosecution Service (CPS) and to date the following has resulted; Social services – I have been successful in obtaining the sacking of one social worker and have also gained two separate letters of apology from two county councils. The police – As expected they failed to address their own failings and saw fit to blame the CPS for this. As a result I have raised my complaint higher now naming a specific inspector citing professional misconduct and failure to follow the principles of their own code of practice (of which I obtained from the CPS). The Crown Prosecution Service – Following my complaint to them about the unequal processing of the law I received a very informative letter highlighting how they make a decision based on the same code of practice that the police adopt. However, they also wished to pass the buck and took it upon themselves to blame the police. As a result I took the liberty to use their own principles to identify their own failings.

So how does this fit with the title of this chapter? Well, for all you regular news followers you may be aware of the recent case of Liam Allen (22). For my American and other nation followers of whom may not be aware of this case, I wish to furnish you with the details. Liam Allan, was on bail for almost two years and spent three days at Croydon Crown Court in the dock before his trial It is fair to admit that my case pales in comparison to Liam Allan's case on the level of potential outcome and seriousness of the case. However, it took a judge to identify the institutional failure of a system that was created to protect the public Liam Allen was wrongly charged with rape and 'dragged through hell' for two years due to a police blunder. Liam Allan's trial was eventually thrown out of court after lawyers discovered his alleged victim texted him suggesting she wanted to have more sex after the alleged attack. She had also clearly stated within these texts that the sexual activity was consensual. It transpired that the texts related to this case had been held by police and should have been made available to both the defence and the prosecution teams almost two years ago but were not due to (and I quote here directly from the judge) 'sheer incompetence.' Liam Allan's lawyer further stated that '[Mr Allen] should never have been charged and was needlessly put through two years of turmoil.' Liam Allen, after his acquittal publicly stated a number of key factors but a key quote was certainly food for thought;

'It's made me realise that something needs to change. There are things that go on behind closed doors that you can't even imagine and that a lot of people are probably going through the same sort of thing.'

In essence, I am sure we can all agree on the fact that the present system is not fit for purpose when it can fail at so many levels. The prosecutor (yes that's right, the lawyer who was employed to attempt to prove Liam Allen's guilt) stated that; 'Sheer incompetence' by police meant that texts about his alleged victim's fantasies of violent and casual sex were kept secret. Thus they were knowingly withholding important evidence from the legal experts to tried to obtain the truth. The prosecutor also highlighted the fact that 'the defence quickly saw the information (held on a police file) [that] blew the prosecution out of the water. If they had not been seen this boy faced 12 years in prison and on the sex offenders' register for life with little chance of appeal. This was a massive, massive, miscarriage of justice, which thank heavens was avoided'. The police attempted to defend this approach by claiming that the 'sexual messages sent by the woman to Liam Allan and her friends were 'too personal' to share' (!!!!???)

So what is this telling us? It is telling people like you and I that the police cherry pick their evidence to support a positive outcome for themselves (not in the true spirit of public interest is it?) The CPS was also asked to explain why it did not demand full disclosure of evidence including phone records before the trial started. The texts revealed that the woman asked Liam Allan for casual sex and fantasised about rough and violent intercourse and even being raped despite telling police she didn't like being intimate with men. It eventually took Judge Peter Gower to stop the trial. Judge Gower was also quick to note that [having this] hanging over his head for years... could have had his life totally trashed. That was awfully wrong'.

So, how can we interpret the final outcome of this case? It is, therefore, reasonable to state that Liam Allen had been betrayed by the system. And it still stands in this country (contrary to false belief) that people are treated as 'guilty until they can prove they are innocent'. Further research on achieving goals over the truth came to light when Chief prosecutor Alison Saunders had made a high profile push to bring more sex attack cases to court. She had asked her lawyers to trawl through a man's relationship history to boost conviction. As a result, the number of rapes reported to police had gone from around 13,000 in 2002 to 45,000 last year but in 2014 it emerged a quarter of sex offences – including rape – were never recorded as crimes. As a result Alison Saunders was eventually accused of inflating rape conviction figures and having little idea of how rape trials work. Ms Saunders has also repeatedly come under fire over the CPS handling of sex allegations. In effect innocent men have had their lives destroyed on the basis of spurious claims later rejected in court. In August this year (2017) she said that men accused of rape will have more of their relationship history put under the microscope during trials in a bid to increase convictions rates. As a result Ms Saunders was warned that the hugely inflated figures in a report on violence against women were 'misleading'. From my point of view it appears that this is a criminal justice system which is not just creaking, it's about to croak. The legal system seems to have been swaggering around without fear of reproduction or justification of its actions. In effect Liam Allen's case has proven that the present system is just not fit for purpose.

I am sure that every person reading this book would agree that any form of sex crime is abhorrent. Yet if we are now aware that the police and CPS are getting it so wrong and appear to be withholding crucial evidence, a jury may automatically have 'reasonable doubt' before the trial begins. This is a concern. As a result of this the real criminals will assume acquittal based on the fact that the evidence set out before them may not be honest enough to secure any form of truth.

So, let us analyze this case more closely. Police officers failed to hand over evidence proving Liam Allan's innocence. This evidence included a computer disk containing copies of 40,000 messages – including ones sent to Liam Allan by the woman pestering him for sex both before and after the accusation of rape. The woman was also reported to have told the police that she didn't enjoy sex. Together with these facts the lead detective had been accused of failing to review these texts. For a reason that cannot be justified, Liam Allan's lawyers were denied access to the woman's telephone records after police insisted there was nothing of interest for the defence or prosecution. Meanwhile, when Jerry Hayes took over the case on the day before the trial started – he demanded that the police hand over the phone records. A computer disk containing copies of 40,000 messages were taken from the handset, revealing that the woman had continuously pestered Liam Allen for 'casual sex'. She also told her friends that she enjoyed sex with him and even spoke about her fantasies of having violent sex and being raped by him. As a result of the collapse of the trial the judge called for an inquiry at the 'very highest level' of the Crown Prosecution Service (CPS) and a review of disclosure of evidence by the Metropolitan Police. As we are now aware, Judge Peter Gower found him not guilty and set him free. But within the judge's summing up he further stated that;

'There is something that has gone wrong and it is a matter that the CPS, in my judgment, should be considering at the very highest level... 'Otherwise there is a risk not only of this happening again but that the trial process will not detect what has gone wrong and there will be a very serious miscarriage of justice... He [Mr Allan] leaves the courtroom an innocent man without a stain on his character'.

The judge further heard that documents were not always sent to defence lawyers in order to keep costs at a minimum. What!!!??? So, money comes before the damage to innocent people's lives? It is now clear that this is the case – and now undoubtedly seems to have been the case for perhaps generations before. Following the criticism of the CPS by Judge Gower, a spokesman for the CPS said:

'A charge can only be brought if a prosecutor is satisfied that both stages of the Full Code Test in the Code for Crown Prosecutors are met, that is, that there is sufficient evidence to provide a realistic prospect of conviction and that a prosecution is required in the public interest'...All prosecutions are kept under continuous review and prosecutors are required to take account of any change in circumstances as the case develops.

Now, after reading my last chapter we all know how those rules can be misinterpreted or used for their own ends. Rightly or wrongly, I would like to think that it is better for a real criminal being found not guilty and set free, rather than an innocent person being punished for a crime that never actually happened. As I have previously stated any potential jury members in the future will not hold an automatic response of 'reasonable doubt' both before, during and after the court case has been heard. Therefore, based on this new principle of 'burden of proof' as set before a jury convictions will always be questionable. Furthermore, this could potentially galvanize any public mistrust of both the police and the CPS. I am sure that at some point in the near future the police will create a new initiative and be told to say to all suspects that;

"Anything you say or do will be written down in pencil and rubbed out at a later date to suit our own purpose"

It's bad enough realising that the police are useless but it's worse to know that the police know it but chose to do nothing about it Is not the rule of law the principle behind a civilized society? Yet the law and all of those set to operate and work within it, are now seen as uncivilized and perhaps even morally bankrupt.

CHAPTER 22
Legal (F)Aid

I would never claim to be a socialist, but I have read the works of Karl Marx (1818–1883). I would also not claim to be a revolutionist, but I have read the works of Jean-Jacque Rousseau (1712–1778). Although I may not fully agree with their works and ideologies, I do appreciate the problems they revealed and the results they suggested. Even now, much of what they said back then is still, if not more so, relevant today.

Karl Marx discussed the shackles associated with class struggles and Rousseau stated that; *"Man is born free, and everywhere he is in chains."* The French Revolution in 1789 devised the concept of; "Liberté, Egalité, Fraternité" (Liberty, Equality and Fraternity). In fact I am adamant that if you stripped away much of the aged descriptions and tone of these philosophers and event, they could happily sit amongst modern people talking and experiencing modern problems and difficulties. Wars have been declared under the banners and mantra of 'freedom'. The English Civil War was fought to combat Royal tyranny. The American civil war was fought for the freedom of slavery from the shackles of the land owner (I am aware there were also other reasons too). Both World Wars and the Cold War were fought to stop the spread of ideologies that halted freedoms of individuals and states. In fact, the lies associated with the Iraq War were eventually and conveniently twisted to eventually argue that it was to free the Iraqi people from the brutal regime of Sadam Hussain.

But there is a tyranny alive and well within every democratic and civil society. It is the tyranny of money (or the lack of it in many cases). The power and rule of those who have it and those of whom don't and never will. In England the development of the Welfare State was, and has been, hailed as a great success. But who for exactly? The English aristocracy had always been scared and wary of the rising and revolutionary poor following the French Revolution. Trained and armed men returned from the trenches after World War 1, and found the golden promises made to them to sacrifice their lives had not born fruit. So, the welfare state was created to keep the poor in check (and ultimately in their place). From the 18th and 19th century, the authorities had been aware that the people would rise if hunger was evident and felt across the population. As a result, the state gave 'just enough' to feed the poor and stave off hunger to secure their place at the top of the social scale and the poor to remain in blissful ignorance of the trick that had been played.

It has often been said that 'money is the root of all evil.' Even George Orwell (1903–1950) implied that the 'tramp on the street is dictated to by money – he has none, thus, he is forced to live the way he does, when he said; *"Poverty frees them from ordinary standards of behaviour, just as money frees people from work."* (Down and Out in Paris and London [1933]). (27) Even from Orwell's perspective in his book '1984' (1948) he could recognise that the poor or working classes would allow empathy because it is the easier option when the alternative is not recognised.

"It was not desirable that the proles should have strong political feelings. All that was required was a primitive patriotism which could be appealed to whenever it was necessary to make them accept longer working hours or shorter rations. And even when they became discontented, as they sometimes did, their discontent led nowhere, because, being without general ideas, they could only focus it on petty specific grievances. The larger evils invariably escaped their notice."

Yet the state finds a reason to keep access to legal services a privilege exclusively for the rich. Access to a lawyer is accomplished via two means. Either paying for a service (which I will discuss further) or via Legal Aid (in the UK). However, access to this benefit has been shrunk beyond any form of grasp. If your income was considered to be low and you met certain criteria you could make a claim for legal aid to assist you find and employ a solicitor to tackle, discuss or direct you on legal matters. To be fair, I too was able to take advantage of this many years ago whilst obtaining custody of my children. Yet, due to government cut backs access to this 'Aid' has become almost impossible to the point of almost non-existence. The reality and dawning of this emerged a few years ago when the highly paid lawyers decided to strike because it effected their pay packets and not for the legal protection of the poor (28). The second way of accessing a lawyer is by directly paying for them. But let's look at this a little bit closer. I recently employed a lawyer (and will need to again) at £200 per hour. That's right 5 hours work equates to £1000. Many of my friends and colleagues have not had a pay rise in many years and the cost of living is constantly putting a squeeze on any available cash that one requires at the end of the month. And any disposable income, alas, is rapidly shrinking at an alarming rate. Homes are being re-possessed and the use of food banks are beyond stretched. Yet, lawyers are reaping the profits of the miserable state of affairs we are in. And they still demand their high fees regardless of the rights of people to seek legal protection and rights. God forbid morality have a higher precedence than commerce.

I have recently fought social services, the police and the Crown Prosecution Service but I have only been able to gather information myself by trawling the internet or books. But what if I was not able to do this? What if I did not the ability or knowledge to pursue this myself. Well, put simply, I would need a lawyer. But not coming from an affluent background or have an over-inflated income, I would not be able to afford one. Thus, the people and authorities I have challenged would get away with their unprofessionalism, arrogance and failings managing to hide behind the unreasonable price of the law. In effect to get justice you need to be wealthy. Thus, law is not fair, equal and blind. It is expensive, discriminatory and (as a result) biased. How can this be allowed? Well, put simply, in my view it has been allowed to prosper because it keeps the working people in check. How dare the little person challenge the authorities whether right or wrong. How dare people question the great and good. Or, as it was once put to me by a social worker; "how dare I challenge him when he is a social worker". It is common sense to state that money does not buy you intellect or common sense. It buys you privilege and opportunities that others do not have. By not being able to pay the astronomical fees associated with lawyers or having access to Legal Aid we all fail to have access to the real protection of the law and what it claims to uphold. And as a result, we are constantly at the mercy of the heavy handed, unchallengeable and (I hasten to add) public funded (hence endless pit of money) authorities. So, the battle against tyranny and police states (historically the police are not the only force to have worn black in the execution of their duties) has never really been won contrary to what we have all been told. It has conveniently been re-wrapped in a fancy wrapping called 'human rights' or 'constitution' with a constricting bow and ribbon only allowing the people with means the access to its contents. The fact is this, normal working people cannot afford lawyers. The disabled, sick or the needy cannot obtain the Legal Aid they need. But the rule makers and imposers, the policy makers and implementers, the rich and ill informed, all have access to push their wishes with the full force of the law both wrongly and now, it appears, unchallenged.

Karl Marx was right when he highlighted the class struggles 170 years ago. The French revolutionaries were right when they extinguished the excesses of the elite. But what has really changed? Okay, people are now better fed and housed. But who is really benefiting if it stops the majority from speaking out or seeking the protection that our ancestors believed in and fought for? Rousseau suggests that the original Social Contract, which led to the modern state, was made at the suggestion of the rich and powerful, who tricked the general population into surrendering their liberties to them and instituted inequality as a fundamental feature of human society. Rousseau's own conception of the Social Contract can be understood as an alternative to this fraudulent form of association. You may say that the beauty of living in a democratic society ensures a level of liberty. If we don't like a certain politician we can vote them out. But what do we get in return? Another narrow minded, ill informed individual who is corruptible in the den of snakes. Perhaps Oliver Cromwell (1599 – 1658) was right when he dismissed the Rump Parliament in 1653. Oliver Cromwell was recorded as saying;

It is high time for me to put an end to your sitting in this place, which you have dishonored by your contempt of all virtue, and defiled by your practice of every vice.

Ye are a factious crew, and enemies to all good government. Ye are a pack of mercenary wretches, and would like Esau sell your country for a mess of pottage, and like Judas betray your God for a few pieces of money.

Is there a single virtue now remaining amongst you? Is there one vice you do not possess?

Ye have no more religion than my horse. Gold is your God. Which of you have not bartered your conscience for bribes? Is there a man amongst you that has the least care for the good of the Commonwealth?

Ye sordid prostitutes have you not defiled this sacred place, and turned the Lord's temple into a den of thieves, by your immoral principles and wicked practices?

Ye are grown intolerably odious to the whole nation. You were deputed here by the people to get grievances redressed, are yourselves become the greatest grievance.

Your country therefore calls upon me to cleanse this Augean stable, by putting a final period to your iniquitous proceedings in this House; and which by God's help, and the strength he has given me, I am now come to do.

I command ye therefore, upon the peril of your lives, to depart immediately out of this place.

Go, get you out! Make haste! Ye venal slaves be gone! So! Take away that shining bauble there, and lock up the doors.

In the name of God, go!

I know that without doubt he would (if he had one) be spinning in his grave if he could see the mess that this country has become. At the loss of virtue and decency that had never been afforded to those of whom needed the protection from the state and its corrupt operatives. The law is not for you and I. It is a tool for the authorities to keep the lies and corruption going. You may think we have rights but you try and get access to them when your money won't stretch that far.

PART VI
REFLECTIONS

CHAPTER 23
The meaning of it all

For these following few pages I want to concentrate on a couple of people who have also had a 'life changing' experience. I won't mention their names mainly out of respect, but I want them to recognise who they are through my words.

I had the luxury many years ago to have studied philosophy. Although it was heavy at times it really made me think about everyday things. I was once told that the art of philosophy is to 'look out of the window and see what is going on.' There is some truth in this but I also think that philosophy can also require you to look at yourself and your emotions. Both during and following my study of philosophy I had always been drawn to two particular philosophers. Firstly, I would like to draw your attention to Schopenhauer. His main motivation of thought was his investigation of individual motivation. Schopenhauer believed that humans were motivated by their own basic desires, (aka "Will to Live"), which directed all of mankind. These desires can be simplistic like the longing for food and shelter. Or it could be more complicated like the desire to be loved. Schopenhauer directed us to the philosophy of 'love' and its purpose. Love still drives many people into the lunatic asylum. There is a case of some sort every year of two lovers committing suicide together because material circumstances happen to be unfavourable to their union. This was also illustrated within Shakespeare's tragedy on the suicide within Romeo and Juliet.

Looking at the chaos of life from this standpoint we find that we become occupied with its want and associated misery. Since first discovering Nietzsche I have found him to be fascinating. He has (and is still) often been misquoted and his thoughts have been used in error. But this man should be recognised more for an everyday thought that we have all heard at some point in our lives.

It was Nietzsche that coined the phrase – "we need the bad times to appreciate the good". I was recently told by someone that "if we had constant sunshine then we would be left with deserts". This holds the same qualities of what Nietzsche said and it still holds true from whatever angle you look at it from. I know I am stating the obvious, but sometimes bad times can be so dense and thick that it becomes difficult to see through it. No, almost impossible to see any other alternative than what we are experiencing in the present.

I have a good friend who is presently trying so hard to battle with his demons. We have had a range of conversations in the past that have stemmed from the down-right stupid to deep and meaningful. Recently, his demons took a greater hold and he found life to be very difficult. Thankfully, he was given a lifeline before it became too late and he is finding the time to recover. I know he doesn't know it (but he will be reading these pages) he really is precious to so many people. In our daily lives, we never stop to take the time to tell people these things. It is only really done when it is either too late or our thoughts are concentrated on that individual following a difficult period. We are not guilty in our negligence. We just assume people know what we are thinking. Or, we may see it as a weakness to stop and tell these people what we think of them in a positive way. However, we are all very quick to say negative things in the heat of an argument. I recently had some correspondents from a local friend who had been delighted to share her good news with me. I was informed that her life is heading in a new direction. She had made positive steps to shut down and liquidate her old life to replace it with a new hope. My friend had suffered terrible abuse and accepted it as a part of 'normal life'. She craved love and attention and received counterfeit examples of this amongst bad people. For her, this desert had now started to flower and offer an oasis amongst a shaded area. This outcome had only come about because she put a stop to what she now didn't recognise as being right.

So, you may be asking, how does this link with depression and abuse? Well, all events and outcomes stem from things we say or do or the actions of others. Whether this is because of ill health or abuse, I think it is immaterial. But for me, having had bad periods in my life has given me a philosophy of its own. I know that by surviving events I now have the strength to fight on. I hope things will never be as bad as they have been. But if they do, I know I can fight it.

If our lives were one of 'milk and honey' then life would have no value. I am rich in the value of my experiences and knowledge and this currency makes me know that things will get better. It has to because things can never remain bad forever. That's life. It has its ups and downs. For my friend who was having a difficult period. I hope you now realise that it wouldn't last.. Believe me, I know. But as you want to survive this then you would have to because you are too big to drown in this nightmare. Things were bad but your life is too valuable to be beaten by these demons. Now you have survived this you would become a greater person carrying the scars of mental health. Everyone has had moments, it's just that some scars are deeper than others and so take longer to recover. For my other friend who has come through it and about to find a new home. Never lose the focus on what you set out to achieve. But equally important is to remember why you needed to do the things you have done to get this far.

I would never consider myself to be a philosopher within a classical sense. But I would like to suggest that our lives are not a pamphlet but a thick book with contents and chapters. It's just that we are all on a different page to each other.

CHAPTER 24
Keeping a record

It is typical of men to not want to cause a fuss or to think things, when left alone, will get better. If you are a victim of any form of abuse I want to prove how vitally important it is to keep a record of what you have experienced. My employer was aware that something was not right. Initially, I was dismissive of what I was experiencing. My realization that something was not right at home came when I attended a male victim of assault by his female partner. This patient was an utter mess and was clearly suffering at the hands of his wife. On that same evening when I arrived home after the shift I realized that I too met many of the characteristics that this patient met to be labelled and recognised as a victim My senior supervisor kept a formal written record of what I had divulged once I realsied that things were not right or harmonious at home. This document, at a later date, had become a highly valued piece of evidence. If it did not exist it would have been my word against hers, and therefore, not have been considered as a solid defence against her allegations. As I have just stated, this evidence became useful within my defence and my solicitor also appreciated its value. As a result I received a copy of a letter from my solicitor which was sent to the court prior to my hearing.. I have removed any identifying details but I wish to share the main features.

Dear Sirs

We write regarding the case of Mr xxxxxxxxx which is due before the Court on xxxx August 2017 for trial.

Mr xxxxxxxxx had provided us with 3 statements from defence witnesses which he wishes to adduce at trial and also some evidence regarding his reporting of domestic abuse to his employers. ...

With regard to the domestic abuse material, Mr xxxxxxxxxxx would be seeking an agreed fact with the prosecution that he had historically reported his concerns of domestic abuse regarding his partner. The evidence would plainly become relevant if it were suggested that Mr xxxxxxxxxxxxx had only raised this issue following his arrest.

And so on....

I hope that you can see from this, the importance of reporting or at least recording, anything you believe to be wrong. I was not suggesting that you run to the police at every opportunity. But at least share your information in a formal way. As stated, if I had not done this then I would have had no defence against her allegations. As my health was starting to improve I was certainly becoming a creature of habit. When I climbed into bed I followed a usual routine. Firstly, I turned the television on, popped a pill then checked my phone. Sometimes I would read or hear something that would inspire me and I would make a note of it for the morning.

However, one particular night was slightly different. I always checked Social media. Yet I had found Social media to be a double-edged sword. It had been a fantastic outlet for me to be heard. During my online conversations I had come across some absolute amazing, people of whom I would never have met otherwise. At this point I want to pay particular praise to my American friend Hal H for giving me feedback and common sense theories on what I had to say. He is an extremely intelligent man whose points of view I still hold in high regard. I also want to heap further praise to Jan S. Although she lacks confidence she holds so many good values that only she can't see. Which is such a shame. I want to say thank you to Tracy R too. Little does she know that the few words of encouragement she gave me in the early days of my writing were immeasurable. Liz (you know who you are). You have been more than a rock to me. Words could never fully explain how grateful I am to you for just about everything. In fact. there are so many more people I could thank. And I will at some point. But look at the list of people above, it contains both men and women.

In fact, when I looked at the demographics of my readership it is predominately read by females. And I embrace this. This book was to talk about my experiences as a male and I am pleased to see that it had not become a beating stick against women. That's just not my style. Depression doesn't discriminate and neither does domestic abuse – and neither shall I. Like I have said, Social media is a double-edged sword. But I have discovered that it has a side I am getting deeply concerned about.

I had joined a number of groups that are supportive in their approach to people either with depression or difficult break-ups. I had found them to be fantastic with both sharing and understanding other people and their experiences. But I became deeply concerned about a constant point being raised that is ignorant, offensive and I would consider to be very abusive. Time and again I had read comments blaming all men for abuse and time and again I commented that abuse is not gender specific. Yet this same view about male perpetrators of domestic abuse is still allowed to continue without being formally challenged. When I seriously think about it most of my woes had stemmed from females. I had a violent and abusive mother. I had also left an abusive relationship and so on. But I know fully well that these individuals do not represent a gender as a whole. That would be ignorant and foolish to argue so. I accept that there are some very nasty men out there, but please recognise that some women can hold that label too. To put this another way, I once saw a white sheep in a field. But this does not mean all sheep are white. So how dare some people post on-line that they either 'do not trust men' or 'men abuse' to even at one point (and I read it on a so-called support group page) that 'all men are potential rapists?? How does this work? Had this specific individual met every male on the planet to consider such a view as valid? We all know the answer to that one don't we. In essence, the person who spouts this kind of poison really needs to be re-educated because their education to date is somewhat lacking. If these individuals insist that abuse is gender specific then society will never be able to tackle the problem. Abuse is not a gender problem, it is an individual's problem. By insisting that all men are abusers then they are abusing a specific group themselves. Therefore, they become the abuser. Perhaps these people need to have a damned good look at themselves before they throw these words around like confetti without forethought or care of the consequences of such stupidity. All they are doing is showing the world their level of ignorance and perhaps they are not the victim they, therefore, claim to be.

If I took the approach that all women are abusers (and based on my personal history it could be justified) then I would have missed out on meeting, talking and working with some amazing females.

During my lifetime, I have been both blessed and lucky enough to meet some amazing women. I work with some great females who are utterly amazing at their jobs. Also, I have had some amazingly life changing conversations with females. I can equally say that I have also had the same experiences with males.

If people are really serious about ending domestic abuse then they must stop abusing others based on their own shallow and erroneous points of view. I know I have faults, I'm sure I have many. But I object to being judged by someone who judges people based on gender. All you are doing is making your own gender look stupid, ill-informed and ignorant. In a harmonious world there is no room for such comments to make any sense. By continuing this rhetoric these people will find themselves lonely, bitter and ill-informed. But most importantly, they will miss out on the richness of what life has to offer (regardless of what gender you are).

CHAPTER 25
Being male

I have had this conversation so many times with female friends who have tried to work men out. The answer is simple – we are just not as complicated as women. All we want is the quiet life. Men just like the simple things. We like a routine that we can recognise and plod on with. Men don't like complicated things that women seem to enjoy. We can be showered and dressed in a matter of minutes whereas women take hours. Women like lots of choices which can over complicate things. Men just like 'yes' or 'no' answers. I can go into a shop and purchase a single item, whereas women can spend all day visiting every shop in the town to buy the first blouse they found 8 hours previously. Women can bitch for hours about other women. Men and boys either ignore other men and boys or have a fight and it's over with. Simple. Men and women are so different that it's amazing that we get along at all. However, this difference is killing men and yet we fail to recognise it. And why is that? It's because it's easier not to admit that there is a problem than to address the problems head-on.

I didn't know when it happened but men seemed to have lost their way. I had previously mentioned, in earlier pages, that my father acted in a way expected of his generation. Whereas, my son acts in his. The two are very opposite but they seem to be equally as happy about it. But somehow, my generation has found itself squeezed into the middle. I am 45 and its seems that my generation are stuck between the stiff upper lip, hard and unemotional view of my father and the more liberal open mindedness of my son. So, what do we do? Well it appears that men of my age group just sit there and do absolutely nothing. because we don't actually know what to do – and it's the easier option to take rather than make a fuss. My observations have found that men are rubbish at; taking medications and rubbish at admitting any form of medical conditions (especially depression and anxiety – it appears that society does not allow men to have depression, therefore to be seen as weak). Furthermore, men are also rubbish at admitting problems at home and even worse at realising and admitting that we are victims of domestic abuse. There are two sides to what I had just said. Firstly, as stated, men fail to either admit or recognise when they are the victims of domestic abuse. But equally, I have unfortunately, met men who also fail to admit when they are the abusers. Both stances are dangerous and toxic. It is no surprise, therefore, that there is an absolute lack of male refuges or support for men because, it appears, (because of our lack of admittance) that the problem does not exist. I am telling you now it does exist and it is as real as that experienced by our women folk. When I was planning to escape I initially found no-where local that was willing to take me because I was a male victim of domestic abuse. Perhaps men need to speak up about the abuse we experience at the hands of a violent partner. We equally need to accept that there is no shame with suffering depression. Yes, it is a mental health problem but I would have no problem admitting to you if I had broken my arm. As a male I have no shame telling you that I was a victim of domestic abuse by my female partner. And yes, I have depression and PTSD. However, I would never have admitted that 12 months ago. But I have, and it feels good to share it with you.

Doris Lessing (29) also seems to suggest the same when she stated;

"I find myself increasingly shocked at the unthinking and automatic rubbishing of men which is now so part of our culture that it is hardly even noticed," declared Doris Lessing, whose novels turned her into a feminist icon in the 1960s, in a speech earlier this year. "Men seem to be so cowed," she continued, "that they can't fight back, and it is time they did."

According to a recent British government report (30), men are more likely than women to commit suicide, suffer from coronary heart disease, have a serious accident or drink too much alcohol. But even though we all know this, men are still willing to sit back and do nothing about it. If I ever visit my doctor it is only because a woman has told me to go. The only reason I am taking anti-depressants is because a female told me to consider them.

Therefore, the only reason I am still alive is undoubtedly because of a woman (and she knows who she is). I therefore, thank women for being what they are. Perhaps us men need to take a leaf out of their book.

Females have become proficient at their art. Along with their developing successes in the work place, women have also won social acceptance for their right to reject work in favour of motherhood. In other words, women can hold the briefcase, or the baby. But at least they can choose whereas men can't. Men are having to be encouraged and bribed into becoming teachers for very young children. Obviously, this is because men fear being suspected of having paedophile tendencies. Yet there is a rise of women being charged with sexual offences against children. But we still see no problem having female teachers in younger years classrooms.

Several years ago I won custody of my sons (from a previous relationship) when they were still very young. One of the first things that was asked of me was how was I going to manage both working and being a single father? The reality was that I had no choice; I had to do both because that was expected of me as a male. I attended 'mother' and toddler groups, only to be told that it was for mother's only!!!. I am pleased to see that this has changed and that my son (who is now a father) never faces the prejudice I felt. There is nothing new in the idea that men are conditioned to suppress emotions. Generation after generation of men have been taught not to show their feelings. This was also expected of me during my period of growing up. I can never recall my father crying, even at his own father's funeral. Yet, 3 months after my wrongful arrest, I had shed buckets full of tears. I was taught to suppress any feeling or emotions as this 'gave something of my identity away' and was, therefore, an element of weakness that as a male was unacceptable. But I am now questioning this self-sacrifice as I had fallen into an abusive relationship and expected it to be okay. This lack of emotion also led (I would argue) to my long history of depression and ultimately self-doubt. As a father, I don't want any of my children (both sons and daughter) to feel second class as a parent or partner. Equally, I didn't want them to be weak and to become an abuser or the abused. But I also want them to celebrate their differences. I am proud to be a male and equally proud of my female friends.

CHAPTER 26
Privilege

Why is it some people never grow up? Okay, people do grow up in a physical sense, but the same playground politics still exists in so many people beyond leaving school and its child centred understanding. Let me give you an example. There are two children in the playground who fall out (it happens) and one child says to the other "my house is bigger than yours" or "my dad is bigger than your dad" and so on. It's almost laughable in its simplicity and innocence. Yet I am bereft and incensed that it does indeed carry on into adulthood. I have lost count the amount of times I have heard or read terms and ideas based on 'male privilege'. I don't know if I am actually missing the point, but where can I find this privilege because I've looked for it and it only seems to be found in fairy tales, feminist agenda propaganda, narrow minded and flawed media stories or certain sections of society with a negative plan aimed at promoting their own ideology at the expense of another.

In an organic way I want to start at the very beginning.

Whilst studying emergency medicine I came across an article about miscarriages, cot deaths and infant mortality. Baby boys are more likely to die than baby girls and medical advances have actually increased the gender gap, a study recently released found.

An analysis (by VR Sreeraman on March 25, 2008 at 11:22 AM Child Health News) of infant mortality in 15 developed countries (The 15 countries analysed include Sweden, France, Denmark, England/Wales, Norway, The Netherlands, Italy, Switzerland, Finland, the United States, Spain, Australia, Canada, Belgium and Japan). The study found that baby boys are 24 percent more likely to die than baby girls. This is down from a peak of 31 percent in 1970, but double the rate in the days before the development of vaccines and public health measures like improved sanitation dramatically improved infant mortality rates. During the great historical improvements in infant mortality, the rising male disadvantage in infancy revealed a level of unexpected male vulnerability," the study published in the Proceedings of the National Academy of Sciences concluded. Girls have a stronger immune system while boys are 60 percent more likely to be born prematurely and to suffer from respiratory problems, among others. Boys are also more likely to cause risky or difficult labour because of their larger body and head size.

When poor sanitation and nutrition weakened all babies and mothers the male disadvantage was less noticeable: from 1751 until 1870 the gender mortality gap was about 10 to 15 percent. But the development of the germ theory dramatically cut infectious disease rates, making complications of childbirth and premature birth more common causes of death. Writing in the journal Proceedings of the National Academy of Sciences, the researchers at The University of Southern California, said baby boys are more vulnerable because their bigger size raises the risk of a difficult birth, they are more likely to be born prematurely and they also have weaker immune systems. The study of three centuries of birth and death data in countries spanning three continents clearly showed boys to be more vulnerable in the early months of life than girls. In the 1750s, baby boys were ten per cent more likely to die than girls, but by the 1970s the gap had widened to over 30 per cent, despite major advances in public health. The University of Southern California researchers said that while both sexes had benefited from modern healthcare, girls had benefited more than boys. Before 1950 poor hygiene and nutrition weakened all babies and mothers, making the gender gap less visible because death rates were high for both girls and boys. But by the 1970s vaccination, antibiotics and better hygiene had cut deaths from infection, which made birth complications and premature babies the leading cause of death, and these potentially fatal problems are more common in baby boys. Since then improved treatment of premature babies and increasing use of Caesarean sections for risky births have narrowed the gap to 24 per cent in 2000.

Nature also works against the trend of male infant mortality by selecting more males. In western nations 105 boys are born for every 100 girls. However, stress can affect the gender ratio, with studies showing fewer boys are born after stressful events, for example in New York after the September 11 attacks, or to mothers with stressful lifestyles. It has been suggested that higher levels of stress hormones may make it more difficult for male embryos to implant in the womb, or somehow increase the likelihood that male foetuses are miscarried. The gender gap rose steadily as infant mortality rates plummeted and only began to reverse with the increased use of caesarean sections and improvements in neonatal care. Only about five percent of babies born prior to 1970 were delivered by c-section while more than 20 percent of births in the 15 developed nations studied are now performed by c-section.

2 Women can get away with domestic violence.

Time again I have seen and witnessed a female can hitting a male and, more often than not, will not face any repercussions. Roughly 40 to 50 percent of domestic violence victims are male, as reported in a study by Parity. That being said, only 25 percent of domestic violence arrests are female. The majority of these female-on-male crimes go unreported, ignored, or even result in ridicule towards the man. "Be a man," or "grow a pair," seem to be a common solution to the problem. To be balanced in my approach it has to be recognised that women are three times more likely to be killed or seriously injured by their male counterpart than vice versa. Though those numbers are indeed frightening, they do not mean or even suggest that women are completely innocent when it comes to domestic violence. More than 830,000 men fall victim to domestic violence every year. A man is the victim of domestic abuse every 37.8 seconds (this is according to statistics provided by the Domestic Abuse Helpline for Men). These numbers are not inconsequential, and the frequency is far from insignificant. What is of further concern is that these numbers are only of those of whom are willing to report the abuse in the face of dismissal or ridicule. Jan Brown, executive director and founder of the Domestic Abuse Helpline for Men, stated that "domestic violence is not about size, gender, or strength. It's about abuse, control, and power, and getting out of dangerous situations and getting help, whether you are a woman being abused, or a man." In 2001, the National Longitudinal Study of Adolescent Health collected data about the health of a nationally representative sample of 14,322 individuals between the ages of 18 and 28. The study also asked subjects to answer questions about romantic or sexual relationships in which they had engaged during the previous five years and whether those relationships had involved violence. From this information researchers found that of the 18,761 relationships, 76 percent were non-violent and 24 percent were violent. Of the 24 percent that were violent, half had been reciprocal and half had not (reciprocal meaning there was violence inflicted by both partners). Although more men than women (53 percent versus 49 percent) had experienced nonreciprocal violent relationships, more women than men (52 percent versus 47 percent) had taken part in ones involving reciprocal violence. This statistic was undoubtedly the most striking: in committing acts of domestic violence, more women than men (25 percent versus 11 percent) were responsible. In fact, in the 71 percent of nonreciprocal partner violence instances, the instigator was the woman. This flies in the face of the long-held belief that female aggression in a relationship is most often predicated on self-defense. Further, while injury was more likely when violence was perpetrated by men, in relationships that featured reciprocal violence men were injured more often (25 percent of the time) than women (20 percent of the time). Great Britain's Office of National Statistics also showed that while 1.2 million women experienced domestic violence, 800,000 men did as well — in the U.K., men comprise 40 percent of those who suffer from domestic violence. The Department of Psychology at California State University, Long Beach, compiled a bibliography that examined 286 scholarly investigations, 221 empirical studies and 65 reviews and/or analyses demonstrating that which we are reluctant to discuss — the uncomfortable reality that women are as physically aggressive, or even more so, than men in their relationships with their spouses or male partners.But let's put this into perspective, a significant amount of the findings regarding male-as-victim intimate partner violence came about as the result of studies and surveys that were aimed at understanding domestic violence against women. These are not studies conducted by rabid anti-women men's groups or right-wing think tanks. They were conducted by organizations like the Centres for Disease Control, National Institutes of Health, the American Sociological Association, Psychology of Women Quarterly and the American Journal of Public Health, to name a few. In essence, no anti agenda was evident from the outset. Just a quest for the truth in a balanced approach. And yet, these numbers seem to have prompt an unqualified backlash. Accusations such as "You're saying abused women are asking for it," or "You're blaming the victim," get hurled. No victim either female or male is asking for it, and no victim female or male should be blamed for what is done to them. I'm merely opening up the conversation to readily available statistics and facts.

If the authorities are serious about addressing domestic violence to its fullest, then they must deal with all of the manifestations of the realities of domestic violence and be seen to pick and choose what is right to feed a politically correct agenda. By feeding the falsehood the imbalence will be allowed to persist. And that kind of conclusion benefits no one – and never will. In recent months we've seen that the police and the CPS have a confused policy with regards to domestic violence and abuse. For quite some time we've known that our court system has had a confused policy about female domestic abuse and the handling of evidence. Their confusion, lack of understanding of male victims and target setting does not reflect our societal misunderstanding of domestic violence and our muddled perceptions about gender. In fact, they have refused to accept the idea that women can be violent as it does not fit an expected stereotype when the reverse does. It is men who are seen as being violent and so the perception and dishonesty continues to exist. It appears easier to state this than to try and re-educate an already brainwashed society. Men are told in one breath to shed their machismo and sexist leanings, and in the next they are told to "man up" and take the blows dealt to them by their female partners. Men are being told that phrases like, "You throw like a girl," or "You hit like a girl," have chauvinistic underpinnings, while simultaneously being told, "It doesn't matter if she hits you because, essentially, she hits like a girl and you can handle it, big boy." So, while we recognize there's often a difference in the physical impact between male and females hitting each other, we completely disregard the emotional and psychological impacts — and often even the physical harm — of a woman hitting a man, whether it be with her hands, feet or objects.

Time and again, in my role as a paramedic I have witnessed the police dismiss an obvious case of abuse for this very reason. Yet, it is only when the man is found with a knife in his back or a hammer hanging out of the front of his head do the police feel compelled to do something. It seems to be all too much of an effort until something gives – and have witnessed the loss of a life to be that catalyst. I am afraid that we are placing people in gender based stereotypical straightjackets. This leads to two very important questions;

1. Is a woman ever responsible for a physical altercation that takes place between her and her male partner?

2. And, does a man ever have the right to tell a woman to not put her hands on him and expect her to respect that?

Statistical and anecdotal evidence says the first question is barely acknowledged, and the second is treated by and large as a joke of which would be foolish to even comprehend.

Everyday observations tell us that the same abusive behaviour and tactics demonstrated by men (physical, verbal and emotional threats and intimidation) are also demonstrated by women. And the fear and shame that is felt as a result of being abused, as well as the excuses made to cover up the abuse, are not gender-specific or equally balanced. Additionally, a fair percentage of men who call the police to report an abusive spouse or partner, are, in turn, arrested for domestic abuse. According to child welfare studies (mainly in the USA), mothers are almost twice as likely to be directly involved in child maltreatment as fathers. I can personally vouch for this having suffered physical punishments at the hands of my 'mother'. Mothers are more likely to abuse their children than fathers. I agree and consider it fair to argue that these numbers are as such because women are usually more involved with their children. But it dismisses the solid idea that mothers are solely loving, caring and protecting of their children. And these abused children, half of which are male, live with that pain and become adults. As men, they are told to not talk about their pain or acknowledge that a woman hurt them. This continues into adulthood and overflows into their own experiences of being abused by their partners. The male privilege rests with the fact that any male at any age cannot be accepted as being a victim at any point. The National Centre for Victims of Crime states that 14 percent of child molestation perpetrators against boys are women. These women are not viewed the same as male perpetrators. Male victims are told to "man up" or are belittled for "not liking it." People will assume that the male victims of molestation "wanted it" or "didn't mind it," resulting in zero or little prison time and far fewer social consequences for the female predator. Rape, in any scenario, is a serious and malicious crime and should be treated as such, regardless of whether the perpetrator is female or male. However, the victimisation of females is hailed, promoted and publicised to its fullest whilst the man is painted as the instigator and perpetrator of such actions and events. The male privilege exposes us to no protection in law to sexual assaults by women.

In terms of domestic violence, the conversation is always overwhelmingly pointing its finger at men and boys. Indeed, I agree that we do need to talk to boys and men about having respect for our partners. Yet, it's only part of the problem. Our girls and young ladies need to be taught what appropriate behaviour is and that any form of violence instigated by them is also equally wrong. It is not and never has been right to proportion blame to a convenient, set of masculine values. In "Are Girls Closing the Gender Gap in Violence?" Meda Chesney-Lind states;

"Between 1989 and 1998, arrests of girls increased 50.3 percent, compared to only 16.5 percent for boys, according to the FBI's 1999 report, Crime in the United States 1998. During that same period, arrests of girls for serious violent offenses increased by 64.3 percent and arrests of girls for 'other assaults' increased an astonishing 125.4 percent. In 1999, the Office of Juvenile Justice and Delinquency Prevention reported that the female violent crime rate for 1997 was 103 percent above the 1981 rate, compared to a 27 percent increase for males, prompting the statement that increasing juvenile female arrests and the involvement of girls in at-risk and delinquent behavior has been a pervasive trend across the United States."

From my perspective I consider that if we talk about female-initiated violence, then it takes away the impetus of addressing violence against women by their male partners. It feels that we can't have one without the other. And as one section has learnt to put up and shut up about it the truth can be hidden easier. The male privilege is one whereby we are not afforded the same protection in law as our female counterpart. Our status is inferior of which is not a privilege at all.

3 Women win the kids in custody battles.

Divorce is alarmingly common in today's world. More alarming than that is how the court system is prone to giving the children of divorce to the mother. A 2009 study by the United States Census Bureau found that 82.2 percent of custody battles are won by the mother. In most cases, the woman is assumed to be the primary caregiver without careful analysis. Just how mothers win custody battles is pretty obvious. Unless fathers can successfully prove that a woman is unfit, the courts will likely award physical custody to a child's mother. Even women who are not the perfect stay-at-home Mom have an advantage over men applying to become a primary caregiver. The nurturing nature of most females goes a long way in convincing a judge that the children will be properly cared for. Since the beginning of time, a mother's love has been acknowledged to be the strongest bond in human relationships. Even in nature, the female of the species will die to protect her young; and so it is with most human beings. From the time a child is conceived, its mother provides physical and emotional nurturing to help the baby thrive. It is no small wonder how mothers win custody battles - they are just presumed to be a better nurturer than fathers. However, we have also previously discussed the fact that children are more likely to be assaulted by their mothers than their fathers. So the presumption is always that 'Mother is best' and it is for the father to prove otherwise. Why cannot the reverse presumption best fit? Okay, there are the obvious biological differences but a fathers love is no less or irrelevant than the mothers. Much of the issue is about access to a safe home. Like domestic abuse refuges there is utterly no chance of securing accommodation after a split. Unless of course it is in privately rented accommodation. Of course, as in my case, once you leave the family home you are often still burdened with the expense of the old home of which you no longer live in. This is further compounded by the fact that the police will always opt to remove the male regardless of what is alleged or proven. According to the Homelessness Resource Centre, 62 percent of the homeless community is male. Men are often viewed as intimidating or as a threat, so other individuals will not feel liable to help them out. Women are seen as vulnerable and helpless.

The only male privilege evident here is the loss of his children and home and the continued abuse from strangers. That is no privilege at all. I believe and have always believed in equality in every form possible. Time and again I have celebrated the achievements of women in the face of outdated and unfair bias. I have also supported organisations that aim to combat abuse in any form. I firmly believe that men and women should receive the same treatment and hold the same responsibilities whilst having the same access to rights protected in law. But we don't. We don't have that privilege at all.

I also want to witness people having the same access to a range of opportunities that our parents didn't have in their lifetime. However, men and women are still being treated differently and the whole argument about gender privilege is an outdated, inaccurate, ill-educated and blinkered view. My privilege is no more or less than most people but, as a man I don't want to be fed inaccuracies based on untruths and privileges that just do not exist when actually exposed to scrutiny. Based on my own experiences (of which in my eyes become facts) I did not have the same access to resources, services or protection that my female counterpart had. I am sorry but if I am missing the point about my male privilege then I would love to know. If the state is going to continually and blindly preach about "male privilege," and blame men for all of women's problems, then they are not pro-feminist. In fact, they are sexist and ignorant. My blame lies with those who flatly refuse to accept there is something wrong with the status quo. The real criminals, abusers, perpetrators of those of whom refuse to address the problems because they like things to remain as they are.

CHAPTER 27
Having the right

We have all put up with being treated badly at some point in our lives. But if it happens in a relationship we are showing our partner that we don't respect ourselves. You are endorsing their view that you are only worthy of the unacceptable way they are treating you. Each time you go back and forgive them, you are reinforcing their bad behaviour. People can only treat you in ways that you allow. In essence, you give permission and furnish people with knowledge of how you want to be treated. So, if you are settling for someone's poor treatment or halfway efforts, you are silently telling them; "Thank you. This is how I want you to treat me, and I like it." They don't understand any alternative other than the messages you are giving them by your silence.

I think the underlying answer is the amount of self-confidence we portray. Lots of nice people are not that self-confident, and it shows in their body language, the way they carry themselves, etc. Those people are the first to be targeted by the abusers. People who appear strong and self-confident don't usually get targeted or abused. The abusers know that these people would stand up to them and their toxic ways. The abusers appear to think that they are better than anyone else, whether they say it or not, and it shows. They create an air of self-confidence. The abusers only target easy prey, because deep down they are not that as self-confident as the image they portray. That's why they bully, so they can feel better about themselves and hold some form of power over their victims.

People are treated in ways they don't like because:

1) They receive the love they want on a rationed basis, and they put up with the poor behaviour in the hope of earning more love at a later date.
2) Their self-confidence is so low, they feel that the poor treatment they receive is all that they deserve. As a result they become thankful for what they receive.

I was being treated based upon how I believed I should to be treated. I was giving away my opinions, freedoms and views to someone who had no business to take control of it. By allowing others to demean and put you down, you are allowing false perceptions that are wrong and not your own. The longer this is allowed to happen the harder it will be to stop it. In my job as a paramedic, I have had the opportunity to meet people from all walks of life. What I have learned from others along with my own life experience is that life is a battle of survival and endurance and we allow people to treat us badly—both consciously and unconsciously. We allow others to criticize, judge, abuse, and diminish us because we can't find our words to defend ourselves as we may feel unworthy or grateful. I believed that at times I deserved it, and felt privileged that someone took the time to highlight my faults. Hindsight is a wonderful thing and I want to share the fact with you that this is wrong. Perhaps my ex was aware of her own inabilities and faults but pointed out mine to hide her own weaknesses and fallibilities. This makes her to be a tragic figure. But she knew what she was doing wrong by allowing it to continue especially when I made it clear that I now knew it was wrong too.

When it comes to image or identity, to a child it doesn't really matter. As a teenager it's everything but as an adult we seek high and low to find it. But identity and acceptance is a major vein of a person's identity.

'Social Acceptance could be defined as the fact that most people, in order to fit in with others, attempt to look and act like them.' – Plato 428 BC – 348 BC

A few of years ago I came across an article about men with beards. It raved about them and went into great detail about what can be done with them. But here I was carrying mine with a sense of individuality. Nobody else had one. Now, however, when I look around it is unusual to see any male without one. Hence, had I lost my identity as an individual within the crowd? I can never consider myself to be a trendsetter – that would just be too hilarious to contemplate. Yet the dead opposite is the case for teenagers. They try so hard to be a part of their sector or group. I remember wanting the same trainers as my mate. I had the same school bag as everyone else. It was what we did then and I am fully aware it's what teenagers still do now. They all want to look the same – perhaps it's a primeval behaviour that we try and revert to a tribe mentality and wish for a uniformity. As an individual I hate going into certain high street clothing shops as I try to avoid looking the same as the next person. Individuality for me is essential. Both physically, in the way I look and mentally by the way I think and speak. It may be difficult to understand what it is I am trying to say. But I think I could feel my own recovery as it developed. For the first time in my life I could recall feeling comfortable in my own skin. I have made great efforts to banish what people expected from me and took a long time to look at my inner self and reassess my values and principles. I appreciated that I didn't want to be like the next person. I was embracing what and who I was. Between you and I, I had discovered that generally the next person is more screwed up than me. And that can be refreshing to know. I had now given up being the enabler to fit other people's profiles and expectations. I was comfortable with that. It suits me because it is me. The problem with being what I wasn't was that I had, therefore, lost my identity. When I was falling into the crowd I actually didn't want to be there. Instead I wanted to sit in a corner and happily watch as opposed to partaking in various misadventures. Of course, I would find myself trying to emulate the confident person, it's a matter of survival at times. And to be honest a part of me doesn't want to give up that character I had created. He is funny, sociable, and confident. I mean it was who I wanted to be for most of my life and now what? Now I was struggling more than ever with identity. It feels like an evolution instead of a revolution.

Going back to creating an identity I had often spent many hours looking around at other people around me. It made me feel mostly like failure. But this isn't a sob story or anything but was how I felt when I was trying to build a level of confidence. I would look around at people of my age and see that they were better at their jobs than I, they would be in great relationships, having nice holidays, beautiful homes and so on. But here sits the irony that I have only just realised. I know these people have their own battles to deal with. In all of its formats life is tough and I know everyone has their own difficulties to deal with. This was why I felt so guilty about being ill. It explains why I beat myself up about the situation I found myself in and struggled to get better quickly. That was why I rushed back into work before I was ever ready to return. But this was why I tried to hide my illness from everyone. To everyone I knew I just wanted to be seen as normal. Just what my understanding of normal was being misrepresented. Consciously, I can now sit here and see the problems and how they manifested themselves over time. I try hard to write my points down and share them with others (such as yourselves) to try and get some perspective on it all. But the reality at the time was that I could talk the talk but I struggled to walk the walk. Why? Because I tried too hard to be what I wasn't. If we take an extensive look at the how this misconceived social expectation is fuelled. I can point my finger directly at social media, adverts, magazines, television programmes, and so on. But it's obvious to everyone the pressures we are under because it's constantly and unwittingly, shoved down our throats. There is an artificial expectation to succeed, to look good (although for some strange reason everyone wants to look the same), to eat more salads, to look good the gym (although the majority who go don't), to have money (but this equates debt) and to have a fulfilling career. But this false failure is always around us. You just have to open your eyes to see it. For example, whilst I type these words an advert is running in the background. It's for a sports shoe. The reality is that if you buy this shoe it would not make you into a super athlete as soon as you put them on. No, it requires pain and commitment not being lazy and over-spending on a false hope that the advert appears to offer. The reality is that it won't change my life by not owning them. In fact I would probably save myself a couple of hundred quid by not doing so. So, in effect its 1-0 to me for not bothering to be fooled. My mind boggles that we who consider ourselves as the superior species on the planet are so easily fooled by other humans using a few words. It's a cruel irony really – when you actually think about it.

I have tried hard most of my life to fit into a category I am comfortable with. I have no idea why I used so much energy on this meaningless task but I have/had. In adolescence, I can understand why we do this. At this point in our lives we are trying to create and shape an identity of our own, and that is part of the process of becoming an adult. We desire to be attractive and popular. Perhaps this is a primeval survival technique. But as an adult, I struggled to accept the fact I didn't feel I had an 'identity' (or whatever that means). I consider now that I never really had the opportunity to finish what I had started. I never really had the opportunity to create an identity of my own because my home life was such a mess. This environment and how it shaped my consciousness, therefore, became my identity and would be for a number of years. Now that I realise this error I am enjoying starting again. It's actually quite exciting.

Acceptance of poor mental health is still slow. Suicide is still the biggest killer of men under the age of 45 and therefore a tremendous amount of work still has to be done so that people feel more comfortable with opening up and talking about their problems and who they really are. Writing this book and its associated notes has helped me identify a whole lot of things. I have said things on these pages that even now I would never verbally say and have never been said before. But I've said them. And I am glad that I have. I am also glad to know that people read what I have to say. And that for me is the most important thing. The fact is this. There is nothing to make sense of. Our concerns are a product of fake hopes. I know I would never have the body of a god, or be filthy rich. Together with this I won't have fantastic holidays on heavenly beaches. But what is important is self-contentment and happiness. Those are things that you can't buy. You just acquire them – eventually.

One day I had a realisation that I may have been responsible for most of my problems. I have always found it difficult to say "no". I've never really liked to say "no" before. This had been mainly due to me trying to be agreeable and accommodating. It is often easier to say "yes" than to deal with the stresses of offering the negative. I had also done things because it had been nice to do rather than me needing to do. In effect, it appears that I've been a people pleaser most of my life. I've done what I think I was supposed to do to make the people around me happy rather than what I wanted to do and be seen as negative by those same people. My logic in thinking this is that I would be happy if the people around me are also happy. But here lies the irony. The more you try and make people happy the more they want and so become less happy because of it. As a result, true happiness is never achievable. Even if this pursuit had cost me my own happiness.

As an adult I can see that happiness is about being able to make choices. And a valid choice is actually being able to say "no" without any form of inner conflict. Trying to please others takes an awful lot of energy to maintain. Perhaps this is why I had considered that I had never been 'fully at my best'. I have tried to please bosses, partners, children, strangers, ex's and so on without my own considerations. But like I have said, this pursuit of other people's happiness may be an impossible achievement but I still unconsciously tried to achieve it at the cost of my own. When I consider work for example, I always arrived early not because I had to, but because I felt it was nice to. Again, my uniform (or suits when I wore them) were always pressed and immaculate. Again, not because I had to but because it was nice to. Well, where had this got me? Nowhere. I had been constantly over-looked for promotions (when lesser people with fewer qualifications and experiences had got them) and have had little support from my managers following my abuse and depression. Well what have I gained from this? Nothing. And why? Partly because I didn't want to let other people down and couldn't say "no". I kept my mouth shut because I didn't want to be seen as a problem and never said no because I wanted to be seen as reliable. In fact ladies and gentlemen, it transpires that every single one of us is expendable. So saying no would not have been detrimental to my career at all. In fact it might had improved it because my treatment couldn't have been any worse. With this in mind, it had dawned on me that I am aware of people 'stuck' in relationships that they don't want to be in. They didn't want to break things off or cool things down because they don't want to hurt their partners feelings. I don't see any nastiness in this frame of mind but the status quo is hurting yourself and taking away your freedom of choice and other types of liberty. Furthermore, by prolonging this agony would only make it more painful for the other person later on. You are also taking away their chance of happiness if it is built on a false hope. This upset would cause pain to them and to you as you are guilty of putting off the inevitable.

When I think about my upbringing which was built on faith and religion (which has no part in my life at all now) I became programmed to believe that pursuing my own happiness was selfish. Yes, it probably is right to think that way as no one likes a person who is considered to be selfish. But there needs to be a line drawn somewhere as this train of thought means that we're not supposed to be happy until we make everyone else around us happy first. As an adult with responsibilities I now see this a wrong philosophy to try and maintain. By putting myself first for once now means saying 'no' much more often than I was probably used to. It's a new concept to consider and it will be strange to apply after all of these years. But it has to be a step in the right direction. Not just for me but for everyone else around me. At least by being honest with myself I can be seen as being honest with other people too.

Perhaps if I start saying 'no' to more people (in a diplomatic way of course) or not volunteering to assist, I may feel bad thinking I was letting people down. But I am sure we will all get over it and it would be eventually forgotten. Especially if it makes us all better people. It has to be worth a try didn't you think? If I set a boundary it would show a line between helping because it makes me feel good and helping because others expect it of me. If we look back at the example of me arriving at work early – it eventually became expected and therefore, became a duty rather than a nice thing to do. It's a bit like living in an abusive relationship. If you choose not to reject the abuse it then becomes the norm and acceptable in the abusers' eyes. Alas, I must admit that I allowed the abuse to happen because I never said "no". Perhaps by exercising my mindset of saying "no", the more people may start to respect my decisions and appreciate those moments when I say "yes". I will say 'no' to things that don't support my values or I just disagree with. In fact, when I think about it I am sure every person who is reading this has done things against their better judgement or will. Perhaps this world would be a better place for everyone if we used the word 'no' more often. If I say 'no' it may mean "not now," or it may mean "absolutely no way." Either way, I will be clear or you might even know the answer before you ask it. But by being free to say 'no' would mean that I have the freedom to say "yes" in a liberating way. The things I choose to do will have a greater value not only to myself but to those around me because it would be done with pleasure or love or commitment. Surely this is a better option than doing things because they are expected, taken for granted or done through gritted teeth. I know that if I had had the courage to have said "no" before I would not have suffered at the hands of an abusive ex and all that came from it. I may have achieved more at work and gained a better outcome and respect from my managers. Who knows, but it's exciting to find out if anything will change.

"Regrets". It's such a simple word that holds so many meanings but it appears to be a word of self-reflection. I consider that most regrets stem from the things we didn't do, rather than the things we did do. Regardless of the life we've lived, whether we struggled with addiction, depression or have had a substantial amount of time in recovery, it turns out that most people regret the same things. I think people who have been through what we have been through or how we have felt will always be hard on ourselves. Often, I had found myself saying "I wish I hadn't" or "if only" and so on. But like so many of us I was sure we acted with the right intentions at that specific point in our lives. As a father, I wish I could have done better but I could only do what I could with the resources available or with the opportunities I had. As a partner I could, it feels, only fire fight by trying to keep things under control. I was sure many of us know the feeling of trying to spin plates by keeping everything in some form of order whilst dealing with outside issues. It's difficult but it doesn't require regrets. It actually requires stamina and we all get tired at some point. Of course, on reflection I regret having found myself in that relationship but let's be clear. No one comes with a label. Furthermore, no one sets out to say, 'let's give it a go although it may end up being the worst experience of my life'. If we all did that I wonder what kind of world we would live in. We may never venture out of the house in case we get run over. We might not get dressed in case our clothes clash or match someone else's outfit in the office.

I have briefly touched upon this train of thought earlier on in this book when I mentioned Nietzsche. His philosophy has stuck with me since I first read him many years ago. He devised the idea that we need to have bad experiences to appreciate the good. As a result, I have now learnt to embrace these regrets although I don't want to go out and find myself repeating them again.

We only seem to have regrets when we are reminded of what we have been through. There are times I regret not telling certain people what I thought of them. But the reality is that either someone else would tell them at some point. Or, they may be so up their own backside that whatever I may have said would not have penetrated their thick skulls anyway. Some people may call it karma I just call it time. All good things come to those who wait. As a student many years ago, I was often told to reflect on things I had seen, done or experienced. I found this whole concept a complete waste of time as I considered that if I was doing my best at that specific moment how could I consider improving. But I am going to give this idea a new, more logical explanation. If I found myself in a similar situation would I handle things differently? What if I had different opportunities at that specific moment, would I still take those chances? Have I changed my views on things or why things happen? The reality however, is not as rosy as the romantic idea of everything being in its place. To explain this better I consider that many things are actually out of our control. If there had been better support for men in these situations then I may have had more opportunities available to me. If the police were more proactive with complaints then issues may have been resolved better. If the ex was more willing to comprehend what I was telling her then she may have addressed her own failings. We will just never know because those options were not available at that moment (and may never be). My regret is that I think I had too much faith in a failing system rather than finding myself in that position in the first place. I have spoken to a few people about regrets but the common denominator is based around reaction rather than being pro-action. Time and time again we may have forgiven or developed an explanation for other people's actions (I know I had) but it is important not to judge everyone by the nasty experiences we have experienced by that one person. Of course, I now recognise the signs better and I am now in a position to question my first thoughts. But I have no regrets about my experiences. I only have regrets for other people or other agencies. I regret that there is no greater support but that's not my fault. I regret not divulging more information (but when I did, very few differences were made). Ultimately though, I regret having too much faith in a system that did not work. But what is most frustrating is that the system doesn't want to improve because it does not see (conveniently) its own failings and this is a worrying factor in the times we now find ourselves in. Following my experiences, I have uncovered so many fake people. But equally I have also met and spoken to some of the most amazing people that I would never have had the opportunity to speak to otherwise. So a regret seems to have its own rewards. I am also equally happy not to forgive other people for their actions – pity is much more appropriate. Yes, I do regret many things. I regret things from my childhood but I was too young to have dealt with it at that moment. I regret telling my children off about certain things, but they have matured into fantastic adults. I regret being in an abusive relationship but I have learnt self-worth and what is right from wrong. Surely these must be seen as positive outcomes from poor experiences. I have read that an abuser is never really sorry for their actions. Do they ever have regrets about the people that they've damaged or hurt? Even if they won't admit it, do they ever feel sorry for the way they had treated other people? I very much doubt it. But I refuse to carry the burden of regret for people who do not see the errors of their own ways. Why should I/we? Life is and can be difficult as it is without trying to explain and justify our actions when dealing with a situation that you had not intended to find yourself in in the first place.

I awoke one morning recalling a moment many years ago that happened when I was at school. Yes, it was just a moment but it has lived with me ever since. Even now the thought of it still makes me angry. But this behaviour is allowed to persist, and in some quarters, it is actively encouraged. The moment I mentioned happened when I was 15 or 16. There was a specific teacher who (for some reason or other unknown to myself) did not like me. I had never attended any of his classes but he always aimed for me in the corridors or the playground. He was a vile little Welshman who clearly had some issue with his height (nearly every child in year 7 was taller than him and he clearly hated it). And so with the excessive weight (for a little man) he tried to throw it around as much as he could. Anyway, one morning he targeted me whilst entering the assembly hall. He shouted right across the hall for me to get out. Well I didn't have a problem with this because I really didn't want to endure his pointless dialogue and rantings anyway. So I stood outside the head's office whilst he preached some kind of pointless ideal to the rest of the poor unfortunates left in the school assembly hall. Once he had finished in the hall and the pupils had been dismissed his little chubby legs made their way towards me still standing outside of the heads office. He accused me of doing something that I had not done and without listening to my protestations he issued a detention. In the scheme of things getting a detention was not a major issue but it was the fact that he had refused to listen to me before issuing his injustice. He was wrong and he knew it but he clearly got off on the idea of pissing me off. In fact this little man enjoyed pissing nearly everyone off he came into contact with. He was a bully who would never have survived in the real world of work outside of a school because I was sure someone would had flattened him otherwise. Many years later after leaving school I bumped into this excuse for a little man whilst he was out with his family. This vile creature had the audacity to approach me with a smile on his face and say "hey, how are you doing, it's good to see you". Well it must have shown in my face because I knew I was filling up with rage. I had the greatest pleasure in telling this little man (in front of his family) how vile he had been to me whilst at school and how dare he approach me in such a manner. I finished the conversation with "now f...k off". It was a great feeling. There was nothing he could do about it. Although even now at the age of 45 I still don't feel the injustice had been addressed. So how does this relate to today? Well it appears that those who persist in creating an injustice are encouraged and certainly don't offer any form of retribution for their actions. Therefore, injustice is allowed to grow and flower. It strangles the decent folk who are left behind to lick their wounds.

I have made it clear throughout my writings on how much I have been disillusioned by the English justice system. But it doesn't end there. The whole system actually appears to support liars and bullies. Let me explain this more. Whilst in court I had proven that my abusive ex was a liar. Her own words and that of her daughter contradicted each other whilst claiming to give evidence. The evidence was proven to be false. Even their statements were riddled with contradictions and her own lawyer told them to think carefully whilst they separately spoke in the dock. It was nice to eventually have the opportunity to be heard after months of remaining silent. At no point had I been afforded the decency and respect to put my story across. One person had made an accusation and therefore, it must have been true in the eyes of the police and other authorities. What utter rubbish. I had always considered that guilt needed to be proven before guilt was established. But no. This is a fallacy. This concept is a lie allowed to persist because it fits a stereotype. Therefore, beyond the rhetoric the opposite is allowed to remain. I was angry that my innocence was not allowed to be heard or tested. The longer the enforced silence was imposed upon me the more I wanted to shout out. I was innocent, in fact I had been the victim but I was anxious because I was not (and still not) allowed to speak out and be heard.

I was always told to be wary of the quiet man when in fact it is the loud ones you need to watch out for.

Once the trial had been concluded I spoke to my solicitor about the evidence that had been put forward. The facts that I had been assaulted and the fact that she had been proven to be a liar. Evidence had been provided to show that she had a track record of false allegations against other men. In fact so much evidence had been provided that it transpired her youngest daughter had moved in with her father because she couldn't live with her mother anymore. I was advised to drop it. To leave it be and let it become an 'experience'. But this is wrong. This injustice was allowed to go unpunished. Her poor behaviour was/is not allowed to be addressed. Her law breaking is, in effect allowed to actively continue without fear of punishment and retribution either now or in the future. I had, whilst living with her and after leaving, been living in utter hell. In so many ways I had lost what is sacred to everyone, I had lost my identity. I had further lost my dignity and potential freedom. The system allowed my ex to throw her weight around without any fear of retribution or punishment. She knew how the system worked against the disadvantaged and she played it to its full effect. She knew how to use her Trump card and play the maiden in distress of whom would be protected even though a sight movement would have exposed the true face behind the mask.

The injustice arises that any wrongdoing such as abusing, assaulting and making false allegations is unpunishable for certain sections of society. She made the allegation first and so was protected by the law. I was proven to be the victim yet I was not afforded the respectability of an apology, a reckoning, or an attempt to balance the wrong doings. I suppose the only solace I have is that the truth finally came out and she was exposed in a small room for being what she is. But what about her next victim? Would she continue until she gets what she wants to the cost of another innocent person? And here lies the injustice. The law is not blind and fair. Yes the truth may come out but punishments are not given out to those of whom deserve it in equal measure. How many times have I read about women who make false allegations of rape. Their punishments are never equal to those of whom have been wrongly accused. And so yes, a victim will always remain the victim as the system is too idle to address these imbalances. Individuals should never be considered as being insignificant people. When cut we bleed and when we have been wronged we continue to bleed in so many different ways. We had been victims in an abusive relationship and our victimization is perpetuated by social services, the police, the courts and in some cases by our own employers.

As I have constantly stated within the pages of this book, everyone is supposedly innocent until proven guilty. This theory does not stand up to scrutiny. It is so much easier to point a finger at an innocent person than to admit the whole system is wrong. And why is this? It's because your existence is meaningless to people with power. I know of someone who took his life because of a false allegation at work. Following investigations by a coroner nothing was changed within his work place. It was easier to allow the status quo to remain than to get people of authority to answer for their actions. And no question has been raised about their subsequent inactions. I now realise that the vile teacher I had many years ago held all of the cards because people fear a false authority. People would rather believe lies because it is often more sensational than the truth. But victims will remain victims because no-one is prepared to hear the truth no matter how loud it is shouted.

When we read a gripping novel we are always keen to know what happens next. If you are a writer we are often perplexed about what to put into the next chapter. Life has its similarities. Very often we don't know what comes next. Even though we have some control over our lives many things happen because of consequences or actions of others. In my case I wanted to get some form of control back. The previous few months had been very much in the lap of the gods and I had to just roll with the events as they unfolded. Once one event had been concluded and I had brushed myself down it was then on to the next event and so on and so forth. As a result, starting again was the step I was striving for. I had lost my home because of a consequence of someone else's actions. I became ill because of a culmination of events that I had not desired. And now, once the dust had started to settle life and its steps had become a little more clearer. It was only a matter of a few months ago whereby I could not see the wood for all of the trees. As a result I often (and still do) took a step back and asked myself the importance of each and every action I was going to take. For example, clearing my name was more important than considering finding a new home and so on. By doing this everything became more digestible than trying to tackle all the problems at once. This approach would have left me engulfed and certainly overwhelmed. Looking back I can see now that the footsteps had become stepping stones that I would repeat if the past events (or something similar) ever happened again. My first step was the realisation that something was wrong. It then led to keeping records and then everything else that followed from those moments. But what I am trying to tell you is that (and I know hindsight is a wonderful thing) even the greatest of walls that are blocking our paths can have each brick chipped away to reveal new paths ahead. For me, I knew I was in a relationship that was wrong. And to keep it in check I supported myself by considering how I could tackle the problems piece by piece. However, throughout all of this I knew that all the wrongs had to be corrected. Above all I had to prove my innocence as this was the most important step to take. Once this was done everything else would fall into place. I always considered that the truth or 'rightness' would always shine through. But I now think this is a little naïve as I had come into contact with people who have had it a lot worse than I. And this is where perspective comes in. Although things were bad, they could always have been so much worse. So what is my next life chapter? Well taking back control gives you more options than you give yourself credit for.

Our lives can be complicated but they all boil down to simple things. For me (other people have their own priorities) it has been family, mental health, work and home. These are not in any particular order but each one has a special consideration that very often overlap.

Work has been at the forefront of my mind for a while. I had been torn between doing a job I had deeply loved but had also recognised the impact it had had on my health and family. My job left me tired and forced me to make decisions on my work life balance. Regardless of what people would say, working shifts covering seven days a week does have an impact upon family life and as a consequence, in the long term, creates issues with your health. As a result, I now know that something has to give. I am in the right frame of mind to consider finding alternative employment to now suit the new person that I now find myself as. I don't really want to go into the 'what for's' as this has already been covered, but I now realise how little value I am to the service I worked so hard for.

My biggest step was finding a new home. A home is much more than a house. When we travel or commute we pass so many houses but each house is a home to someone. It is here that memories are made (good or bad). I do miss my old house, but it is only the construction that I miss. It was a very old house and the historian in me loves that kind of thing. But the ghosts within those walls would never leave if I had remained there. It was an unhappy house and so would never be a happy home. For me my new home is a blank page whereby each stroke of my pen creates a mark which can be shaped into whatever I want it to be. A new home doesn't judge you on your past, but it wants to become a part of the family whereby it would be loved and taken care of. Just like the people of whom live within it. When I first saw this house, I wouldn't say it was love at first sight as I wanted to be as far away from society as I could be. I didn't want a neighbour for as far as the eye could see. But living in the real world this would have been a difficult task to complete. But this house is rural and has a few houses dotted along its (at times busy) road. And that is forgivable especially as the views all around are beautiful. In the morning I am awoken by the horses playing in the field of which my bedroom over looks. But most importantly, it feels like a home. There is room for grandchildren to come and play and space for children to stay (although they are fully grown adults now). The walks can be long with so much to find and discover along the way. But importantly, as this is a new start we are both getting used to each other's faults (the boiler needs a PhD to work out) and I have had my off days whereby I want to be embraced by its warm and comforting walls. This really is a fantastic new beginning. With the comfort of having a new home my next steps are to tackle work and as a consequence I hope my health will improve. I think it will, because it has to. But a home is never where the heart is because so many homes can have negative memories. But a home is what you feel inside and where you feel comfortable within yourself. Whether this is a cave or a mansion a home can reflect where you want to escape to once the door is closed behind you. That probably doesn't make sense, but my new home will not allow or tolerate abuse or assaults within. It is a haven from all of those kind of things, because my experiences would never allow such nastiness to filter through these new walls, doors or stairway ever again.

CHAPTER 28
Dystopia

English literature is littered with fantastic novels. We have been fortunate to have access to books that have been written over many centuries and, I hope, we will be exposed to future books or stories of equal magnitude over time. One particular genre has gripped generations of readers over many years. I would never consider dystopian works as science fiction, but they are very often set in the future. Dystopian societies appear in many artistic works, particularly in stories set in the future. Some of the most famous examples are George Orwell's *1984* and Aldous Huxley's *Brave New World*. From the outset of cinematic history directors were quick to cash in on this theme by creating films such as *Metropolis* and films based on Victorian works such as HG Wells, *War of The Worlds*. Dystopias are often characterized by dehumanization, totalitarian governments, environmental disaster, or other characteristics associated with a dreadful decline in society. The art of considering a Dystopian story is when it is often used to draw attention to real-world issues regarding society, environment, politics, economics, religion, psychology, ethics, science, or technology. In effect the idea of a dystopian state is not one built up on the dreams of those living in the present. It is the idea of the nightmare made flesh. It is the realisation that society is fragile and has been removed to a state that we no longer recognise. In our own ignorance and self-centred interpretations, we have missed the developments associated with the predictions of Orwell and HG Wells. HG Wells wrote about killing machines that attacked from the sky decades before the first manned flight had ever taken place. He even discussed the use of poisoned gas attacks prior to trench warfare. George Orwell introduced the concept of a Big Brother state that was forever watching its subjects. And this was before the invention of the CCTV.

But we often use words that are now taken for granted but are, I hasten to add, words of warning from the past. Big brother is now associated with cheap television entertainment. Even the word Kafkaesque is often misunderstood in it's literal meaning. Franz Kafka (1883-1924) was a Czech-born writer whose surreal fiction vividly expressed the anxiety, alienation, and powerlessness of the individual in the 20th century. Kafka's work is characterized by nightmarish settings in which characters are crushed by nonsensical, blind authority. Thus, the word Kafkaesque is often applied to bizarre and impersonal administrative situations where the individual feels powerless to understand or control what is happening.

Time and again, I have been given the advice that very often 'ignorance is bliss'. But who for? I assume the masses As ignorance protects people from the shaping and manipulation of the world around us. Even Plato (427 – 348 BC) desired us to 'open our eyes' once we are set free from the darkness of 'the Cave'. The example of the Cave contains many forms of symbolism used to describe the state of the world. The cave is the world we live in and the prisoners are those who inhabit the world, in effect it is us. The chains that prevent the prisoners from leaving the cave represent ignorance, meaning they interfere with the prisoners seeing the truth. The shadows cast on the walls of the cave represent what people see in the present world. Last, the freed prisoner represents those in society who see the physical world for the illusion that it is.

So how does this fit with society now? Well, many nightmares don't hit us straight away. If we look at German Society following the First World War, the German people were looking for a guide or leader to rescue them from the plight that the Treaty of Versailles had inflicted upon them. Little did they know then that their 'saviour' would finally smash Europe and result in millions of lives lost. Like a domestically abusive relationship the soft tender love slowly develops into assaults and violence. It doesn't just happen. It is a slow, organic process that appears slowly over time.

The nightmare for many continues after the domestic escape. Our elected representatives sell us both and idea and a solution with conveniently placed sound-bites and marketing to buy our votes. The reality is a nightmare perpetuated by enforcing the status quo of the present situation. Let me give you an example, we all know about the Big Brother state whereby our movements are monitored both physically and electronically. Our emails are scanned, and texts monitored clandestinely. But we were warned about this many decades ago in George Orwell's 1984. Kafka warned us about being arrested and tried by a state that holds no logic or explanations. Therefore, nothing improves it only intensifies under a wrong regime that continually fails to address the nightmares of society. We vote our leaders in who do not concern themselves with everyday problems once they have secured their seats in Parliament.

It transpires that the police and the CPS now pick and choose the evidence they require to arrest and charge individuals. This is nothing new, dictator states such as Nazi Germany or Stalin's Russia arrested, sentenced and executed individuals based on what did not fit into their idea of society. There was no chance or option of appeal or defence. Your only crime was if you met certain criteria. Or a member of a particular group. This doesn't make you a criminal it makes you a victim. And a target setting state system does not make sense, it makes victims. In fact Stalin coined the phrase 'one death is a tragedy, many deaths are a statistic'. And here lies the similarity with what I find today. Because men represent a large part of society each individual is a statistic. Our claims for equal treatment in courtrooms around the world are ignored. Our legal claims are rejected in the favour of either the state or the convenient lies of a false accuser who fit the states 'targets'. It works well for them both (the state and the accuser). This present dystopian state has a legal system that protects the untruths because it works well for the state. Every state throughout history has needed a scapegoat on which to off load its failings onto and it has been convenient to blame men for societies evils. Men have been unable to defend themselves because we are either labelled as being sexist, racist, homophobic, violent, abuser and so on. But we are too scared to deny it (as being further labelled) or too under supported to fight it (lack of legal recognition, state protection or equality in the eyes of the law). In effect, men are having to fight the fight with both hands tied. We are none of the above, and yet we are not allowed to question the state or have our cases heard without preconceived ideas or prejudice and silence equally valid voices of which need to be heard. It is wrong, it is a state supported dictatorship. As a 'modern man' I support the ideas of feminism. I love the idea of an equal, fair and just society. But I cannot support a form of ideology that attempts to trample on a section of society to enhance their own. I see this as the equivalent of the Book Burning incident in Nazi Germany that attempted to eradicate the sharing of ideas. Yes, women are victims and require protection from abuse. But men are victims too but are not afforded the same decency, honesty or protection. And this is now the dystopian state that we all find ourselves in. It is only recently that the abuse of power by the police and the CPS has come to the forefront of the news. But what will happen? People will be moved on to be replaced by new fresh faced 'yes' people. The embarrassment will be moved but the facts and actions cannot be erased. Peoples lives have been ruined and the stains on their lives are indelible. This state simply washes its own errors in tainted waters that continues to cover up without actually cleaning.

If we look at corruption in the police force it has been a well known feature for generations. My great grandmother warned me about their actions and characteristics many years ago. The 1980's exposed a corrupt unit in the West Midlands Constabulary yet nothing has changed. The state made promises that it would 'change' its ways, yet the same things have happened again and again. Nothing has changed and nothing will. People raise a concern and then forget it when a new story hits the headlines. Perhaps society is full of ignorant people – because it is better to live that way than see the nightmare we are in. That is, until it happens to them. From an age whereby, I knew right from wrong I was fed the state propaganda that we are protected equally and without prejudice. In fact we were all taught this because our predecessors also believed this, and so the fakery continued. But I am now free from the Cave and can see the light for what it is. This dystopian state has fed us as children to believe in a state and a system that just does not exist. The nightmare future that so many authors and philosophers predicted is, alas, here now. And living in

Plato's cave does not protect us from the facts as they are. It just hides them well. Unfortunately, our warnings may not protect our children from the future nightmares yet to come.

CHAPTER 29
A Happy Goodbye to 2017

I recall a conversation many years ago whilst studying for my A levels. During this conversation we were discussing a psychology experiment that had a long-term effect upon the patient. This particular patient had been brought up to believe the opposite of what was indeed fact. For example, this child (we shall call her 'XY') was told that black is white and vice-versa. Unfortunately, I just cannot recall the name of this experiment, but the eventual outcome was that XY ultimately killed herself in her early adulthood. But what was even more tragic was that XY was the daughter of the man carrying out the experiment. Okay, so what has this got to do with the dawning of a new year? Well the comparison is very similar to the last few years and in particular the year I have just bid a farewell to. We are all growing and adapting to the changes and developments around us in one way or another. Like XY you assume the world around you is how it is because we have been led to believe that this is so. If we marry this thought process with the famous quote by Josef Goebbels stating the value of a lie we can probably understand better.

"If you tell a lie big enough and keep repeating it, people will eventually come to believe it. The lie can be maintained only for such time as the State can shield the people from the political, economic and/or military consequences of the lie. It thus becomes vitally important for the State to use all of its powers to repress dissent, for the truth is the mortal enemy of the lie, and thus by extension, the truth is the greatest enemy of the State."

For me I have spent the majority of 2017 realising fact from fiction. Perhaps fiction is too weak a word because fiction in this sense is an untruth and not just a story. The facts were there for show and did not suit the purpose of which they had been created for. 2017 has exposed that the English Legal System is corrupt and innocents does not secure your rightful freedom. 2017 has also opened the casket of recognising that men also suffer with depression as recent television documentaries have shown willing to touch upon such subjects. It has often been said that there is a book within each of us and 2017 has been that story for me. The start of 2017 was a slight discomfort culminating into a rush of events leading from other events. Yet who would have thought that twelve months later I would be sitting here analysing what the last year had been like? For many it is another year but for me it has been a revelation. Like child XY I had been led to believe over so many years that the democratic and liberal society I was born and raised in does not actually exist. What else was there to learn? I learnt that as a male victim I did not have the same rights or protection as my female equivalent. Yet, even as a victim I was not afforded the same consideration, protection and, as I found out the same equality in law. Perhaps 2018 will afford me greater riches of knowledge. I am more aware now that the streets that I walk and the thoughts that I have are no longer the same as they were before. I have confidence in saying that male victims are at a disadvantage. It doesn't make it right, but I am not fooled by the 'smoke and mirrors' that have been created by the authorities to paint a picture that doesn't resemble the facts as they are.

The issues associated with mental health have also had a clean sweep. I have managed to stand tall and inwardly scream that it is okay. I have come to accept that the reality of having depression is as real as the size of my feet or the colour of my eyes. They are what they are and I am who I am. And for people to accept these factors I need to accept them within myself. And for once, 2017 has allowed this to happen. And it's good, it works well. I suppose that the start of a new year can sweep away old thoughts of what I perceived to be right. I am certainly stronger in the knowledge that if any victim of abuse or depression approached me I could afford to give them the knowledge that 2017 gave me. And although the facts are far from pretty the strength I have gained from it could make anyone cope. 2017 has given me new friends with the same backgrounds and experiences that I had endured. And these are good friends I would not have met otherwise. I have also learnt to pick and choose who I want in my life and this factor will last into

2018 and no doubt, beyond. So yes, 2018 is going to be a better year. Because it has to be. I've never been one to make new years resolutions as I am fully aware that the changing of a date should never come with unrealistic or (perhaps) unobtainable goals. But, whilst I reflect I think I have made plans for 2018 way back in May when everything I knew had turned on its head. So if we recall child XY. We have both had a realisation that things were not so. I am also sure that child XY also attempted to gain some form of perspective. And alas, death became inevitable. Child XY took her own life in a terrible and tragic way. But for me the demise of 2017 has created a funeral pyre of false realities, unrealistic expectations and fake beliefs. But I am actually okay with this because whatever outcome or result that 2018 will bring I know it has been my own efforts that have achieved them – it has not been done with the support of (a lack of) male refuges or (the lack of) police support and help. I have also accepted that there is nothing offensive about taking medication.

So what am I saying to you, the reader? Well regardless of how 2017 has been I am sure that it has educated you into finding a new element about yourself – whether good or bad. Any form of learning has to be seen as positive. 2018 will ensure (I hope) that we will have learnt from those mistakes we have made, said or done. So yes, I wish you all a happy new year. I hope that 2018 will furnish you with a better understanding thus making you a better person.

CHAPTER 30
A letter to my older self

When somebody mentions the 1990's it feels like 5 years ago, but it isn't, its nearly 30 years ago. And I find this a shocking revelation. I can still recall the songs played on the radio and I probably still own a few shirts from back then buried deep in my wardrobe. Time has passed so quickly, too quickly in fact. It almost seems unfair to think about the time I have wasted or the positive things I could have done. I probably won't have another 30 years left (who knows). But I want to take the time to talk to my future self. I want to be able to, one day, look back and read this letter and say "oh yeah, I remember that".

Or "that problem seemed so massive at the time". Better still, I hope to say the following; "I survived it all" and "I am happy now.". This letter had taken a while to consider. Undoubtedly, I have probably left some important things out, but that's okay. I can always write another. A part 2 if you like. But below is my letter addressed to my older self. I want to be in my mid 60s when I read this letter. I can picture myself now. Balder, thinner (I hope). But I want to remain gentle and loving. I want to be warm with a wealth of knowledge to share and appreciate. But most of all I want to be content with who I became and I want to have buried the evils that have plagued my life at present. Did the abuse turn me into a better man than I could ever have envisaged or did it finally take a hold of me which could not be shaken? I want to live and be strong. I have a whole lot of love to give in its many forms. Perhaps I just want to know that I eventually had the opportunity to reach my full potential. Anyway, here is my letter to myself…

Hello

I was glad you've taken the time to read this letter. It has been a long time in the making, but was very hard to submit into words. After all, how do you talk to yourself in an unknown situation, at an unknown time? Of course, you are older now and I hope that you are well.

Firstly, if you are reading this I want to congratulate you. I was pleased that you never took your life. I know the depression was hard and although you didn't want to give in to it, the option of 'ending it all' was always there, over-hanging your every thought and action. If you recall you never feared dying and that was always admirable. But it never stopped the pain of your past and present. Yet this has been my biggest fear. When I was ready to die, I really was ready to go. But it's all about what came next. Would I have scored an own goal and missed out on the best years of my life yet to come? Would the pain of those left behind been too heavy a price to pay for my weakness? Perhaps it's easy to suggest, as an alternative, that I may not even have been missed. Do you recall the months of planning and researching the best way to go? If you remember you did indeed discover the painless way and you were happy to keep it a secret for many years. I just hope that you put those thoughts down and picked up new revelations.

Things that had a bigger and better meaning. Would I see them too, soon? I am trying to seek them out, but I just need a bit of direction at the moment.

I just hope the future is brighter and gave you everything that you ever desired. I know you never hunted for financial riches, but you spent all your life searching for other riches in life such as acceptance, warmth and love. Please tell me you found them? Are you happier now? If so do you measure your happiness in a different way to how I do it now? Most importantly though, did you learn anything from those awful years? I keep telling myself that within these grey clouds a silver lining must be found. I must admit, it is only now that I do see a glimmer of hope and it's a warm feeling to know it is there. It's a happy feeling and I hope to feel its full embrace very soon.

Do you remember how much you loved animals and how you would go out of your way to show them affection. Animals for you gave you the unconditional love that you had always wanted. You knew it was easier to love animals than people at times. I just hope that your affection for animals remained and that you have a loving dog curled up around your feet as you are reading this. Next to a warm fire with the lights down low. I know that would make you happy.

Your children grew into lovely people I am sure. Did you maintain a good relationship with them? I know that your parents (in all guises) let you down. I am also aware that their style of parenting shaped yours. You never intentionally hurt them and always told them you loved them – this was a characteristic I liked about myself. I was always keen to let them know that parental love was important. And I always grabbed the opportunity for a hug. If you recall, you had recently become a grandfather. We both know that he would be a good father. You would have to let me know how good his parenting skills were. He often called or text with messages on what to do in certain situations. This gave you comfort because it showed he cared for his son. Perhaps I had done right by him. After all he had the makings of a good father – that was all you wanted from him.

I was always drawn to the countryside. The early years were spent living in the city and the first opportunity I had to leave I grabbed it with both hands. Living in the countryside was a liberating experience. I would spend hours walking through fields and down remote country lanes. The air was always so much better and the smells made me feel complete in the knowledge I felt at home there. I really hope that you did finally find your little 'bolt-hole' deep in the countryside. As far away from other people as you wanted. Do you remember that time telling your careers teacher that you wanted to be a hermit in response to his question "what do you want to be when you're older"? I always thought this was a funny response.

I suppose by the time you read this there have been advancements in photographic technology, and you have taken full advantage of your country walks. It would be nice to know that the love for photography never wavered.

Contrary to what you are probably thinking right now, I did not have any massive demands of me, or false expectations or goals that I might have failed to meet. I was just happy to get through each day. I was also glad that I broke down my own barriers to accept the help when it was required. I did it for my benefit really, because I wanted me to grow old surrounded by the important things in my life. Those were the simple goals. One day at a time. Not a big house or a massive car. But self-contentment and self-value. We both know it was difficult to find when the timing was tough but I was glad we saw it through. Did I achieve those things? Did I achieve any of it? If you are not who I imagine now, I am okay with it, I'll support you. Because maybe who I was imagining is someone else, and you are—well you're not someone else, you're me. And what you are now is the product of the decisions I have made today.

For me, at this moment, the biggest lesson I have learnt is the idea of allowing myself to be whoever I am. I am also looking forward to making plans for who I should become. And that for this present moment, is more than enough. Was there ever a time that you were able to lay the ghosts of abuse to rest? I accept that you may not have ever let your younger years go. They were after all your formative years. But what about the failed romantic relationships? I really hope you have now got to the point whereby you struggle to remember her name. I was always adamant that I would never forgive her but only feel pity. Was this option the best to take or did anger and hate consume me further before I could let it go?

Before I go, I want you to heed my words. I want you to love your children even as they are now fully-grown adults. You sacrificed so much for them and they were ultimately your reason for holding on. Really love the woman you may have now. Although you know you could survive on your own, sharing these years with someone special is all that you have desired throughout your life. Let it be. Enjoy her and be what you want to be with her.

I hope you are happy

References

1. Trump says gun violence 'isn't a gun problem' - 08/27/15 M S N B C – J a n e C . T i m m http://www.msnbc.com/msnbc/donald-trump-says-gun-violence-isnt-gun-problem

2. Domestic violence and abuse; Domestic violence and abuse: new definition. 26, March 2013. Home Office. https://www.gov.uk/guidance/domestic-violence-and-abuse

3. Unequal Trapped and Controlled (Marilyn Howard and Amy Skipp). March 2015. TUC Press.

4. Victims No Longer: The Classic Guide for Men Recovering from Sexual Child Abuse. Mike Lew. 2004.

5. Ibid

6. Ibid

7. In the Psychiatrist's Chair. Brian Masters. Radio 4 Extra. September 2016.

8. Healing from Hidden Abuse: A Journey Through the Stages of Recovery from Psychological Abuse. Shannon Thomas. Prime 2016.

9. T h e L o n g t e r m e f f e c t s o f b u l l y i n g (https://www.mentalhelp.net/articles/the-long-term-effects-of-bullying). September 2016.

10. Lupri, Eugene; Grandin, Elaine (2004). "Intimate partner abuse against men". January 4, 2009. Retrieved June 21, 2014

11. "Family Violence Statistics: Including Statistics on Strangers and Acquaintances" (PDF). Bureau of Justice Statistics, U.S. Department of Justice.

12. Gelles, Richard J.; Straus, Murray A. (1985). Intimate Violence: The Causes and Consequences of Abuse in the American Family

13. Ibid

14. Mirrlees-Black, Catriona (1999). Domestic Violence: Findings from a new British Crime Survey self-completion questionnaire. London: Home Office. pp. 17–26

15. Britton, Andrew (2011). Homicides, Firearm Offences and Intimate Violence, 2010/2011: Supplementary Volume 2 to Crime in England and Wales, 2010/2011, London: Home Office. p. 96

16. (Carrado, Michelle; George, Malcolm J.; Loxam, Elizabeth; Jones, L.; Templar, Dale (June 1996). "Aggression in British Heterosexual Relationships: A Descriptive Analysis". Aggressive Behavior. pg 401–415)

17. Carrado, Michelle; George, Malcolm J.; Loxam, Elizabeth; Jones, L.; Templar, Dale (June 1996). "Aggression in British Heterosexual Relationships: A Descriptive Analysis". Aggressive Behavior. 22 (6): 401–415)

18. Do Male Domestic Abuse Victims Get Arrested? 23/09/2013 http://www.huffingtonpost.co.uk/bob-morgan/male-domestic-violence_b_3962958.html

19. Tull, M., Jakupcak, M., Paulson, A., and K. Gratz. The Role of Emotional Inexpressivity and Experiential Avoidance in the Relationship Between Posttraumatic Stress Disorder Symptom Severity and Aggressive Behavior Among Men Exposed to Interpersonal Violence. Anxiety, Stress, and Coping. 2007. 20(4):337-51.

20. Ibid

21. Sleep and Depression. https://www.webmd.com/depression/sleep-depression#1

22. 'When Depression Makes You Feel Guilty For 'Wasting Time'...':https://themighty.com/2017/06/depression-guilt-wasting-time/

23. Edwin Shneidman, The Suicidal Mind. Oxford Press. 23 Apr 1998

24. https://winstonswish.muchloved.org/gateway/stages-of-grieving.htm)

25. https://www.spectator.co.uk/2015/03/the-shocking-truth-about-police-corruption-in-britain/

26. Ibid

27. George Orwell. Down and Out in Paris and London [1933]

28. (http://www.telegraph.co.uk/news/uknews/law-and-order/9731800/Barristers-rake-in-fortunes-from-legal-aid.html)

29. D o r i s L e e s i n g https://www.goodreads.com/quotes/1430634-i-find-myself-increasingly-shocked-at-the-unthinking-and-automatic

30. Dr Clare, the British psychiatrist 2009